SEXUAL AND GENDER DOCTRINAL LANGUAGE

SEXUAL AND GENDER DOCTRINAL LANGUAGE

A Source of Pain and Trauma in the Catholic Church

TODD A. SALZMAN AND
MICHAEL G. LAWLER

FOREWORD BY JAMES F. KEENAN, SJ

Paulist Press
New York / Mahwah, NJ

Cover image by Wow Design Studio / Shutterstock.com
Cover and book design by Lynn Else

Library of Congress Cataloging-in-Publication Data
Names: Salzman, Todd A., author. | Lawler, Michael G., author.
Title: Sexual and gender doctrinal language: a source of pain and trauma in the Catholic church / Todd A. Salzman and Michael G. Lawler; foreword by James F. Keenan, SJ.
Description: New York, Mahwah, NJ: Paulist Press, [2025] | Includes bibliographical references and index. | Summary: "This book discusses doctrinal language on sexual and gender ethical issues and seeks to move the Church forward using synodal ecclesiology and 'new pastoral methods' of Pope Francis"—Provided by publisher.
Identifiers: LCCN 2024036541 (print) | LCCN 2024036542 (ebook) | ISBN 9780809157440 (paperback) | ISBN 9780809189120 (ebook)
Subjects: LCSH: Sex—Religious aspects—Catholic Church. | Gender identity—Religious aspects—Catholic Church.
Classification: LCC BT708 .S2439 2025 (print) | LCC BT708 (ebook) | DDC 241/.664088282—dc23/eng/20250108
LC record available at https://lccn.loc.gov/2024036541
LC ebook record available at https://lccn.loc.gov/2024036542

ISBN 978-0-8091-5744-0 (paperback)
ISBN 978-0-8091-8912-0 (ebook)

Published by Paulist Press
997 Macarthur Boulevard
Mahwah, NJ 07430
www.paulistpress.com

Printed and bound in the
United States of America

This book is dedicated to all those who have suffered indignity,
trauma, and abuse in and from the Catholic Church
and to those who work so hard to promote
their human dignity and healing.

CONTENTS

FOREWORD

In 2010, with the theological ethicist Linda Hogan, I chaired the second international conference of Catholic Theological Ethics in the World Church in the city of Trento, Italy. We had about six hundred theological ethicists participating from seventy-two countries. We had held our first conference in 2006 at Padua, Italy, and now we chose Trento because it was where the field of moral theology was born. The Council of Trent (held in three sessions between 1545 and 1563) mandated the creation of seminaries for the training of future priests in theology and pastoral care. Among their fields of study that the Council argued needed to be taught was moral theology, or what we today call theological ethics.

We opened on a Saturday in July. On Sunday, at the Cathedral of Trento, where the Council was held, our six hundred members attended the regularly scheduled 5:30 p.m. Mass at which the archbishop, Monsignor Luigi Bressan, presided. The church was incredibly packed with several hundred regular Trento churchgoers and ourselves. The archbishop invited me to say a few words to the entire congregation afterward. I explained why we were there and the people of Trento applauded in welcome. And then I said,

> You may notice that there are more than 150 priests concelebrating—they are all moral theologians [applause]. There are also others here who are theologians. Probably most of the faces that you don't recognize are moral theologians. Yes, most of those men dressed like you are moral theologians [applause] and yes, those women you do not recognize are also moral theologians [greater applause]. And you may notice a lot of children here, too. No, they are not moral theologians, but their parents are

[even greater applause]. The face of the moral theologian is changing [thunderous applause].

During those days we heard thirty plenary papers and over 240 concurrent presentations. One of the latter was by the famous team of Todd A. Salzman and Michael G. Lawler, who discussed "The Sexual Person and Virtue Ethics in Dialogue."

I returned to those days in Trento, when I was finishing *A History of Catholic Theological Ethics* for Paulist Press, I began my last chapter with "Changing the Face in the Field," telling how in 1973 Margaret Farley became the first of nearly ten lay Roman Catholic moral theologians who got their doctoral degrees in the 1970s. Like them, Michael Lawler received his in 1975, but in systematic theology.

Interestingly, just about every one of those first lay theologians wrote at some point on sexual ethics, and well they should have. For the most part, their contributions were designed to offer a new way of thinking about sexuality, in particular to think of it not as forbidden or threatening, but as experientially significant. These theologians had an experience of sexuality that was more shared and public than their clerical forebearers. Here sexuality was seen, if you will, in greater complexity, with less emphasis on set biological categories and functions and more as constitutive of relationality. And, assuredly, they did not approach sexuality with any less seriousness; on the contrary, they were able to describe and narrate just how significant sexuality is for the human community.

In that first 1970s cohort were Lisa Sowle Cahill, Christine Gudorf, and Patricia Beattie Jung joining Margaret Farley. Each of them wrote on sexuality *and* gender, bringing even greater awareness of the overlooked complexities of both topics. In particular, they explored gender as less defined by complementarity but more by a broader set of issues than had hitherto been brought to the field by priestly men. Women were seen not as the complement of men, but in their own embodied, relational natures.

When lay men and women theologians began their work, they were not entering already existing spaces. Obviously, in the newness of their projects, they were considering what went before them, but the ambit of these lay investigations broadened exponentially, and along the way they were constructing spaces for all of us to consider their findings.

For instance, I studied theology from 1979 to 1982 at Weston Jesuit School of Theology in Cambridge, Massachusetts. In 1980, I learned that Cahill was teaching in Boston College and enrolled in her course. It was a terrific experience. The most striking recollection I have is how familiar she was with the tradition, how easily she wore her intelligence, and how welcoming and encouraging she was as we explored the fullness of theological ethics.

Before studying with her, I thought that a lot of moral theology was about gatekeeping and about figuring out what issue belonged to what category. In her class I was struck by her hospitality, by the way she was bringing us graduate students on board and into the project. It was not so much a field I was entering, but a community of scholars. True, moralists who were priests were also hospitable, especially the uncanny Charles Curran, but Lisa's style was hers and different from Charlie's.

Each of these four women wrote notably on sexual ethics and like them, so did Lawler and Salzman as they began their collaborative work between a systematic theologian and a theological ethicist. Not only were these lay theologians making contributions, they were becoming leaders in the field, and they proposed a sexual ethics that was more interested in understanding sexuality well and living sexually joyfully and responsibly.

It is noteworthy that they were not responding or reacting to particular magisterial teachings on sexuality. Rather, they were trying to expand the field, to follow Pope John XXIII's admonition to open up the windows. They wanted to let in experience, shared understanding, dialogue, shared decision-making, maturation, relationality, and a host of other insights to help develop the agency of people as sexually alive and loving. Effectively, they were, like Cahill in her class, evoking greater participation and thought of others. A discourse about sexuality and ethics was developing.

As the discourse developed there was need to develop a language. The turn to values and virtues naturally emerged. When talking about virtues in the moral manuals, the virtue of chastity held pride of place, but these lay theologians, like Lawler and Salzman in their earlier work at Trento, were trying to hold up the broad spectrum of the virtues for the sexual person to appropriate. Thus, besides chastity, they added to the discourse on sexuality, the virtues of love, justice, mutual respect, fidelity, self-care, and prudence. Indeed, in their footsteps followed others elaborating values, virtues, and practices: Cristina Traina, Jason King, Julie Hanlon Rubio, Megan McCabe, Craig Ford, Elizabeth Antus, Emily Reimer-Barry, Bridget Burke Ravizza, Mary Doyle Roche, Jennifer Beste, Victor Carmona, Christine Hinze, and many others. The discourse broadened and deepened and aimed to be inclusive and hospitable.

Unlike earlier moralists who instructed the faithful on sexual morality, these newer voices were looking to engage readers and listeners as agents who through virtue might be able to realize their sexuality lovingly, responsibly, generatively, justly, carefully, honestly, wisely, happily, and of course, morally rightly.

Their influence was broad and extensive and in fact one could say influenced not only their fellow theologians, but the laity, the clergy, and hierarchy as well. This is not to say that there are not those—lay, clergy, or hierarchs—who still prefer the more direct, instructive, "traditional" model, but this newer appeal to virtue-seeking agents is in full force and has after fifty years hit a remarkable level of maturation. Its mature influence is palpable especially if you read Pope Francis's apostolic exhortation *Amoris Laetitia* (2016).

It is at this point that Lawler and Salzman present a critique of past exercises of moral instruction. Rather than building up what has been said, they raise the issue of language to explain how particular ways of teaching can harm others. Again, the issue of language arises, but now after fifty years of developing a more critical yet hospitable language, method, and framework for a Christian sexual ethics, they demarcate what should not be said or taught, even if it has been.

Notice, however, the attention to the agents. This work highlights precisely how harm to the people of God is a sure sign of problematic teachings. The teachings are not conceptual connections with other teachings; they are Christian truths as life guides for Christian agents, dare we say, disciples, and, our authors argue, such harm to the agents challenges the truth claims of the instructions.

With this work, Salzman and Lawler, while invoking the style and language of *Amoris Laetitia*, take these critical steps of critique.

Only in time will we know whether they convince those within the various sectors of the church of their arguments.

Note by working with *Amoris Laetitia*, for instance, they are not seeking to replace the magisterium, rather they are interested in shaping the teachings so that the teachings are virtuous, and not, on the contrary, vicious. In a manner of speaking, they argue that the teachings need to be at least as virtuous as the call to discipleship itself actually is.

Of course, there is a certain boldness here, but readers of Lawler and Salzman are familiar with their courage and claims.

After Trento, after meeting six hundred ethicists from around the world, I reflected on who we theological ethicists are and found that we are by nature critical: our vocation is based on the premise that we are ethicists because things are not as they should and could be. As the critics and reformers of society and church, we seek to practically bridge the gulf between who we are and who we can be. We always begin, then, with the premise that we are not where we ought to be yet. We need together to find a way of improving.

Often when church leaders or church laity hear presentations by ethicists, they wonder why we are not more positive. Still, we believe that we *are* positive. We believe that people can do better and that the church can do better. We therefore try to highlight where we need to go and how we ought to get there.

By nature, we are teleologists: we aim at a better end or future. We believe that Jesus Christ wants us as a people to move forward. Here then we follow in the footsteps of Thomas Aquinas, who taught *Stare in via Dei retrocedere est* (to stand on the way of the Lord is to move backward). Pope Francis echoes him as well every time he insists that we need to move forward, not backward.

We ethicists believe that we must find the truth, and in part that means naming not only what is lacking, but what was not virtuously expressed. In this work, Lawler and Salzman offer their insights into the ongoing discourse to find virtuous pathways for contemporary Christians on the way of the Lord.

James F. Keenan, SJ
Canisius Professor
Boston College

PREFACE

The most egregious violent attack in the United States on members of the LGBTQI+ community occurred on June 12, 2016, in Orlando, Florida, at the Pulse gay nightclub, where a single gunman brutally murdered forty-nine people. This senseless and violent act was a clear manifestation of the extreme homophobia directed against LGBTQI+ persons, maybe specifically against Latino LGBTQI+. This homophobia is based, not on any understanding of the dignity of such persons as human beings or of their relationships to family, friends, social and religious communities, but solely on ignorance, hate, and a distorted view of who LGBTQI+ persons are. Many spoke out against this violent act, including many Catholic bishops. Although those bishops decried the senseless violence and violation of human dignity, only a few, such as Bishops Gerald Barnes and Frank Caggiano, acknowledged that the attack was specifically directed at gay and lesbian people. It is unclear why the United States Conference of Catholic Bishops (henceforth USCCB) did not issue an official document acknowledging this fact. In his statement on the shooting, Bishop Robert Lynch honestly and courageously makes a clear connection between the violence and religion: "Sadly it is religion, including our own, which targets, mostly verbally, and also often breeds contempt for gays, lesbians and transgender people. Attacks today on LGBTQ men and women often plant the seed of contempt, then hatred, which can ultimately lead to violence."[1] His statement draws a correlational, if not a causal, link between Catholic language about LGBTQI+ persons and the homophobic attitudes and violence that language on occasion promotes. Although the Pulse attack is the most extreme case of physical violence directed against LGBTQI+ persons, it is not an isolated event and Catholic doctrinal language has led to other forms of spiritual and sexual violence, pain, and trauma.

The clerical sex-abuse scandal and its cover-up by church leadership is a clear violation of human dignity. It was enabled by the Catholic language about the so-called ontological change that takes place in ordination to the priesthood and has threatened the trust of Catholics in their church. The sacramental language of ordination and the "ontological change" that is claimed to occur through ordination has created a caste system and a hierarchical ecclesiology in the Catholic church that promotes clericalism, hierarchism, entitlement, authoritarianism, and the potential for the type of sexual abuse and cover-up that has been exposed but still continues despite Pope Francis's efforts to correct it. A culture of clericalism endures in the Catholic Church, and this culture is influenced and perpetuated by language that continues to promote that clericalism.

In addition to this abuse, there are other, more subtle and not so subtle, forms of sexual trauma promoted by Catholic doctrinal language regarding human sexuality. Not-so-subtle forms include Catholic teaching on LGBTQI+ issues, which promote so-called just discrimination and, as we have seen, even violence against LGBTQI+ people. More subtle forms include doctrinal teaching that does not recognize any parvity of matter in sexual sins, which means that all sexual sins are potentially mortal sins. These require grave matter, and church teaching on sexual sins can cause spiritual trauma to believers who have discerned, through well-informed consciences, that their acts and relationships are not sinful, but live nevertheless with the trauma of church condemnation. Whether the issue is the use of artificial contraception, masturbation, nonreproductive homosexual or heterosexual marital sexual acts, premarital sex, or artificial reproductive technologies, and even though a firm doctrine of the Catholic Church asserts the authority and inviolability of a well-formed conscience, Catholic doctrine, which absolutely prohibits all such acts as potentially mortally sinful, can have a damaging impact on the emotional, psychological, relational, and spiritual lives of the Catholic faithful.

English theologian Adrian Thatcher correctly notes, "Connexions are not being made between abusive behaviour in the churches and the abusive [doctrinal] teachings and practices that tend to legitimize it."[2] This book is an attempt to make those connections clear. It first proposes revised language, grounded in a revised anthropology, ecclesiology, and sacramental theology, to move the church forward in promoting human dignity in all areas, including sexual human dignity. It then explores Catholic sacramental, ecclesial, and moral language in detail and critically analyzes that language using psychological and scientific resources that detail the pain- and trauma-producing impact of religious language on human beings.

We develop our argument as follows. Chapter 1 makes proposals for the reformation of doctrinal language in the church, a reformation that will include anthropological, theological, ecclesiological, and ethical methodological language. Chapter 2, co-authored with Dr. Julia Feder, defines various types of trauma and their physical, emotional, psychological, and spiritual effects. We then explore both the power and authority of language to enable, cause, and justify personal trauma, and how the language of Catholic sexual ethical teaching functions to cause sexual trauma. Chapter 3 examines the violence, pain, and trauma caused by the clerical sex-abuse scandal and its cover-up. This clerical abuse, we argue, can be traced in large part to a culture of clericalism and hierarchicalism that is enabled by sacramental language that teaches a so-called ontological change through priestly ordination and, therefore, the superiority of priestly life over lay and married life.[3] We argue that it is this sacramental language of priestly ordination and the ecclesiological structures and culture that it creates and perpetuates, in large part, that enable ongoing sexual abuse and cover-up in the Catholic Church. Chapter 4 explains, and critically analyzes, the anthropological doctrinal language that is the foundation for all Catholic teaching about sex and gender. We address the psychology and meanings of sexuality and propose what we call a holistic complementarity as an approach to the unions of female and male.

Chapters 5 and 6 investigate the Catholic doctrinal norms guiding human sexuality and the pain and trauma such norms create and perpetuate. We deal with the teachings on contraception, divorce and remarriage, cohabitation, homosexuality, transgender, and intersex, and how these teachings impact vulnerable populations. The traumatic impact is perhaps most clearly reflected in doctrinal teaching against homosexuals and their sexual acts, and in the so-called just discrimination against LGBTQI+ persons, which we address in chapter 7. Catholic sexual teaching claims that it *is* just to discriminate against LGBTQI+ persons because their sexual orientation or inclination is "objectively disordered,"[4] and the USCCB has sought legislation to permit so-called just discrimination against them. Catholic social teaching, however, absolutely opposes such discrimination. This inconsistency in Catholic sexual and social teaching illustrates underlying problems with Catholic sexual teaching, its language, and the damage it does to LGBTQI+ Catholic faithful and to members of the broader community. Chapter 8 concludes with a consideration of the doctrine of the human equality of female and male and how this equality is lived (or not) in the sacraments of marriage and holy orders. We consider specifically the ordination of women to the diaconate.

Throughout the book, we illustrate the spiritual pain and trauma done to Catholic believers with anecdotes from vulnerable individuals and groups who have suffered such pain and trauma. These narratives, along with sociological data that demonstrate alienation and a growing exodus from the Catholic Church, substantiate a correlation, if not a causal relationship, between doctrinal language and its negative impacts on the religious and spiritual lives of faithful Catholics.

1

FOUNDATIONS FOR REFORMING CATHOLIC DOCTRINAL TEACHING

In his 2023 *motu proprio, Ad Theologiam Promovendam,*[1] Pope Francis challenges theologians to open up to the world and to humanity, "with its problems, its wounds, its challenges, its potential." He affirms that theological reflection must make room for, and construct, "an epistemological and methodological rethinking," and that "good theologians, like good pastors, also smell of the people and the street and, by their reflection, pour oil and wine on the wounds of men [and women]."[2] The analyses and critiques in this book deal largely with the wounds of the faithful, the violence, pain, and trauma occasioned by the doctrinal language of the Catholic Church. To somehow soften the negativity involved in those analyses and critiques, this chapter offers "epistemological and methodological rethinking" and positive proposals for the reformation of that language. That reformation will require a revised anthropology, theology, ecclesiology, and ethical methodology. The church, we argue, must embrace and integrate scientific and experiential understandings of human sexuality into its theological anthropology and formulate doctrines that reflect these understandings. This integration calls for a reform of the doctrines themselves, and in what follows in the book, we will propose such reforms. No reformation of any Catholic doctrine, however, will happen in this book; that is for the discerning church to do through Pope Francis's recovered synodal process. What we propose is a comprehensive methodology and a holistic anthropology to facilitate that reform.

The trauma that Catholic sexual doctrines can and do cause to Catholic faithful can be direct, indirect, complex, chronic, or religious. Sacramental doctrinal teaching on ordination, clericalism, and a hierarchical ecclesiology enable priests and bishops to inflict trauma and sexual violence on children, women, and men. The same language enables bishops to cover up that violence. Doctrinal sexual teaching causes various types of trauma among many Catholics, especially LGBTQI+ Catholics who experience discrimination, homophobia, and exclusion from the Catholic community. These trauma-inducing doctrines have led to a call for foundational reform from Pope Francis, some bishops, and laity. Pope Francis has condemned clericalism as one of the sources of trauma and sexual violence in the Catholic Church. "Clericalism" he states, "is a thorn. It is a scourge. It is a form of worldliness that defiles and damages the face of the Lord's bride. It enslaves the holy, faithful people of God."[3] Cardinal McElroy of San Diego disagrees with the doctrinal phrase "objectively disordered" to label LGBTQI+ people, arguing that disorder "is a terrible word and it should be taken out of the *Catechism*."[4] Other church leaders have gone further. Cardinal Hollerich of Luxembourg argues that "the sociological-scientific foundation of Catholic teaching on homosexual people [and acts] is no longer correct." It is, he believes, "time for a fundamental revision of the doctrine" on homosexual acts.[5] Bishop Helmut Dieser of Aachen asserts that "same-sex feelings and love are not an aberration, but a variant of human sexuality." He maintains that church thinking on homosexuality in particular and human sexuality in general is "too simple." Homosexuality, he argues "is—as science shows—not a glitch, not an illness, not an expression of any kind of deficit."[6] Cardinal Marx of Munich and the majority of the German bishops have made similar statements.[7] Bishop Georg Bätzing, the president of the German bishops' conference, emphasizes the reform of doctrine based on viable arguments, which include "fundamental truths of faith and morals, progressive theological reflection, and also an openness to new results in the human sciences and the life situations of people today."[8] We propose progressive theological, anthropological, and ethical methodological reflections to reform Catholic sexual doctrine.

FOUNDATION OF CATHOLIC ETHICAL DOCTRINE: HUMAN DIGNITY

Many years ago, distinguished German theologian Karl Rahner emphasized the importance of anthropology for doing theology. "Today, dogmatic [and moral] theology must be anthropology and such an 'anthropological turn' is necessary and fruitful."[9] His insight remains and is perhaps even more essential today with respect to sexual anthropology. Catholic theology is grounded in human dignity.[10] What facilitates attaining human dignity is good and right, what frustrates attaining human dignity is evil and wrong, and knowing what facilitates or frustrates sexual human dignity requires a theological anthropology.

Catholic doctrinal teaching defines sexual human dignity as heterosexual, male-female natural complementarity that is principally intended for procreation. All artificially manipulated and non-reproductive sexual acts, it teaches, frustrate human dignity and alienate a person from God, others, and self. There is no small matter in sexual sins; according to Catholic tradition, all sexual sins are grave matter and are potentially mortal sins. In addition, sex and gender are intrinsically linked, though culture can impact our understanding of gender, and there is a strict sexual binary to which every person conforms.[11] It is this anthropology that defends absolute Catholic sexual, gender, and ethical doctrinal teaching. There is strict heterosexual complementarity between male and female and only reproductive sexual acts between them in marriage facilitate human dignity; all other intentional sexual acts frustrate human dignity. There is a strict division between male and female human nature, so that only male human nature, the Catholic Church teaches, can reflect *persona Christi* in priestly and diaconal ordination.

To reform Catholic doctrine, then, requires first and foremost the reform of Catholic theological anthropology. This reform depends on, and has implications for, reforms in ethical method, sacramental theology, ecclesiology, and pastoral theology. Before exploring and explaining this reform, however, we explain the sources of ethical knowledge for defining human dignity and formulating and justifying doctrines that facilitate, not frustrate, attaining it.

SOURCES OF ETHICAL KNOWLEDGE

There are four universally acknowledged sources of theological and ethical knowledge, the so-called Wesleyan Quadrilateral: scripture, tradition, reason/science, and human experience. All four of these sources contribute meanings to Catholic sexual ethics and all four need to be carefully listened to in any reform of Catholic sexual doctrine to discern either the truth in those doctrines or whether they need to be revised. Reigning Catholic doctrinal teaching emphasizes tradition, narrowly defined as church teaching, prioritizes this source, and uses it as a hermeneutical lens to select, interpret, prioritize, and integrate all the other sources. We emphasize the need to complement this narrow definition of tradition with a broader understanding that includes the *sensus fidelium* and the other three sources. We further emphasize that human experience demonstrates that human sexuality is not reducible to an exclusively or primarily biological meaning. Human meaning, Joseph Selling argues, "is the result of personal-social construction that is attributed to experience uniquely by human beings."[12] He cites with approval the assertion of the Congregation for the Doctrine of the Faith's (CDF) *Persona Humana* on the findings of the sciences with respect to human sexuality: "According to contemporary scientific research, the human person is so profoundly affected by sexuality that it must be considered as one of the factors which give to each individual's life the principle traits that distinguish it…[and] make that person a man or a woman, and thereby condition his or her progress toward maturity and insertion into society."[13]

Reviewing the scientific meanings of human sexuality uncovered by modern psychiatrists, psychologists, sociologists, and sexologists, Selling concludes that it necessarily includes, among other dimensions, "not only intimacy ('unitive') and fertility ('procreative') but also pleasure, recreation (play), relief, affirmation, receptivity, self-acceptance, forgiveness, reconciliation, gratitude… respect."[14] Discerning all those meanings and their interrelationship, we point out, is always a historically contextual task to be achieved not only by clerics but by the whole Church, informed by the lived experience of people in relationship. Those meanings are essential to a revised anthropology from which we can formulate and justify revised sexual doctrines.

A revised anthropology that recognizes differing priorities and nuances includes at least six dimensions.[15] First, it judges the biological-procreative definition of human sexual dignity offered by the church's anthropology as overly reductionist. Second, it fully accepts John Paul II's invitation to theologians and scientists to search for truth through "critical openness and interchange,"[16] and additionally accepts that this process of open dialogue may yield positions that challenge the church's definition of human sexual dignity and the sexual doctrines deduced from it. Third, it urges the inclusion of other voices besides the magisterium's and its "approved authors" ongoing discernment of the four theological sources (scripture, tradition, science, and experience) and of any selection, interpretation, prioritization, and integration of them into any definition of sexual human dignity. Fourth, it engages in an ongoing dialectic among all the sources of ethical knowledge, rather than prioritizing tradition narrowly defined as the magisterium as the hermeneutical lens for evaluating the insights and contributions of the other sources. Fifth, it manifests a greater degree of humility and tentativeness toward the conclusions of the magisterium, theologians, and scientists about human sexual dignity. Sixth, this humility and tentativeness demand that all theological and scientific judgments about human sexual dignity, including the church's, be subjected to confirmation or disconfirmation by human experience and the *sensus fidelium* of the entire body of the faithful.[17] The result of this process, we believe, will produce a holistic sexual anthropology that expands the church's biologically focused and ontologically prioritized anthropology.

ANTHROPOLOGY: SEXUAL, SOCIAL, HOLISTIC

There are inconsistencies in the Catholic doctrinal definitions of human dignity depending on whether the definition is supporting sexual or social doctrines. We consider these inconsistencies and propose holistic human dignity that integrates those two anthropologies and serves to reform Catholic sexual doctrines.

In chapter 4, we discuss John Paul II's ontological complementarity and propose holistic complementarity as a corrective for reforming Catholic anthropology and the doctrines deduced from it. Here we expand on that discussion to include Catholic social anthropology and Pope Francis's contributions.

Pope John Paul II's Sexual Anthropology

Pope John Paul II developed the most comprehensive definition of Catholic sexual human dignity in light of both past teachings, notably Pope Paul VI's encyclical *Humanae Vitae* and its prohibition of the use of artificial contraception in every act of sexual intercourse, and contemporary ethical issues, such as reproductive technologies and the social and cultural move to recognize the legality and morality of same-sex relationships. His introduction of ontological complementarity, which includes the biological and relational dimensions of human dignity, is a foundational concept in contemporary Catholic teaching that defines sexual human dignity and defends the church's absolute sexual ethical doctrines.

John Paul attempted to move the Catholic tradition beyond a biological, procreationist ontology and to develop the unitive, relational ontology of human sexuality by more fully developing personalist insights into human relationality. Sexuality, he argues, "by means of which man and woman give themselves to one another through the acts which are proper and exclusive to spouses is by no means something purely biological but concerns the innermost being of the human person as such." This is said to be a sign of "a total personal self-giving."[18] John Paul develops his philosophical personalism in conjunction with a reading of scripture to construct a theological anthropology, which others have called a "theology of the body."[19] This theology is grounded in a theological anthropology, developed from an interpretation of Genesis, of the communion between woman and man. Masculinity and femininity are "two 'incarnations' of the same metaphysical solitude before God and the world." These two ways of "'being a body'...complete each other" and are "two complementary ways of being conscious of the meaning of the body."[20] It is through the complementarity of female and male that a "communion of persons" can exist and that the two "become one flesh."[21]

Following John Paul's approach, complementarity has become a foundational concept in Catholic anthropological, sexual, and gender doctrines. Complementarity means that certain realities belong together and together produce a whole that neither can produce alone. We note the following characteristics of John Paul II's idea of complementarity. First, complementarity is nearly always classified along masculine and feminine lines.[22] Second, complementarity is often formulated as a "nuptial hermeneutics" in terms of bridegroom and bride.[23] Third, this nuptial hermeneutics reflects the relationship between Christ (bridegroom) and Christ's church (bride), and also leads to an argument for a male-only priesthood. Fourth, in his theological anthropology, John Paul II posits an "ontological complementarity" whereby men and women, though fundamentally equal and complete in themselves,[24] are incomplete as a couple.[25] Sexual complementarity completes the couple in marriage and reproductive sexual acts by bringing the masculine and feminine biological and psychological elements together in a unified whole. All intentional nonreproductive sexual acts, such as contraceptive and homosexual acts, damage this complementarity and frustrate human dignity. All three characteristics of complementarity—male/female, nuptial, and ontological—are evident in John Paul's and the church's teaching on sexual anthropological complementarity and have become foundational for Catholic sexual doctrinal teaching.

Pope John Paul II's Sexual Anthropology: A Critique

John Paul II's personalist anthropology and the church teaching based on it are good examples of how there can be a shift in terminology—for instance, human nature to human person—and still fall prey to neo-Scholastic conceptual and terminological baggage. It is putting new wine into old wineskins. While John Paul's works are laden with references to the person, personal dignity, and personal responsibility, these are frequently explained and defined in terms of "nature"[26] and more often than not ignore the lived human, relational experience of married couples.[27] He notes that "in the order of love a man can remain true to the person only in so far as he is true to nature. If he does violence to 'nature' he also 'violates' the person by making it an object of enjoyment rather than an object of love."[28] Contraception is a violent act against "nature" and it has a "damaging effect on love."[29] Love and procreation are intrinsically linked in John Paul's theology of the body and his teaching on complementarity, but in this relationship there is a clear prioritization of the biological over the personal and relational.[30] Heterogenital complementarity is the sine qua non and primary consideration for whether or not personal complementarity can be realized. If heterogenital complementarity is not present, as it is not present in homosexual acts, the sexual act is by definition "intrinsically disordered" and there can be no personal complementarity in it, regardless of the relational meaning of those acts for the two persons involved.

In a personalist-based theology, however, one must ask whether or not the biological can serve as an adequate foundation for the personal and relational. John Paul II and church teaching cite Genesis 1:27 to defend the prioritization of biology in their anthropology: "Christian anthropology has its roots in the narrative of human origins that appears in Genesis, where we read that 'God created man in his own image…male and female he created them.'…These words capture not only the essence of the story of creation but also that of the life-giving relationship between men and women, which brings them into intimate union with God."[31] That is not the contemporary Catholic understanding. The Second Vatican Council abandoned the focus on sexed bodies and replaced it with a focus on related persons. In marriage, a man and a woman enter into a personal covenant in which "the spouses mutually bestow and accept each other,"[32] not each other's bodies as was stated so biologically and physically in the 1917 Code of Canon Law.[33] This focus on interpersonal covenant brings marriage and all friendship relationships into line with the rich biblical traditions of covenant between God and God's people and Christ and Christ's Church.[34] John Paul II's and the Catholic Church's prioritization of biology over personal relationship in their interpretation of scripture and tradition to construct their anthropology is theologically outdated. Personal, covenantal relationship between God and women and men, not biology, is dominant in scripture.

All peoples, females, males, and the sexual varieties embraced in LGBTQI+, can enter into such covenantal relationships, each imaging the infinite God in her or his own unique way.

Creation's form and shape flow from God's relationship to it, they do not preexist that relationship. Relationship to God is primary; creation's materiality flows from that relationship. Even in God's creation of *'adam*, humankind, "God created humankind [*'adam*] in his image" (Gen 1:27). God creates humans through relationship first, and biological, sexed bodies are a manifestation of that relational creation. John's Gospel affirms this relational prioritization. It begins with the relationship between God Creator and God Savior. "In the beginning was the Word, and the Word was with God, and the Word was God....All things came into being through him, and without him not one thing came into being" (John 1:1, 3). The preferred Jewish masculine pronoun is used to designate God as spiritual, relational being, not as male-sexed, relational being. The relationship between God and God's Word is at the root of all creation, including the creation of female and male, which first flows from and manifests that relationship and only then reflects it in biological materiality. The shape and form of human beings derive from God's relationship with them. Just as Jesus's relationship with God the Creator was established before Jesus's sexed humanity, so too humans' relationship with God is established before their sexed humanity as female, male, or LGBTQI+. Relationship is primary; biology is secondary. In a wonderful way the reality of intersexed people, though statistically a human minority, confirms and privileges this relationality. It disrupts the biological, heterogenital complementarity that is foundational for Catholic sexual human dignity and the absolute doctrines that follow from that definition.

Therefore, we ask, should not personalism begin with a holistic understanding of the human person in all her or his psychological, emotional, relational, spiritual, and biological complexity? If it should, and we insist that it should, then the biological is only one dimension of the person, and it should not be given inordinate importance in the hierarchy of being as a foundation for sexual anthropology and doctrines deduced from it. Authentic personalism takes the particular human person in her or his sexual complexity and formulates doctrine for sexual relationships and identities out of a profound appreciation of that complexity, not on the primacy of heterogenital complementarity and biology. John Paul II's and the church's notion of complementarity lacks an appreciation and integration of the whole human person, biologically, psychologically, relationally, and spiritually. To the extent that Catholic sexual doctrine is based on Catholic sexual human dignity when it addresses sexual ethical issues, it also lacks this appreciation and integration of the whole person.

Catholic Social Human Dignity

The definition of Catholic sexual human dignity is foundational for the church to deduce Catholic sexual doctrines. It is not, however, the only definition of human dignity reflected in church teaching. Catholic social teaching links human dignity with the Catholic social principle of the common good and introduces a distinct definition of human dignity grounded in that social teaching. Citing its document *Economic Justice for All*, for example, the USCCB's *Ethical and Religious Directives for Catholic Health Care Services* notes that "the common good is realized when economic, political, and social conditions ensure protection for the fundamental rights of all individuals and enable all to fulfill their common purpose and reach their common goals."[35] Catholic social teaching is founded on two basic principles: human dignity and the social nature of human persons.[36] Catholic social human dignity is quite distinct from Catholic sexual human dignity in its emphasis on the principle of the common good as an essential anthropological dimension.

The social nature of human beings recognizes the interrelationship of, and the balance between, human dignity and the unique person created in the image and likeness of God and the social, political, economic, and environmental relationships in which that person exists. Theologian John Coleman labels the anthropological core of Catholic social teaching "communitarian liberalism," which consists of several interrelated dimensions: individual human dignity, the common good, human solidarity, a preferential option for the poor, distributive justice, subsidiarity or participatory justice, and stewardship.[37] As noted, individual human dignity is defined differently in Catholic teaching depending on the specific ethical issue. Catholic sexual human dignity prioritizes a biological ontology over a relational ontology; Catholic social human dignity considers the whole complex unity of social, relational, and biological dimensions of the human person and, depending on the ethical issue, may prioritize one dimension over another. For example, poverty and socioeconomic considerations, according to Pope Francis, can drive couples into de facto unions, which cannot be condemned, he argues, without due consideration of the existential context and circumstances. People's socioeconomic reality, over which they may not have control, impacts their sexual and relational decisions. Ethically evaluating such situations does not allow for a one-size-fits-all approach to sexual ethical issues, which it would require if Pope Francis was following a strict application of sexual doctrines deduced from a traditional Catholic sexual anthropology.

A fundamental epistemological question about the nature of the common good, similar to the question about human dignity, is whether there is a single definition or plural definitions of the common good. Different perspectives may define the common good differently and allow for plural responses to specific ethical issues. The common good and, therefore, Catholic social human dignity, recognizes and accepts pluralism. The CDF's International Theological Commission asserts that "in the context of pluralism, which is ours, one is more and more aware that one cannot elaborate a morality based on the natural law without including a reflection on the [subjective] interior dispositions or virtues [or perspectives] that render the moralist capable of elaborating an adequate norm of action."[38] This process of elaboration is evolving and pluralist: "The vision of the common good evolves with the societies themselves, according to conceptions of the person, justice, and the role of public power."[39] Pope Francis approvingly cites the ITC's document in *Amoris Laetitia*: "Natural law could not be presented as an already established set of rules that impose themselves *a priori* on the moral subject; rather, it is a source of objective inspiration for the deeply personal process of making decisions" (*AL* 35). Brian Stiltner accurately notes that "pluralism is central to the common good because different communities center on the pursuit of different components of the complex human good; because institutional diversity facilitates extensive participation in social life; and because no one association [including the Church and its noninfallible moral teachings] can claim to be a perfect community."[40] The challenge for the ongoing discernment of the meanings of the common good is to engage in what theologian David Hollenbach calls "social solidarity across cultures" in order to "attain a greater degree of shared moral vision."[41] This process takes time, patience, and a commitment to the "dialogue in charity," that Francis calls both "the first law of Christians" (*AL* 306) and "the highest and most central value of the gospel" (*AL* 311).

Just as church teaching recognizes plural definitions of human dignity, so too does it recognize plural definitions of the common good. Catholic teaching, in fact, is inconsistent in its definition of the common good. It assumes a narrow definition of the common good when it teaches absolute prohibitive doctrines on sexual ethical issues and it assumes a broad definition when it teaches more flexible doctrines on care for the poor and the environment. For example, the USCCB opposed the Respect for Marriage Act, passed by Congress in 2022 to protect legalized same-sex marriage, "in light of the [sexual] teaching of the Catholic Church and considerations for the common good."[42] The USCCB's narrow definition of the common good suggests, without any supporting evidence, that same-sex marriage threatens the common good. It, therefore, opposed such legislation and promoted discrimination against members of the LGBTQI+ community. The *Catechism of the Catholic Church*, however, following Catholic social anthropology, recognizes a broad definition of the common good that condemns discrimination of any form. "Social justice," it teaches, "is linked to the common good" (1928). Therefore, "every form of social or cultural discrimination in fundamental personal rights on the grounds of sex, race, color, social conditions, language, or religion must be curbed and eradicated as incompatible with God's design."[43] This inconsistency in Catholic teaching and its approach to the common good and discrimination depends on whether the church adheres to its biological sexual anthropology, which promotes discrimination against LGBTQI+ people, or its social anthropology, which condemns discrimination against them and all other human beings.

Catholic teaching embraces a broader definition of the common good when it treats social issues such as climate change and care and concern for the poor. This broader definition allows for plural analyses and ethical judgments about how a decision impacts, not only biological dimensions of human persons, but also their personal, social, economic, and political relationships. There is a clear tension in Catholic doctrinal teaching between Catholic social human dignity, which posits broad and pluralist definitions of the common good based on the discernment of conscience in community, and Catholic sexual human dignity, which posits a narrow and single definition of the common good as interpreted exclusively by the church's teaching authority. The mandate in *Gaudium et Spes* seems to be applied only to social issues and not to sexual issues: "In fidelity to conscience, Christians are joined with the rest of men [and women] in the search for truth, and for the genuine solution to the numerous problems which arise in the life of individuals from social relationships."[44]

Solidarity, and the conversion necessary to realize it, is a second dimension of Catholic social human dignity. Solidarity is at the heart of the theological foundation of Catholic social human dignity, and Pope Francis calls for "authentic solidarity" in social relationships.[45] He notes that "the suffering of others is a call to conversion, since their need reminds me of the uncertainty of my own life and my dependence on God and my brothers and sisters."[46] He proposes that solidarity is a virtue that fundamentally challenges and transforms indifference to the poor and is at the heart of the gospel and Catholic social teaching. Pope John Paul II provides a concise definition of the virtue of solidarity: "It is a firm and persevering determination to commit oneself to the common good; that is to say to the good of all and of each individual, because we are all really responsible for all."[47] The common good broadly defined includes all God's people, including LGBTQI+ people, where discrimination that alienates persons from the community based on their sexual orientation and identity can never promote human dignity or the common good. He further explains that solidarity is undoubtedly a Christian virtue. Indeed, "many points of contact between solidarity and charity, which is the distinguishing mark of Christ's disciples (cf. John 13:35),"[48] can be identified.

Subsidiarity or participatory justice is another essential anthropological component of the common good and Catholic social human dignity. The changing demographics of laity and clerics within the Catholic Church make it even more critical to engage in dialogue through the synodal process at all levels, to discern the formulation, interpretation, and application of Catholic sexual doctrine. The word *synod* is instructive; it derives from two Greek words, *syn* which means "together," and *hodos*, which means "journey." A synod, therefore, is journeying together, a church synod of all the members of the church, laity and clerics together, journeying together toward doctrinal and ethical truth.

Intimately related to the principle of subsidiarity is the process of consultation by church officials *before* formulating authoritative doctrines. Pope Francis has provided a model for this consultation in the processes of the Synods on Marriage and the Family. At its fall meeting of 2019, the German Bishops' Conference voted to establish what it called "the synodal way," which was inaugurated on the first day of Advent 2020, with a meeting of German Bishops and Germany's largest lay organization, Zentralkomittee der deutschen Katholiken. In synodal dialogue, together they voted to approve blessing same-sex relationships,[49] which Pope Francis later approved.[50] It is a very good start in a church that is essentially a communion of believers. Pope Francis has himself modeled commitment to a synodal way of dialogue. Dialogue, he teaches, "is born from an attitude of respect for the other person, from a conviction that the other person has something good to say. It assumes that there is room in the heart for the person's point of view, opinion, and proposal. To dialogue entails a cordial reception, not a prior condemnation," of those with differing theological visions. In order to dialogue, Pope Francis teaches, "it is necessary to know how to lower the defenses, open the doors of the house, and offer human warmth."[51] Dialogue should embrace not only "approved authors" but also all the competent members of the church, both those who agree and disagree with church teaching on specific ethical issues. Bishop Georg Bätzing, the president of the German Bishops' Conference, emphasizes the development of doctrine based on viable arguments, which include "progressive theological reflection."[52]

Bishops must learn to appreciate theological diversity and the importance of consulting laity, to consider their contributions as a manifestation of the Spirit at work in the church, not as a threat to be silenced or excluded from the table of discernment. It is telling that, to our knowledge, no theologian who promotes neoliberal capitalist theory, which is antithetical to Catholic social teaching, has been censured or silenced. However, numerous theologians who have theologically challenged Catholic sexual doctrine based, in large part, on the experiences and voices of the faithful, have been silenced, removed from tenured teaching positions, or fired from administrative positions. This inconsistency in how the church addresses *disagreements* with church teaching, a word Pope Francis prefers to *dissent*, is telling and highlights inconsistencies in subsidiarity and "dialogue" in the church when addressing either social or sexual ethical issues. Although the introduction of ideas that challenge official teaching may cause tension, that is no more than a way for a synodal church to move toward a fuller possession of the truth about the infinite God it believes in and what the Spirit of God may be asking of it in a pluralistic world.

Stewardship, the responsible use and allocation of limited resources, has a predominant and necessary place in Catholic social and sexual teaching. Discerning the responsible use and distribution of resources requires dialogue, where all people affected by stewardship decisions, especially the poor and most vulnerable, have a voice in the dialogue. Socioeconomic realities have a profound impact on human, sexual relationships, and this impact is often overlooked in church teaching that proposes one-size-fits-all sexual doctrines. An example of this oversight that further reflects the tension between sexual and social anthropology is Pope Francis's visit to the Philippines in January 2015, where a former homeless girl, Glyzelle Palomar, gave a heart-wrenching address to the pope and some thirty thousand young people gathered for Filipino youth Sunday. In that address, she burst into tears recounting her experience of homelessness. "There are many children neglected by their own parents. There are also many who became victims and many terrible things happened to them like drugs or prostitution. Why is God allowing such things to happen, even if it is not the fault of the children? And why are there only very few people helping us?"[53] Pope Francis responded to her with the compassion that has characterized his papacy, imploring Christians to learn how to weep in solidarity with those who suffer, especially the most vulnerable in society.

What was left unaddressed in both the pope's and the Philippine bishops' responses to Glyzelle's plight, and that of countless others like her, is the correlation between poverty and homelessness, especially among children, and the rigid stance of the Philippine bishops who stridently resist the legalization of birth control in the country. A Guttmacher Institute study indicates that 50 percent of all pregnancies in the Philippines are unintended and 90 percent of these unintended pregnancies are due to a lack of access to birth control.[54] Only in 2012 did Filipino lawmakers pass a bill for free family planning and access to contraceptives, legislation that the bishops of the Philippines fiercely resisted and continue to resist.[55]

There seems to be a surprising unawareness on the part of the pope and bishops worldwide of how patriarchal culture, gender norms, familial relations, and socioeconomic and political factors impact reproductive decisions in marriages. This lack of awareness reflects the fundamental methodological distinction, which we address in detail below, between Catholic social teaching and Catholic sexual teaching. The former prioritizes moral principles and criteria for careful discernment and personal judgment of an informed conscience; the latter prioritizes absolute moral proscriptive norms for submissive obedience. An integrated social and sexual ethical methodology would offer a general, formal principle, responsible parenthood, for example. An integrated social and sexual anthropology would allow a married couple to discern and judge in conscience a particular doctrine or norm to realize this formal principle in their contextual, relational, social, economic, and gender circumstances.

To summarize, Catholic teaching vacillates on its definition of Catholic social and sexual human dignity in relation to the common good. A narrow definition of the common good depends on a biologically prioritized sexual anthropology and emphasizes adherence to absolute proscriptive sexual norms. Following these absolute norms, it is suggested, realizes the common good and facilitates human dignity; violating these absolute norms violates the common good and frustrates human dignity. Individual conscience is made subservient to absolute norms and the church's authority. A broad definition of the common good depends on a relational, complex social anthropology and recognizes and embraces pluralism and its impact on the definition of human dignity. It prioritizes the authority and inviolability of a well-formed conscience to interpret relevant doctrines to make an ethical judgment of conscience, a process that may or may not coincide with absolute proscriptive sexual norms. In a broad understanding of the common good and social human dignity, differences are respected and engaged through the process of dialogue. In a narrow understanding, differences are suppressed by institutional authority. Pope Francis provides a roadmap for resolving the tension between a narrow and broad definition of the common good and its anthropological implications for human dignity by integrating the best of Catholic sexual and social human dignity in what we label Catholic holistic human dignity.

Catholic Holistic Human Dignity

In his apostolic exhortation *Amoris Laetitia*, Pope Francis has demonstrated an integration and expansion of Catholic sexual and social human dignity, and we call this integrated anthropology Catholic holistic human dignity. *Amoris Laetitia* recognizes the impact poverty has on human relationships and ethical decisions. Francis offers the example of a couple that cohabits "primarily because celebrating a marriage is considered too expensive in the social circumstances. As a result, material poverty drives people into *de facto* unions" (*AL* 294). He does not focus on these unions as a violation of the norm prohibiting unmarried sexual intercourse, but recognizes that socioeconomic realities profoundly impact human relationships, decisions, and morals. This real impact is often overlooked in church teaching that proposes one-size-fits-all moral norms in its prioritization of the biological over the relational in Catholic sexual human dignity. Francis focuses on relationship and the need to offer cohabiting couples constructive responses, seeking to transform them into opportunities that can lead to the full reality of marriage and family in conformity with the Gospel. These couples, he teaches, "need to be welcomed and guided patiently and discreetly" (*AL* 294). The integration of Catholic social and sexual teaching marks a profound shift in Catholic theological ethics.

We now present Pope Francis's Catholic holistic human dignity and compare the doctrinal implications of this anthropology with Catholic sexual human dignity as reflected in current Catholic doctrines. *Amoris Laetitia* reflects a holistic anthropology that draws from the relational emphasis in Catholic social human dignity and a relationally focused personalist anthropology in Catholic sexual human dignity. It closely reflects, in fact, the dimensions of the human person that moral theologian Louis Janssens developed over forty years ago in his exegesis of *Gaudium et Spes* and its preparatory document, Schema 13.[56] In *Amoris Laetitia*, the human person is a free subject, not an object (*AL* 33, 153); in corporeality, the physical and spiritual are integrated (*AL* 151); in relationship to the material world (*AL* 277), to others (*AL* 187–98), to social groups (*AL* 222), and to self (*AL* 32); created in the image and likeness of God (*AL* 10); a historical being (*AL* 193); fundamentally unique but equal to all other historical persons (*AL* 54). There are, however, fundamental sexual anthropological developments in *Amoris Laetitia*. In its absolute proscriptive norms, Catholic sexual human dignity prioritizes the biological function of the sexual act over its relational meanings; Francis emphasizes the relational and spiritual in ethical decision-making. *Amoris Laetitia* informs and complements Catholic sexual human dignity with insights from Catholic social human dignity and, in so doing, tempers and qualifies absolute sexual norms.

AMORIS LAETITIA AND ETHICAL METHODOLOGICAL DEVELOPMENTS

Amoris Laetitia introduced anthropological and methodological developments in Catholic teaching, leading Cardinal Schönborn of Vienna to judge that it "is the great text of theological ethics we have been waiting for since the days of the [Second Vatican] Council."[57] Vatican Cardinal Parolin notes that it indicates a "paradigm shift" that calls for a "new spirit, a new [method]" to help "incarnate the Gospel in the family."[58] *Amoris Laetitia* notes that the dialogue during the 2014 and 2015 Synods raised the suggestion of "new pastoral methods" that are tailored to different communities and the marital, familial, and relational realities of those communities (*AL* 199). It not only affirms but also develops the anthropology of Catholic social and sexual teaching and incorporates social teaching's methodological developments philosophically, focusing on inductive reasoning, historical consciousness, and an appreciation of culture, experience, and the sciences.

A major methodological shift in Catholic sexual teaching in *Amoris Laetitia* is from a deductive to an inductive ethical method. Deductive reasoning, which traditionally characterized both Catholic social and sexual teaching, begins with a universally accepted definition of human dignity and universal principles and doctrines that facilitate or frustrate its attainment. Inductive reasoning, which is a central methodological development in Catholic theological ethics since Vatican II, begins with particular, cultural, social, and contextual definitions of human dignity and formulates and justifies doctrines that facilitate or frustrate its attainment. Inductive reasoning begins with particular situations to attain universal insights.[59] "It is reductive," Pope Francis notes, "simply to consider whether or not an individual's actions correspond to a general law or rule, because that is not enough to discern and ensure full fidelity to God in the concrete life of a human being" (*AL* 304). We must begin with the particular, contextual reality of human persons to discern what old doctrine applies or what new doctrine needs to be formulated to address their reality. He cites with approval the International Theological Commission's statement that "natural law could not be presented as an already established set of rules that impose themselves *a priori* on the moral subject" (*AL* 305). This is the only time, in fact, that Francis mentions natural law in *Amoris Laetitia*, and it is mentioned in the context of a warning against a deductive approach to moral decision-making and promotes natural law as "a source of objective inspiration for the deeply personal process of making decisions" (*AL* 305).

Amoris Laetitia cites with approval, for the first time ever in Catholic sexual teaching, Thomas Aquinas's warning that, although there is necessity in general principles, the more we descend to matters of detail, the more frequently we encounter defects. "In matters of action," Aquinas writes, "truth or practical rectitude is not the same for all as to matters of detail, but only as to the general principles; and where there is the same rectitude in matters of detail, it is not equally known to all....The principle will be found to fail, according as we descend further into detail."[60] The devil, as the old saying goes, is in the details. Catholic theological ethicists often cite Aquinas's principle to refute claims to absolute sexual doctrines. By citing this text from Aquinas, at the very least, Francis is both cautioning against a deductive, one-norm-fits-all approach to ethical decision-making and emphasizing the importance of context and circumstances and an inductive approach.

Second, *Amoris Laetitia* recognizes historical consciousness in its law of gradualness, borrowed from John Paul II. This law acknowledges that the human being "knows, loves, and accomplishes moral good by different stages of growth."[61] This is illustrated best in Francis's discussion of the morality of cohabitation. Nowhere in his exhortation does he condemn cohabitation in blanket fashion, as he surely would have to do if he were following Catholic marital and sexual doctrines. Contrary to the *Final Report* from the synods that condemns all cohabitation, he makes a distinction between "cohabitation which totally excludes any intention to marry" (*AL* 53) and cohabitation dictated by "cultural and contingent situations" (*AL* 294), like poverty. He teaches that the latter cohabitation requires a "constructive response" that can lead to marriage when circumstances permit it. We have named the former nonnuptial cohabitation and the latter nuptial cohabitation.[62] Borrowing from Jesus's encounter with the Samaritan woman (John 4:7–30) and applying the law of gradualness, Francis accepts the latter "in the knowledge that the human being knows, loves, and accomplishes moral good by different stages of growth" (*AL* 295). The church must never "desist from proposing the full ideal of marriage, God's plan in all its grandeur" but, aware of all the historical, cultural, psychological, and "even biological" mitigating circumstances, she must also never desist from accompanying "with mercy and patience the eventual stages of personal growth as these progressively appear" (*AL* 308). Acknowledging the law of gradualness, Francis recognizes that some types of cohabitation may be genuinely loving relationships that, given the right circumstances, can grow into marriages. The same law of gradualness may be conscientiously discerned to apply to other ethical issues, communion for the divorced and remarried, for instance.

We note a third shift, dependent on the first and second ones, in philosophical method. Prior to the Second Vatican Council, ethical method and the approach to ethical questions, both social and sexual, were primarily classicist and deductive. They started with traditional abstract ethical principles, formulated absolute doctrines from those principles in Catholic sexual teaching, and then applied those principles and doctrines to every sexual situation and act. *Gaudium et Spes* opened the church to a different approach, a historically conscious, inductive approach that starts with the human person and the human situational experience and works upward to specific ethical doctrines and general ethical principles. It emphasizes that, "thanks to the experience of past ages, the progress of the sciences, and the treasures hidden in the various forms of human culture, the nature of man himself is revealed and new roads to truth are opened."[63] This trilogy, human experience, culture, and science, is paradigmatic for an inductive approach to ethics and is widely reflected in *Amoris Laetitia*.

First, *Amoris Laetitia* is based on "the joy of love experienced by families [that] is also the joy of the Church" (*AL* 1). It is grounded in experience and bases its reflections on both the experience of actual married life and the human sexuality complexly reflected in it, along with socioeconomic factors like poverty and hunger that so impact it throughout the world (*AL* 25). Relating human experience to the formulation of doctrines, ethicist Margaret Farley asserts, and we agree, that doctrines cannot become effective in the church merely "from receiving laws or rules," for reception "entails at the very least a discernment of the meaning of laws and rules in concrete situations."[64] Such discernment requires reflection on human experience—personal, social, and religious—and the social sciences throw revealing light on that experience. We agree wholeheartedly with Farley's further assertion that "it is inconceivable that moral norms can be formulated without consulting the experience of those whose lives are at stake."[65]

Second, *Amoris Laetitia* recognizes and embraces the importance of particular cultural contexts. This concern for the import of experiential and cultural particularity was initially evident in the two Synods that presented surveys to, and requested feedback from, Catholic faithful on their lived experiences in relationship to church teaching. Taking these reflections to heart, *Amoris Laetitia* notes that "each country or region...can seek solutions [to moral and/or pastoral issues] better suited to its culture and sensitive to its traditions and local needs" (*AL* 3). The sciences, finally, can be helpful for the education, growth, and development of children in families (*AL* 273, 280).

Amoris Laetitia demonstrates some theological development in its use of scripture and ecclesiological perspective when approaching marital, familial, and sexual ethical issues. First, there is a shift to virtue, highlighted best in chapter 4's beautiful reflection on Saint Paul's paeon to love in 1 Corinthians (13:4–7). There is a fundamental shift from proscriptive norms to virtues and to scripture as a pedagogical source for virtues in a marital and ethical life. *Amoris Laetitia*'s use of scripture on issues like marriage and divorce, however, is at times selective and incomplete. It presents Matthew's teaching on the indissolubility of marriage (Matt 19:6), for example, but fails to mention his permission of divorce in the case of *porneia* (Matt 19:9). It also fails to acknowledge the reality that the church has granted and continues to grant divorce via the Pauline Privilege, based on Paul's teaching in 1 Corinthians 7:12–15, and has historically also granted them via the so-called Petrine Privilege, based on marital situations caused by slavery.[66] It does not cite any scriptural text to condemn same-sex relationships and avoids much of the proof-texting of scripture that earlier church documents utilize when addressing specific ethical issues.

Much like Catholic social teaching that empowers local bishops' conferences to formulate and apply teaching on the basis of their particular cultural and socioeconomic contexts, *Amoris Laetitia* refers extensively to bishops' conferences and how they have responded to particular ethical questions with respect to married and family life (Korean bishops, *AL* 42; Spanish bishops, *AL* 32; Mexican bishops, *AL* 51). Pope Francis has made a concerted effort toward subsidiarity and decentralization of power and has attempted to empower bishops' conferences. The consultation of the laity before and during both synods shows his commitment also to *sensus fidelium* and church synodality. Some theological explanation is needed here. *Sensus fidelium* is a theological concept that denotes "the instinctive capacity of the whole church to recognize the infallibility of the Spirit's truth."[67] It is a charism of discernment, possessed by the whole church, that receives a teaching as apostolic and is, therefore, to be held in both faith and *praxis*. *Lumen Gentium* is clear:

> The body of the faithful as a whole, anointed as they are by the Holy One [cf. 1 John 2:20; 2:27], cannot err in matters of belief. Thanks to a supernatural sense of the faith [*sensus fidelium*] which characterizes the people as a whole, it manifests this unerring quality when, "from the bishops to the last of the faithful,"[68] it manifests universal agreement in matters of faith and morals.[69]

Any effort to evaluate a church teaching will automatically include open dialogue, uncoerced judgment, and free consensus. That is the way genuine, authentic, and universal *sensus fidelium* is formed. Surveys of laity leading up to the synods, which attempt to include the voices from those surveys, clearly reflect a useful process for discerning *sensus fidelium*.

This discernment is a complex process, which takes time, patience, and a commitment to the kind of honest and charitable dialogue that Pope Francis so appreciated at the 2014 Synod on Marriage and the Family and characterized as "a spirit of collegiality and synodality."[70] Some see a defining characteristic of his papacy as seeking to realize synodality, the ecclesiology of Vatican II that focuses on seriously journeying together and listening to the input from all quarters of the church, laity and clerics alike, to engage in charitable, honest, and constructive dialogue to discern God's will and the path the church must follow to live according to that will. The two synods that laid the foundation for *Amoris Laetitia* modeled this dialogue in a way that synods in the past have not done. Synodality is a central and defining dimension of Pope Francis's papacy and will open the door to further dialogue and doctrinal reform.[71]

Amoris Laetitia and New Pastoral Methods

Pope Francis notes that the two synods preceding *Amoris Laetitia* "raised the need for new pastoral methods…that respect both the church's teaching and local problems and needs" (*AL* 199). The proposal of new pastoral methods draws from both philosophical and theological methods and lights a pathway to greater methodological consistency between Catholic social and sexual teaching. *Amoris Laetitia* makes some progress in integrating the two methodological perspectives of Catholic social and sexual teaching, especially in its reflection on economic-driven cohabitation, but more integration is needed.

This integration has profound implications for how we consider ethical truth and how we formulate and justify doctrine to guide human consciences. First, it is the role, function, and inviolable authority of a well-formed conscience to determine whether or not a doctrine has anything to say about a person's particular life situation. Highlighting irregular situations, Francis seems to indicate that not only is the situation irregular but the doctrine guiding the situation is also irregular, and conscience must discern which doctrine to select and how to interpret and apply it in any given situation. In the case of the divorced and remarried without an annulment, for instance, it is not the case that a couple may be permitted to take communion as an exception to the general doctrine; it is that the doctrine itself does not apply to the different situations of all divorced couples. Second, as irregular situations gradually become regular, as is now the case with cohabiting couples already committed to marry one another, our nuptial cohabitors, and couples practicing artificial contraception in their marital relationship, there may need to be a reform or "organic development of doctrine,"[72] perhaps similar to the development of the doctrines on slavery, usury, religious freedom, and capital punishment that fundamentally changes the doctrine. Even though *Amoris Laetitia* changes no specific Catholic doctrines,[73] its anthropological and methodological developments lay the foundation for doctrinal change, in much the same way that Pope John XXIII's encyclical *Pacem in Terris* laid a sure foundation for the Second Vatican Council's *Dignitatis Humanae* and its entirely reformulated doctrine on religious freedom.

On the basis of *Amoris Laetitia*'s anthropological focus on conscience, discernment, and a virtue-based approach to communal decision-making, we can anticipate some doctrinal development on sexual ethical issues in the Catholic church and a reform of many absolute proscriptive sexual norms that many of the faithful, via discerning consciences, have already revised and are at peace with. These developments will be supported by Francis's methodological focus on inductive reason, historical consciousness, appreciation of culture, integration of the sciences, explicit concern for the impact of socioeconomic conditions on relationships, critical use of scripture, a communion-synodal ecclesiology, and the introduction of new pastoral methods that acknowledge the reality and legitimacy of a well-formed conscience. We consider many of the sexual doctrinal teachings that need to be reformed in the chapters that follow.

2

TRAUMA, LANGUAGE, SEXUAL AND RELIGIOUS VIOLENCE*

"All sins of impurity of whatever kind or species are of themselves mortal."[1] It is clear that sexual abuse, including clerical sexual abuse, is a form of sexual violence that induces personal trauma in those violated. What is not so clear is that Catholic doctrinal sexual language continues not only to enable clerical sexual abuse and its cover-up but also to induce the personal trauma of shame and guilt in Catholic believers.[2] In this chapter, we first define various types of trauma and their physical, emotional, psychological, and spiritual effects. We then explore both the power and authority of language to enable, cause, and justify personal trauma, and how the language of Catholic sexual ethical teaching functions to cause sexual trauma.

TRAUMA: TYPES AND EFFECTS

Trauma is the state of being overwhelmed, physically, emotionally, psychologically, or spiritually by an external threat. This threat can originate from individuals, nature via natural disasters, society, culture, laws, policies, and religious teachings. A particularly grave form of trauma is that which originates from a trusted

---

* We are grateful to Dr. Julia Feder, who coauthored this chapter. See her *Incarnating Grace: A Theology of Healing from Sexual Trauma* (New York: Fordham University Press, 2024).

authority, such as a parent, a sibling, a spouse, a friend, or a cleric of any rank. Traumatic experiences objectively and seriously threaten the sufferer, inducing a feeling of being overwhelmed. The traumatic experience must be interpreted by the subject as threatening in order to qualify as traumatic.[3] In addition, the feeling of being overwhelmed remains with the sufferer long after the immediate threat has passed. More than just creating negative stress for the sufferer, "traumas represent destruction of basic organizing principles by which we come to know self, others, and the environment; traumas wound deeply in a way that challenges the meaning of life."[4]

Traumatic experiences associated with religion are particularly devastating, since the very essence of religion is about questions related to the ultimate meaning and purpose of life. When traumatic experiences emerge from religious authorities, institutions, or doctrinal teachings, the impact is not only in the present and future in this life but also is believed to have implications for eternal life. Catholic doctrinal teaching that all sexual sins are potentially mortal sins, for example, has implications for one's eternal salvation. It is not uncommon that LGBTQI+ people are traumatized by religious language that teaches that their sexual identity is "objectively disordered,"[5] and that eternal punishment is a consequence of sexual acts in accord with that identity. Religious trauma is unique in both its present and eternal implications. It adds spiritual components to the standard physical, emotional, psychological effects of trauma.

Effects of Trauma

The effects of traumatic violence are broad reaching, both the spirit and the body are negatively affected in the act of violence. Traumatic wounding can damage the wholeness of the human person on multiple levels: personally, interpersonally, socially, and spiritually. On the personal level, traumatic violence can block the victim's attention to both present and new reality. Because the traumatized individual is giving her attention to the past traumatic event, she encounters difficulties in responding to any new perceptions that are unrelated to the original traumatic event. If the new perception has some relationship to the original traumatic memory, such as a similar smell or sound, the new perception can trigger the past traumatic memory and the victim's response to this new event is really a replayed reaction to the old event.[6] A child who is sexually abused by a priest, for example, can experience the trauma from that event whenever she enters a church and smells incense, since that smell is associated with the original traumatic event.

Some trauma theorists hypothesize that the fixation on traumatic memories at the expense of taking in new information has a neurological basis. Bessel van der Kolk, for example, writes,

> When people develop posttraumatic stress disorder (PTSD), the replaying of the trauma leads to sensitization with every replay of the trauma, there is an increasing level of distress. In those individuals, the traumatic event, which started out as a social and interpersonal process, comes to have secondary biological consequences that are hard to reverse once they become entrenched.... This new organization of experience is thought to be the result of interactive learning patterns, in which trauma-related memories become kindled; that is, repetitive exposure etches them more and more powerfully into the brain.[7]

These biological (mal)adaptations ultimately form the underpinnings of the remaining PTSD symptoms: problems with arousal, attention, and stimulus discrimination, and a host of psychological elaborations and defenses. Underlying van der Kolk's claim is the belief that traumatic memories are qualitatively different than other kinds of memories. "There is a dramatic difference between the ways people experience traumatic memories and the ways they experience other significant personal events.... The very nature of a traumatic memory is to be dissociated, and to be stored initially as sensory fragments that have no linguistic components."[8]

Traumatic triggers can easily so overwhelm people that they become accustomed to "life happening *to* them"[9] rather than actively forging life by their own agency, even in matters as mundane as keeping to a schedule or securing a job. This lack of agency in everyday life mirrors the lack of a sense of agency in the original traumatic encounter(s). Trauma researchers refer to this posttraumatic process of being overwhelmed again as the alternation between the intrusion of the original traumatic event, as triggered by a new sensory event, and the personal numbing as the victim shuts down as a means of coping. These extreme states can present themselves so frequently that their alternation can be mistaken as a permanent and central feature of the victim's personality. Psychiatrist Judith Herman calls this a "costly error" because it can suggest that these symptoms cannot be ameliorated with treatment.[10] The original traumatic event as an experience of helplessness endures in continued experiences of disempowerment throughout one's posttraumatic life. Trauma victims struggle to secure a sense of their own integrity, a foundation for positive self-esteem and a basic degree of autonomy or individual competence.[11] In addition, trauma survivors often suffer from elevated cortisol levels and corresponding diseases related to increased inflammation, like cancer, diabetes, autoimmune diseases, obesity, and allergies.[12]

On the interpersonal level, sexual and other types of trauma can present barriers to healthy adult relationships, especially healthy sexual relationships. Researchers have identified a correlation between sexual abuse in childhood with risky sexual behaviors later in life, including a higher number of sexual partners and less condom use,[13] higher rates of marital separation, and higher rates of self-reported dissatisfaction in sexually intimate relationships.[14] In nonsexual relationships, interpersonal challenges persist. Traumatized individuals often struggle with issues of trust, of maintaining healthy boundaries with others, and maintaining a sense of their own desires as distinct from, and in some cases conflicting with, the desires of another.[15]

On a sociopolitical level, trauma can work to dismantle trust in the fundamental structures of human social organization, family, education, and religion. In traumatized individuals, it is perhaps truer than in any others that the personal is the political. Judith Herman argues that "rape and combat might thus be considered complementary social rites of initiation into the coercive violence at that foundation of adult society."[16] The habitual violation of the bodies or minds of those who are vulnerable in society creates a sense of normalcy surrounding grave acts of injustice such that they become part of the fabric of the ordinary social order.[17] Institutions—familial, educational, or religious—are no longer seen to be safe zones that protect and promote justice and security, but are perceived as threatening and destabilizing.

Medically diagnosable traumatic stress is typically classified by psychologists as PTSD. This classification, however, can give the false impression that trauma is homogenous. In reality, trauma is a "spectrum of conditions rather than a single disorder" united by "family resemblances."[18] The *kind* of traumatic violence experienced; the *context* in which it was originally experienced; and the *profile* of the victim, age, sex, prior mental health, genetic predisposition,[19] all influence the degree of persistent traumatic wounding. Subjective characteristics of the perception of the event contribute to the degree of traumatic wounding along with the reaction of others when the victim tells what has happened to her or him.[20] A particularly damaging reaction in the case of clerical sexual abuse occurs when the victim is not believed by parents or family members, is punished for making what trusted others label a "false accusation," or is personally blamed for the abuse.

On a spiritual-religious level, sexual trauma inevitably transforms the way its victims understand the relationship of God to created reality. This is often labeled "spiritual abuse" by survivors of clerical sexual abuse. It is "a form of emotional and psychological abuse" that "is characterized by a systematic pattern of coercive and controlling behavior in a religious context." It "can have a deeply damaging impact on those who experience it."[21] Where perhaps individuals had once perceived the world as a safe place, after an experience of abuse they may question their safety and the safety of those they love. Where perhaps individuals once perceived God as a protective figure, they may now perceive God as indifferent to human suffering or even as one who punishes unatoned sins with violence. For some who have never experienced a safe environment, a threatening or distant vision of God shapes their spiritual imagination and is reinforced by trauma.

Sexual trauma can affect religious belief in a multitude of ways, but at least one study shows that only a *small* percentage of individuals become *more* religious following sexual trauma. It is much more likely that sexual trauma generates greater secularization.[22] Because strong supportive relationships are critical to the recovery process, secularization, particularly if it is accompanied by increased social isolation, can create barriers to recovery. For the minority who react to sexual abuse with intensified religious practice, it tends to be only a source of external engagement rather than a tool for deeply examining the self.[23]

Types of Trauma

The most obvious form of traumatic experience is an experience of "direct trauma"—one in which the traumatized individual directly experienced sexual abuse, interpersonal violence, war, a natural disaster, genocide, or the like. The destruction of one's cultural community or an experience of dislocation are also direct traumas.[24] Individuals can also suffer from "indirect" or "secondary trauma" when a traumatic event is caused by a close relational other or when an individual directly witnesses violence happening to another. Therapists can often suffer from secondary trauma as they listen to and absorb the experiences of their patients.[25]

"Complex trauma" occurs when an individual does not experience only one traumatic event but is exposed to repetitive, prolonged stressors. Over time, the cumulative effect of repeated exposure to traumatic experiences of sexual abuse or ongoing discriminatory language puts individuals at increased risk of developing traumatic symptoms in response to a traumatic experience. Notably, a family history of trauma exposure—not directly experienced by the individual herself but experienced by her parents or grandparents—can put an individual at increased risk. Children of Holocaust survivors, for instance, have been discovered to be at high-risk for developing PTSD themselves.[26] Some researchers suggest the risk for developing severe PTSD is better predicted, not through exposure to a single traumatic experience, as much as through cumulative exposure to trauma,[27] including the more insidious forms of "cumulative stress."

The cumulative stress of living in a sexist, racist, homophobic society or religious tradition puts women, people of color, and gays and lesbians at greater risk of developing traumatic symptoms. To describe this negative effect of cumulative stress endured over time, trauma theorists have developed the terms *chronic trauma* or *insidious trauma*.[28] In chronic trauma, social environments, victim-blaming, isolation, and loss of social status are maintained through everyday experiences of discrimination and dehumanization.[29] Rather than a dramatic interruption of violence that shatters an otherwise intact worldview, insidious trauma often shapes one's worldview from birth following experiences of constant violence.[30] Philosopher Theresa Tobin argues that doctrinal misogyny in the Roman Catholic Church functions as a chronically traumatic kind of "quiet violence" that erodes women's agency, beginning at birth and building momentum over the course of life.[31] One could extend such not-so-quiet violence to Catholic bishops and doctrinal language that actively and publicly promotes discrimination against members of the LGBTQI+ community. Such discrimination is justified by what Johanna Stiebert labels "abusive theology":

> As with other kinds of abuse, power relations play a key role in abusive theology. Consequently, groups disenfranchised in terms of representation and agency—women, children, LGBTQI persons, persons with disabilities—are disproportionately targeted in spiritual abuse. Such abuse is predominantly perpetrated by hegemonic men in positions of authority: be that in faith communities, the family or the public sphere.[32]

Such abusive theology and not-so-quiet violence is evident in recent sexual policies for Catholic schools in many dioceses in the United States that specifically target and discriminate against LGBTQI+ persons.[33] Insidious trauma is experienced by individuals, but it is directed at whole groups of people, like women, people of color, gays, and lesbians, whose intrinsic identity is socially devalued.[34]

Most people assume that we are all vulnerable, to a certain degree, to traumatic events. Indeed, humanity on the whole possesses a "universal vulnerability" to car accidents, illnesses, and natural disasters. Traumatic violence, however, whether direct, complex, or chronic, which involves malicious intent, like rape, child sexual abuse, discrimination based on race or sexual orientation or identity, contributes to the perception of its victims as possessing "unique vulnerability" because of their personal identity.[35] The unique vulnerability of women, children, gays and lesbians, religious minorities, and people of color reinforces victim-blaming and can increase the risks of developing PTSD in response to a traumatic event.[36] When survivors come together to share their experiences with each other, this can reduce feelings of isolation and mitigate internalized blame.[37]

SPIRITUAL VIOLENCE AND RELIGIOUS TRAUMA

It is not uncommon for sexually abusive clergy to use religious objects as weapons in predatory activities—for example, using a crucifix to rape children.[38] It is even more common for religious leaders to use religious rituals like the confessional or their own exalted, so-called ontologically changed status to target vulnerable individuals[39] and to groom them for sexual and violent behavior. More common and ubiquitous forms of religious trauma that cause spiritual violence are dehumanizing doctrinal teachings, which claim that a person's very identity is objectively disordered and has a strong propensity toward intrinsically evil acts that can lead to eternal damnation.[40] Such trauma is direct, chronic, and insidious.

Religious trauma, which involves "religious means to violate a person's spiritual self,"[41] has both a religious cause and a religious effect. In instances of direct trauma, and sometimes in instances of chronic trauma, the traumatized self creates a "shattered worldview,"[42] a distorted worldview that hinges on the self as fundamentally disordered and incapable of receiving the fullness of human or divine love. As in all trauma, the subjective interpretation of the traumatized individual matters. Religious trauma is

> a traumatic experience perceived by the subject to be caused by the divine being, religious community, religious teaching, religious symbols, or religious practices that transforms the individual, either epistemically or not-merely-cognitively, in such a way that their capacity to participate in religious life is significantly diminished.[43]

This diminishment can be a persistent subjective feeling of inferiority or sinfulness based on religious teachings or practices that drive people from participation. It can also be objectively experienced through imposed religious sanctions, like denial of sacraments based on a judgment of one's identity, judgment and condemnation rather than mercy and compassion in the confessional, or disciplinary actions, including expulsion from Catholic schools or hospitals. A same-sex spouse or transgender person who is denied a Catholic burial, lesbian or gay teachers and counselors or unmarried pregnant women who are dismissed from Catholic schools, are all examples of objective sanctions.

Spiritual violence can diminish or even destroy religious faith, causing what philosopher Michelle Panchuk calls "non-culpable failure to worship God," or "religious incapacitation."[44] In the case of clerical sexual abuse, this specific type of religious trauma has been described by Thomas Doyle as *soul murder*. Victims of clerical abuse are betrayed by priests, the church, and, from their perspective, God. These betrayals lead to a spiritual death and an inability to find refuge or solace in an all-loving, compassionate, merciful God, or even to imagine such a God, causing additional depression, anxiety, and hopelessness.[45]

Secondary Religious Trauma

Even when individuals have not suffered directly and subjectively from the language or actions of the church and clerics, it is possible to suffer from secondary religious trauma if one closely identifies with one's religious identity and perceives that identity to be hostile to, or the cause of violence in, other's lives. David Turnbloom and his colleagues argue that many Roman Catholic laypersons suffer from secondary religious trauma and spiritual injury in response to the clerical sexual abuse of minors, as their trust in the spiritual integrity of their church leaders has been severely damaged.[46] Participation in the liturgical life of the Church can be retraumatizing for laity, since Catholic liturgical life is centered on the ordained priest who is said to mediate Christ to the worshiping community. To the extent that the liturgical rituals of the church maintain the exalted status of the priest above the people he serves, laity can be overwhelmed by a doubly binding feeling of both powerlessness and guilt for the unethical actions of Catholic clerics. When this occurs, "these liturgical rituals cease to be primarily provocative signs of God's love and are rather experienced as participation in systematic sexual [and doctrinal] assault."[47]

The Catholic Church is implicated in all of these types of trauma and sexual and spiritual violence. Priests and bishops have been accused and prosecuted for the sexual abuse of children and the rape of men and women, including vowed religious women. Bishops have been found to be complicit in the institutional cover-up of such abuse, compounding the trauma suffered by victims and further damaging trust in the church. Doctrinal language has directly enabled this abuse and its cover-up. It also causes trauma by creating a hostile and discriminatory atmosphere for Catholic LGBTQI+ faithful through the ethical sexual teaching, which labels their basic identity "objectively disordered," promotes just discrimination against them, absolutely condemns any and all homosexual acts, and leads to the denial of sacraments to them and their children. In addition, Catholic sexual teaching in general, which recognizes no "parvity of matter" in sexual sins, threatens eternal damnation for anyone who violates those teachings. Finally, Catholic sacramental theology that limits ordination to men is perceived by some as misogynistic and discriminatory and can be a source of trauma, especially for women.

DOCTRINAL LANGUAGE AND TRAUMA: ENABLING AND CAUSING

Doctrinal language often creates extreme instances of the trauma generated by the sexual violence of clerical sexual abuse and rape. In this section, we explore doctrinal language and its use to enable clerical sexual abuse and its cover-up and to cause trauma. We first, however, explore the interrelationship between language, power, and authority that shapes both institutions and their members, both abusers and abused.

Language, Power, and Authority

Irish psychotherapist Marie Keenan has extensively researched the Catholic clerical sex-abuse crisis. She explores the importance of language in constructing social phenomena that contribute to that crisis,[48] and argues that the pathology that led to the abuse is supported and perpetuated, in large part, by an institutional culture constructed and reinforced by the language of religious authorities. She emphasizes the power of language that defines both institutions and their human subjects. This language is evident in the doctrinal language that teaches that the church is the "spotless bride of Christ," in sacramental language that emphasizes the "ontological change" in the one ordained to the priesthood, and in the ethical language that establishes that there is "no parvity of matter" in sexual sins, with the consequent threat of eternal damnation for any sexual transgression. This language promotes a deep suspicion of human sexuality,[49] as well as structures of church governance, and of seminary training that promotes clericalism and the lack of transparency and accountability in order to protect the church's good name. While Keenan's focus is on how language creates a culture that shapes and enables the clerical sex abuser, we argue that language not only *enables* abusers but also, in the case of the Catholic language of sexual morality, *inflicts* trauma on the Catholic faithful. We delve deeper into each of these, ecclesiology, sacramentology, and sexual moral theology in the chapters that follow.

Keenan explains how language is a manifestation of power. Too often, we approach reality as if it is natural and established, and language functions to establish and describe that reality. Scholars recognize a dialogical relationship between language and reality: language first establishes reality and then it is, in turn, shaped by the language-established reality. Language, in plain words, first forms and then is formed by reality. When language changes, reality changes; when reality changes, language changes. We inquire into the nature of the relationship between language and reality.

Michel Foucault explores this question in depth and argues that coercive power shapes and permeates every aspect of reality and is psychologically oppressive for those who do not hold and exercise that power. He argues that knowledge and power are indistinguishable in expert disciplines, such as psychiatry, law, and we add, also theology. These disciplines reproduce, reinforce, and control dominant social relationships through language and knowledge. Commenting on Foucault, Gerald Arbuckle correctly notes, "People who control specialized disciplines, for example, government officials, mass media moguls, and religious leaders, hold extraordinary power in society, power that can rarely be questioned by outsiders."[50] The experts in these disciplines define the reality and truth which is beyond question except by the experts themselves.

There are several important points to note regarding Foucault's theory of power, language, and the Catholic Church as institution. First, analyzing the Catholic Church and power, there is an incommensurability between the expert disciplines of Catholic theology and canon law compared to other expert disciplines. The Catholic Church teaches that Christ's church "subsists in" it[51] and that it has the imprimatur of God himself so that its authority and truth are largely placed beyond question. Even when Pope John Paul II admitted to historical and current failings in the church, it was the failings of "the past and present sins of her sons and daughters," not of the church herself.[52] Maintaining the purity of the church, its holiness, and authority beyond reproach is essential to an institution that claims to be beyond question and whose integrity or good name must be protected at all costs, even to the point of covering up sex abuse by its clergy. Professional disciplines such as law, psychology, psychiatry, and psychotherapy do not have the divine power and authority to support their knowledge claims and, therefore, are subject to the evaluation, judgment, and integration based on how power and authority is exercised in the Catholic Church.

In the Congregation for Catholic Education's (CCE) *Guidelines for the Use of Psychology in the Admission and Formation of Candidates for the Priesthood*, we read, "Inasmuch as it is the fruit of a particular gift of God, the vocation to the priesthood and its discernment lie outside the strict competence of psychology. Nevertheless, in some cases, recourse to experts in the psychological sciences can be useful."[53] Even though other expert disciplines, such as psychology, are said to be "useful," vocation directors, who are very often not trained in psychology, hold the trump card as experts in making judgments about a candidate's suitability for admission to a seminary and subsequent ordination. Given the sexual abuse committed by candidates first admitted to seminaries and then ordained as priests, it seems clear that other expert disciplines should be utilized more fully to screen candidates.

In her presentation to the United States Conference of Catholic Bishops in November 2009, Margaret Smith, a member of the committee that authored the John Jay Report on Catholic Abuse, stated the following:

> What we are suggesting is that the idea of sexual identity be separated from the problem of sexual abuse. At this point, we do not find a connection between homosexual identity and the increased likelihood of subsequent abuse from the data that we have right now.[54]

This conclusion has been replicated by other sources but, despite this conclusion and the expert psychological disciplines that support it, the church continues to teach that seminarians and priests with "a homosexual tendency" should not be admitted to seminary or ordained to the priesthood. This is an example of the power and authority of the church and its nonprofessional experts overriding and ignoring the evidence of genuine professional experts.

Second, the ability to question the power, authority, and truth claims of the Catholic Church is evident not only in extensive professional reports, such as the John Jay Report, but also in the silencing of theological experts who do not enjoy clerical power in the church and argue for changes in church sexual teaching. Charles Curran, Margaret Farley, and the authors of this book are among the expert theologians who have suffered church sanctions for challenging the language, authority, and teaching of clerical authorities on Catholic sexual teaching.

Third, there is a certain church approach to these fields of expertise, such that discoveries in one area of expertise, the science of human sexuality, for instance, is dependent on its acceptance by church theologians and doctrinal language. If any clerics judge that any discipline is threatening the power or authority of the church, that discipline is simply deemed to be inaccurate, false, or irrelevant, not as the outcome of a professional examination but simply as an affirmation of the power and authority of a particular church discipline. We see such a situation in Catholic doctrinal teaching on social ethics versus sexual ethics. The discipline of Catholic social ethics has engaged in dialogue with climate science and integrated science's expertise into its own language and adjusted its own language to reflect that science.[55] However, the discipline of Catholic sexual ethics, which teaches that homosexual orientation is an "objective disorder," has failed to integrate the findings of science and psychology on human sexuality that judge homosexual orientation a normal development of human sexuality and sexual expressions between lesbians and gays as potentially as just and loving as any heterosexual expressions. This exercise of church power and theological language and the ignoring of scientific research on human sexuality illustrate well Foucault's thesis on language and power.

Those with power and authority, clerics in a male-dominated, hierarchical church, use language, especially language about sacramental ordination and human sexuality, to construct a reality that is said to be beyond question because established by God. Foucault argues that "normative judgments," in our discussion "doctrinal language," often do not reflect objective reality. Rather, such judgments or doctrines that are posited as true are deduced from "practices and customs that are reified over time" and become codified through authoritative teachers and repetition that makes them appear to be objectively true. Theologian Bradford Hinze sums up well the interrelationship between power, authority, and normative judgments. "In the process of 'reification,' the 'power relations at play in their creation' are elided."[56] Power structures that are at the root of Catholic doctrine recede into the background and we are left with doctrine that claims to be objectively true and revealed by God, regardless of critical-analytical thinking and reasoned argument from outside voices to the contrary.

How reality is "languaged" and the nature of that "languaged" reality is dictated by those in power and authority and determines whether it is privileged over other realities and defines the core features of that reality.[57] That reality shapes and constructs a subject's self-identity. Drawing from Foucault, theologian Richard Gaillardetz applied his understanding of power as domination to "the harmful structures and habits of power enacted in the Catholic Church, past and present."[58] That power and domination are manifested in the language of sacramental ordination and human sexuality. In the case of priestly ordination, doctrinal language that claims an "ontological change" creates a culture of clericalism that enables sexual abuse and its cover-up.[59] Sexual doctrinal language can cause personal trauma and spiritual abuse by promoting discrimination against LGBTQI+ persons, and poor self-esteem, guilt, and shame in them.

Priestly Ordination: Language That Enables and Inflicts Trauma

Theological language on priestly ordination, believed to be instituted by Christ and part of God's divine plan, is presented as authoritative and beyond question. Hinze emphasizes the power and authority vested in sacred disciplines such as theology and canon law that enable clerical sex abuse and its cover-up. The sacramental theology of ordination and priesthood and the language of the "ontological change" ordination communicates to clerics that divine providence puts them above and apart from the laity and that, therefore, sexual rules guiding human sexuality do not necessarily apply to them. They prioritize a "sacralized hierarchy" that protects the church and avoids scandal by covering up abuse. Such "theological [language] reinforced and supported by a preexisting power arrangement (a hierarchy that sets adults above children, priests above laity, and, in the end, the reputation of the church above the truth) while pretending that it was simply reflecting and defending timeless truths [and reality]."[60] This is how Catholic doctrinal language, whether it applies to sacramental ordination or sexual doctrinal teachings, becomes "a means of control and a method of domination."[61] It is tragic and revealing that clerics, both priests and bishops, who have engaged in sexual acts with boys or young men have been some of the most outspoken critics of homosexuality, alternative sexual identities, and the sexual realities associated with LGBTQI+ people.[62] The hypocrisy of such critics is ironic and tragic. It is revealing and verifies Marie Keenan's observation that such language shapes the identities of subjects, even those in power. It also verifies Foucault's assertion that language is established by authority and reified in spite of experience and evidence to the contrary.

The Congregation for Catholic Education (CCE) issued an *Instruction* on the admission to seminary and ordination in the wake of the sexual-abuse crisis. Rather than focusing on the language of "ontological change" in priestly ordination, and on clericalism, it focuses on sexual norms and homosexuality. It prohibits admission to both the seminary and ordination of men "who practice homosexuality, present deep-seated homosexual tendencies or support the so-called gay culture."[63] Though the CCE began drafting the *Instruction* before the sexual-abuse crisis broke in 2002, many speculate that the document is at least in part a response to the crisis and how to avert it in the future by weeding out homosexual candidates for the priesthood. Similar guidelines against admitting men with an "uncertain sexual identity" and "deep-seated homosexual tendencies" were issued again by the CCE in 2008.[64]

There are several problems with the CCE's *Instruction and Guidelines*. First, Richard Sipe, a former priest and present psychotherapist, estimates that 30–50 percent of Catholic clerics have a homosexual orientation.[65] About 4 percent of clerics sexually abuse children. This means, importantly, that the vast majority of homosexual (and heterosexual) clerics do not engage in any kind of sexual abuse. To ban from seminary or ordination every man who "presents deep-seated homosexual tendencies" is, therefore, neither reasonable nor addressing the more systemic problem. It is merely reifying the doctrinal sexual teaching that all homosexuals are ethically suspect because of their homosexual orientation. Catholic doctrine teaches, "Although the particular inclination of the homosexual person is not a sin, it is a more or less strong tendency ordered toward an intrinsic moral evil; and thus the inclination itself must be seen as an objective disorder."[66] The ethical suspicion surrounding all seminarians or clerics with a homosexual orientation is rooted in doctrinal language to scapegoat homosexual orientation and to reify that language. It does not address the more fundamental structural and ecclesial issues that are responsible for the crisis.

Second, the John Jay Report indicates that between 1950 and 2002, 81 percent of clerical sexual abuse victims were male, 51 percent were between eleven and fourteen, 27 percent were fifteen to seventeen, 16 percent were eight to ten, and about 6 percent were under age 7.[67] Science makes clear that there is no correlation between sexual orientation and pedophilia, the abuse of prepubescent children. Both homosexuals and heterosexuals sexually abuse boys and girls. If pedophilia was related to sexual orientation, the CCE's *Instruction* and *Guidelines* should issue warnings about people with homosexual *and* heterosexual tendencies. Singling out a homosexual tendency as potentially ethically problematic for seminarians and clerics, in and of itself, is scientifically and experientially unfounded. We have found no literature establishing a correlation between sexual orientation and ephebophilia, the abuse of postpubescent adolescents, and the *Diagnostic and Statistical Manual of Mental Disorders* (DSM) does not address ephebophilia as a distinct mental disorder.[68] If there is such a correlation, this would apply to both heterosexuals and homosexuals, but no prohibition is placed on men with heterosexual tendencies entering the seminary or seeking ordination.

Third, and most important, the response to clerical sexual abuse has focused on doctrinal sexual teachings on homosexuality rather than on sacramental teachings about the ontological change produced in clerics by their ordination and the culture enabled by the teaching. Catholic theologian Lieven Boeve speculates that Pope Benedict resigned because of "cognitive dissonance" between his vision of the church as "a beacon of light and truth" and the reality of the church caught up in the sexual-abuse scandal that has irreparably damaged its authority and reputation. Instead of reassessing foundational sacramental and ethical theological language, Benedict's response to the sexual and financial scandals in the church was to resign in order to bring about his personal "dissonance reduction."[69] In Foucault's terms, his resignation leaves in place the power structures and theological language that led to these scandals in the first place, rather than seeking the church's reassessment and the revision of the doctrinal language on priestly ordination and sexual ethics.

Pope Francis has taken a very different approach to the sex-abuse scandal.[70] He has called for church reforms and has promoted "a more humble, poorer and dialogical Church," especially through synodality. Through the synodal process, we have seen many calls from laity, priests, bishops, and cardinals to reform the church, including its doctrines on sexual ethics in general and homosexuality in particular. This attempt to reform the church and its doctrinal language is an attempt to break the historical pattern of reifying doctrinal language and the power and authority that maintains it in spite of the scientific evidence and human experience that challenges it. It also clearly opposes those abusers who attempt dissonance reduction by embracing Catholic teaching against homosexuality and projecting onto homosexuals their own sexual disfunction and pathology. Given the conservative opposition to Pope Francis's church reforms in general and to the process of synodality in particular in the wake of Pope Benedict's death, there is a clear attempt to maintain the institutional status quo of power structures and doctrinal language, which perpetuates reified language and practice.[71]

Doctrinal Language That Causes Trauma

In the pre–civil rights era in the United States, Jim Crow laws and segregation were codified and caused violence and trauma for African Americans. In the post–civil rights era, racist and xenophobic language, such as that used at the Unite the Right Rally in 2017 in Charlottesville, Virginia, and the racism surrounding the murder of George Floyd in 2020 while in police custody, caused similar trauma. A more subtle and insidious language that causes trauma is religious doctrinal language. It is more subtle because it is often not perceived to be explicitly oppressive, discriminatory, or homophobic; it is more insidious because it is institutionalized and (ab)uses God, scripture, and Catholic tradition to justify its truth claims.

Catholic doctrinal language about human sexuality teaches that there is "no parvity of matter" in sexual ethical issues; this means that all sexual sins are potentially mortal sins leading to eternal damnation. The tradition prioritizes sexual sins like masturbation and unmarried sexual intercourse above other types of more egregious and damaging sins like racism and the abuse of the poor. This approach defines the long history of Catholic teaching on human sexuality.[72] Cardinal Robert McElroy of San Diego comments on this problematic history.

> The effect of the tradition that all sexual acts outside of marriage constitute objectively grave sin has been to focus the Christian moral life disproportionately upon sexual activity. The heart of Christian discipleship is a relationship with God the Father, Son and Spirit rooted in the life, death and resurrection of Jesus Christ. The

> church has a hierarchy of truths that flow from this fundamental kerygma. Sexual activity, while profound, does not lie at the heart of this hierarchy. Yet in pastoral practice we have placed it at the very center of our structures of exclusion from the Eucharist. This should change.[73]

That history and the lack of any development of the doctrinal language and teaching about the ethics of human sexuality, despite developments in general anthropological language, reflects Foucault's reification of sexual language and communicates a deep suspicion of sexuality, especially sexual pleasure. It also induces in many Catholics the personal trauma of guilt, shame, and fear about their ultimate salvation.

Michael Patton published a comprehensive, interdisciplinary study that relies on history, theology, law, medicine, sexology, psychology, psychiatry, and anthropology to investigate and document the "mass human suffering and damage caused by Catholic sexual orthodoxy in both the Catholic Mind and the Western Mind."[74] The teaching and the language in which that orthodoxy is phrased has caused, and continues to cause, a deep pathology, trauma, and spiritual violence regarding human sexuality among many of the Catholic faithful. That trauma is driving many from the church and is leading others to self-harm and even suicide.

The language of judgment and condemnation, especially of LGBTQI+ people,[75] that harms people and even drives some to consider suicide, calls for reform. That reform is underway through the vision and leadership of Pope Francis, some bishops and priests, Catholic theologians, and laypeople. Marie Keenan summarizes well the doctrinal language that enables abusers and induces trauma among the faithful. "A Catholic sexual ethic and theology of priesthood that 'problematizes' the body and erotic sexual desire and emphasizes chastity and purity over a relational ethic" is problematic for the faithful and contributes to clerical sexual abuse. "This theology of sexuality," she continues, "contributes to self-hatred, shame, and personal failure, and needs serious theological examination and revision."[76] We agree wholeheartedly and are pleased to recognize that such examination and revision are underway and supported by Pope Francis.

CONCLUSION

A revision of Catholic doctrinal language regarding the sacrament of ordination, ecclesiology, and ethical teaching about human sexuality, and the power structures that have instituted and been instituted by that language, must, we believe, take place to bring healing, wholeness, and the gospel language of God's unconditional love and mercy to the forefront in the Catholic Church. We embrace and support the shifts that are already taking place to revise Catholic doctrinal language. Among these shifts are an emphasis on the authority and inviolability of conscience; Pope Francis's synodal ecclesiology that is participatory and structurally transformative; listening to the voices of the faithful; designating the failure to love as the root of human suffering and the need for church conversion to confront that suffering; experience and the contributions of the sciences and other expert disciplines as foundational sources of ethical knowledge to answer the key question posed by James Allison on homosexual teaching: "Yes, we know this is church teaching, but is it true?"[77] The revisions we have listed in chapter 1 can provide bases for critiquing and revising the church's doctrinal and ethical language. We offer a detailed critique of that language and proposals for its revision in the chapters that follow.

3

SEXUAL ABUSE, TRAUMA, AND DOCTRINAL LANGUAGE

Now the [priest], by reason of the sacerdotal consecration which he has received, is truly made like to the high priest and possesses the authority to act in the power and place of the person of Christ himself [*virtute ac persona ipsius Christi*]. (*Catechism* 1548)

[The church] cannot admit to the seminary or to holy orders those who practise homosexuality, present deep-seated homosexual tendencies, or support the so-called gay culture. (Congregation for Catholic Education, *Instruction: Concerning Criteria for the Discernment of Vocations with Regard to Persons with Homosexual Tendencies in View of Their Admission to the Seminary and to Holy Orders* 2)

Scandal is an attitude or behavior which leads another to do evil....He damages virtue and integrity; he may even draw his brother into spiritual death. Scandal is a grave offense if by deed or omission another is deliberately led into a grave offense. (*Catechism* 2284)

Although the Pulse Night Club massacre is the most egregious violent attack against members of the LGBTQI+ community and an indirect and correlational connection can be drawn between that event and religious, doctrinal language targeting LGBTQI+ people, the clerical sex-abuse crisis and its cover-up have a direct, causal relationship to doctrinal language that enabled it. In this chapter, we investigate the extent of clerical sex abuse, the trauma caused by that abuse, and the doctrinal language that enables the abuse and cover-up.

CLERICAL SEX ABUSE AND ITS COVER-UP

For the past several decades, the Catholic Church has featured prominently in world news because of clerical sexual violence against women, men, adolescents, and children, and the sinful episcopal cover-up of that abuse to protect the church's good name and authority at the expense of vulnerable people.[1] The full extent of sexual abuse in the church worldwide is unknown since such abuse is largely underreported, especially in more conservative Catholic countries that embrace a pre–Vatican II, hierarchical ecclesiology where people do not question the actions of church leaders.[2] Although the United States, Canada, and Europe have been more transparent about the number of cases, more conservative parts of the Catholic world in Asia,[3] Africa,[4] and Latin America[5] lag behind in their reporting due to both the hesitancy among those abused or their families to come forward and report the abuse and the resistance among church officials to acknowledge and address such abuse. Many church leaders knew about the abuse, yet that information was covered up to protect the church. Far from protecting the church, of course, episcopal cover-ups have done as much to tarnish the church as the sexual abuse itself. Donald Cozzens correctly labels the cover-ups by religious authorities forms of violence.[6]

Richard Sipe indicts church structures as a central cause for cycles of abuse, violence, and cover-up. "The scandal of priestly sexual abuse of minors," he notes, "is primarily a symptom of an essentially flawed celibate/sexual system of ecclesiastical power.... Maintenance of the system develops, fosters, and protects sexual [and spiritual] abuse and violence."[7] We will critically analyze the structures of church power and the celibate/sexual system below. The power in clerical and religious sexual abuse is not only gendered and physical but also theological and spiritual.[8] The spiritual violence is clear from the personal testimonies of those who have been sexually abused. A sixty-two-year-old Irishman who had been sexually abused by his parish priest when he was an altar boy made this clear to us. "I was eleven years old," he told us, "and the priest was a man of God with sacred power. He could forgive sins,

I believed, and change bread into the body of Christ. I was in awe of him, and I could not believe he would do anything to hurt me. Looking back on it, I cannot think how I could have acted differently." The problem could not be better articulated. How could an immature eleven-year-old boy, confronted by a man with sacred power whom he held in awe and trusted, have acted differently?

Extent of the Abuse in the United States

The most comprehensive study of clerical sex abuse in the Catholic Church in the United States covers the period from 1950 to 2002 and was conducted by the John Jay College of Criminal Justice between March 2003 and February 2004. It reached out to all 202 dioceses and 221 religious orders in the United States. Of those, 195 dioceses and 140 religious orders responded. The Report found that from 1950–2002 there were 10,667 children who were victims of abuse, and 4,392 priests who abused out of 109,694 who served in ministry. Among diocesan priests, 4.27 percent were accused of sexual abuse and among priests in religious orders 2.7 percent were accused of abuse.[9] Based on the dioceses that reported gender information about the victims, 80.9 percent were male and 19.1 percent were female. The number of females abused increased noticeably after 1994, when girls were allowed to become altar servers. The age of the victims varied: over 50 percent were between 11 and 14, 26.7 percent were between 15 and 17, 16.5 percent between 8 and 10, and 3.6 percent were under age 7.[10]

In 2018, the Center for Applied Research in the Apostolate (CARA) at Georgetown University reported that from 2004 to 2017, there were 8,694 new allegations spanning the period from 1954 to 2017.[11] This is an important statistic since these additional allegations are quite close to the number of allegations reported by John Jay between 1950 and 2002. More recently, Maryland's attorney general identified 158 priests in the Baltimore Archdiocese accused of physically and sexually abusing over six hundred victims in the past eighty years.[12] The Baltimore circuit court notes, "For decades, survivors reported sexual abuse perpetrated by Catholic priests and for decades the church covered up the abuse rather than holding the abusers accountable and protecting its congregations."[13] Due to underreporting of sexual abuse, especially by male victims, and the lack of reporting among some dioceses and over a third of religious orders, this gives credence to clinical psychologist Mary Gail Frawley-O'Dea's estimate that as many as fifty thousand young people were abused over the period of the John Jay Report.[14]

TRAUMATIC IMPACT ON VICTIMS OF CLERICAL SEXUAL ABUSE AND ITS COVER-UP

O'Dea has counseled abuse victims for over three decades and addressed the USCCB in 2002 in Dallas, specifically on the long-term effects of abuse on victims. She subsequently published a book that addresses those effects as well as the perversion of power that led to the abuse and its cover-up. In her preface, she sums up well how clerical sexual abuse victims differ from other types of sexual abuse victims she had counseled over the years. "Priest abuse was different. To someone raised a Catholic, priests were essentially God-on-earth, so their crimes [and bishops' cover-up of those crimes] were even more upsetting to me than the 'usual' sexual abuse stories."[15]

Sexual abuse may include all types of trauma, direct, indirect, complex, and religious. Direct trauma is the personal experience of sexual abuse; indirect trauma is from the experience of others who witness the abuse by the trusted other, "God-on-earth" in the case of priestly sexual abusers; complex trauma is either actual repeated sexual abuse or reliving a single instance of abuse and its impact emotionally, psychologically, and physically; religious trauma is caused by "a traumatic experience perceived by the subject to be caused by the divine being" and that divine being's representatives on earth, the priest who abused and the bishop who covered up the abuse.

Bradford Hinze identifies three of the most key features of the trauma of sexual abuse identified by psychologists such as O'Dea.[16] The first is called *dissociation*. According to Bessel van der Kolk, "Dissociation is the essence of trauma. The overwhelming experience is split off and fragmented, so that the emotions, sounds, images, thoughts, and physical sensation related to the trauma take on a life of their own."[17] O'Dea connects dissociation and the destructive actions that flow from it with soul murder, which effects all dimensions of the human person, body, senses, mind, memory, and imagination. "Sexual abuse survivors may be thrown into a regression by something or someone reminiscent of the earlier trauma. No longer firmly located in the present, survivors dissociate—they think, feel, experience their bodies, and behave as the victims they once were, badly confusing themselves and those around them."[18] Dissociated experience exists as a separate reality, cutting off the victim "from authentic human relatedness" and deadening him or her "to full participation in the life of the rest of the personality."[19]

The impact of dissociation on the victim is profound and widespread. It suppresses the cognitive memory and the processing of traumatic events. Often, victims cannot recall incidents of sexual abuse for ten, twenty, or more years. The experiences are suppressed from consciousness and compartmentalized, but senses or sensations can evoke the trauma without recollecting the actual experiences. Dissociation can be the source of low self-esteem, depression, and even suicidal urges, and it impacts the victim physiologically, causing high blood pressure, insomnia, stomach disorders, and substance abuse. Van der Kolk sums up the physiological impact with his mantra: "The body keeps the score." Most devastatingly, dissociation impacts the ability to relate holistically to oneself, others, and even God due to the religious trauma and violation of trust at the hands of God's representative on earth.

A second form of trauma is sometimes described as a second form of abuse, related to but distinct from the actual physical sexual abuse itself. It is the fundamental violation of trust and betrayal by a member of a respected institution and community. In the aftermath of clerical sexual abuse, when a victim came forward to report the abuse to respected authorities, such as a bishop or his representative, that authority was too often more concerned with protecting the abuser and the church rather than showing care, compassion, and concern for the victim. For example, dioceses spent millions of dollars on lawyers to fight lawsuits and protect the assets and reputation of the church rather than caring for victims and prioritizing transparency and accountability. Abusive priests were often moved to another parish or diocese to protect the priest and the church's reputation. Bishops were active participants in this cover-up and second form of abuse. Although the Dallas Charter of 2002 created a "zero-tolerance" policy for sexually abusive priests in order to restore trust in the church and prevent this second form of abuse, it did not formulate any policy to hold bishops accountable for covering up abuse and sheltering abusers.[20] The Pennsylvania grand jury report summarizes the role of bishops in the abuse scandal: "The bishops weren't just aware of what was going on; they were immersed in it. And they went to great lengths to keep it secret. The secrecy helped spread the disease."[21] Consequently, lack of institutional trust remains an issue.

The impact of this second form of abuse on survivors is complex. First, a victim's act of publicly acknowledging abuse is a highly vulnerable act. The victim rightly expects compassion, empathy, understanding, and an attempt by authorities to restore trust in the church and to affirm one's human dignity and the violation of that dignity by a representative of the church. Instead, victims' accounts were often met with suspicion, skepticism, or denial, the perpetrator was not held accountable for his actions, and the victim's vulnerability and trust were abused and violated. Second, bishops' preferential option for abusers rather than victims furthered mistrust towards them and the church they led. A 2018 survey indicates that only 31 percent of American Catholics rate the ethical standards or honesty of clergy "high" or "very high." This is an 18 percent drop since 2017.[22] Third, the practice of moving abusive priests to other parishes or dioceses endangered other children and adolescents and exposed them to abuse.

The third form of trauma is that victims of sex abuse often experience serious "subjugation of the self." Through abuse and institutional maltreatment, victims have been subjugated sexually, physically, and psychologically to the power and authority of individuals and institutions. This subjugation eliminates a sense of self and prevents, sometimes indefinitely, authentic self-identity, development, and holistic integration. Victims attempt to reconstruct what has been deconstructed and destroyed in terms of their overall self-identity and well-being. Through professional counseling, support of loved ones, family, friends, and perhaps church representatives, reconstruction, self-formation, self-realization, and self-actualization can take place, but this is a lengthy process that requires deliberate and concerted effort. However, the deep trauma experienced by abuse victims often prevents total healing.[23]

ONTOLOGICAL CHANGE, ORDINATION, CLERICALISM, AND HIERARCHICALISM

While the traumatic effects of sexual abuse and its cover-up are tragic and well documented, the doctrinal language that enabled the abuse remains intact. To an analysis of that language we now turn. Referencing Michel Foucault, Irish psychotherapist Marie Keenan notes that religious language becomes "a means of control and method of domination" that enables clerical sex abuse. Control and domination are evident in language surrounding ordination that enabled abuse, a hierarchical ecclesiology that enabled its cover-up, and a distorted understanding of an ethical principle to justify both.

A widespread and demonstrated cause of priestly sexual abuse and its cover-up is clericalism, the idea that ordained ministers in the church, deacons, priests, and bishops, have a privileged place of holiness and power and exercise unquestionable authority over laity. A foundational source of clericalism is what is referred to as the "ontological change" that is said to happen to a man on his ordination to the priesthood. The phrase is technically not doctrinal, but the theology that justifies it is. Hinze comments that theology and canon law both support the idea of an "ontological change" in priestly ordination. "Theological discourse reinforced and supported a preexisting power arrangement...while pretending that it was simply reflecting and defending timeless truths."[24]

The Code of Canon Law of the Catholic Church decrees that "by divine institution, some of the Christian faithful are marked with an indelible character and constituted as sacred ministers by the sacrament of holy orders" (can. 1008). This indelible character, which deacons, priests, and bishops receive through ordination (can. 1009), is often referred to as an ontological change. The John Jay Report to the USCCB refers to this change as an "ontological shift," which means "that when a man is ordained, he undergoes a fundamental change of being."[25] This change of being should reflect the mission of Christ and his love and service to all people.

Unfortunately, it is too often transformed into clericalism and a priestly caste system that views itself above the laity. Julie Hanlon Rubio and Paul Schutz define *clericalism* as "a structure of power that isolates clergy and sets priests above and apart, granting them excessive authority, trust, rights, and responsibilities while diminishing the agency of lay people and religious."[26]

Catholic teaching on the consecrated life has an unfortunate interpretation that can reinforce clericalism and give it theological and traditional justification. Pope John Paul II, for instance, asserts the following: "As a way of showing forth the church's holiness, it is to be recognized that the consecrated life, which mirrors Christ's own way of life, has an objective superiority" to other, nonconsecrated life, including any lay state. "Precisely for this reason," he continues, "it is an especially rich manifestation of Gospel values and a more complete expression of the church's purpose, which is the sanctification of humanity."[27] The objective superiority of priestly life, according to this church doctrine, is presumed to be real and tangible. A priest who is ordained to consecrated life is meant to be really different, a true disciple of Christ who serves the people of God. There are, however, inherent dangers in this theology. As Philip Murnion correctly points out,

> If this is not to mean reverting to differences of status and privilege, to claims of prestige and acts of domination, it will be because we will foster a priesthood whose theology and spirituality, whose sense of shared priesthood with the people, and shared ministry with the women and men in parish ministry, enable him to help people be aware of the presence of Jesus in sacrament, in their community, in family and work.[28]

This real change too often manifests itself in clericalism, where privilege and power are the focus rather than shared priesthood, ministry, and service.

African theologian Agbonkhianmeghe Orobator provides a poignant statement on the role of clericalism in the abuse scandal. "For decades this demonic culture sustained by clericalism violently assaulted the lives and consciences of innocent and vulnerable children" and, we add, equally vulnerable women, men, and adolescents.[29] Pope Francis describes *clericalism* as "an elitist and exclusivist vision of vocation, that interprets the ministry received as a power to be exercised rather than as a free and generous service to be given....Clericalism is a perversion and is the root of many evils in the church."[30] Gerald Arbuckle, a former rector of a major seminary in New Zealand, asserts that clericalism begins in seminary formation, "quasi-indoctrination and voluntary incarceration to foster in candidates for the priesthood and/or religious life submission to the ecclesiastical and pastoral status quo."[31]

The John Jay Report shows a correlation between a seminary curriculum that lacks "training in self-understanding and the development of emotional and psychological competence for a life of celibate chastity" and increased priestly sexual abuse.[32] The Australian Royal Commission affirms this assessment and emphasizes celibacy's impact on sex abuse. "It is clear that inadequate preparation for ministry, loneliness, social isolation, and personal distress related to the difficulties of celibacy have contributed to sexual abuse of children."[33] This statement on celibacy is in direct contradiction to an earlier statement by the USCCB that "it would be a tremendous waste of time and money to conduct a study [on the relationship between celibacy and priestly sexual abuse]."[34] Although some seminaries have attempted to address these issues through revised programs that emphasize "human formation," there is also a trend to attract, recruit, and form rigid young men who embrace a hierarchical and patriarchal ecclesiology, and who are openly critical of Pope Francis's papacy and calls for church reform.[35]

Although clericalism as a manifestation of the ontological change helps to explain and understand the power and privilege that led to violations of trust and sexual abuse, Jesuit James Keenan makes an important distinction between clericalism and hierarchicalism. Whereas clericalism derives more from vanity than power, hierarchicalism indicates "the exclusive power culture of the episcopacy" which "preceded, generated, sustained, and emboldened clericalism."[36] This power culture of bishops protected priests from exposure and criminal sanctions, moved abusive priests to other parishes, exposed hundreds of children and adolescents to further abuse, and enabled abusers to escape accountability for their actions. The appointment in 2004 of disgraced Cardinal Bernard Law of Boston as archpriest of the Basilica of St. Mary Major in Rome might be the epitome of hierarchicalism. Law's installation to that largely honorary position provided him effective sanctuary against criminal investigations in the United States for his role in the Boston clerical sex-abuse scandal and its cover-up.

Remarkably, it was not until 2019, seventeen years after the "Spotlight" reporting in the *Boston Globe* that drew the world's attention to the extent of clerical sex abuse and the USCCB's 2002 Dallas Charter, that Pope Francis issued *Vos Estis Lux Mundi*.[37] This document introduced new procedural norms for addressing the sex-abuse crisis, and explicitly held bishops accountable for covering up such crimes. In the 2002 Dallas Charter, no norms or guidelines were formulated to hold bishops accountable for covering up sexual crimes by priests, which is a striking oversight that highlights clericalism, hierarchicalism, and an ecclesiology in which bishops see themselves beyond accountability and reproach. Although Pope Francis has attempted to address clericalism and hierarchicalism by issuing *Vos Estis Lux Mundi*, removing serial abuser Cardinal McCarrick from ministry, promoting a synodal church, and heavily critiquing clericalism, both clericalism and hierarchicalism remain largely intact today.

HIERARCHICAL ECCLESIOLOGY AND EPISCOPALIST PARADIGM

The ontological change that promotes both clericalism and hierarchicalism is manifested institutionally and doctrinally in a hierarchical ecclesiology, which provides an institutional explanation for why bishops covered up priestly sexual crimes. The so-called ontological change and clericalism, which it creates and sustains, naturally feed into, and support, a hierarchical ecclesiology. Rob Dreher correctly notes that "among…[clericalism's] chief manifestations are an authoritarian style of ministerial leadership, a rigidly hierarchical worldview, and a virtual identification of the holiness and grace of the church with the clerical state and, thereby, with the cleric himself."[38] This hierarchical worldview was fundamentally challenged at Vatican II, though there are lingering remnants in its documents that reflect theological tensions between traditionalist and progressive theologians at the Council. This is certainly the case with *Lumen Gentium*, which advocated a people of God communion ecclesiology but retained remnants of a pre–Vatican II hierarchical ecclesiology. In addition, there has been persistent resistance among many bishops, priests, and Catholic faithful to the Second Vatican Council's vision of the church as a communion of all the faithful, laity, priests, and bishops together. This resistance continues in the ongoing church debate over this conciliar vision and the position the Latin Mass occupies within it.

The pre–Vatican II hierarchical church remnants that remain largely fuel bishops' past and present cover-up of sexual abuse. Thomas Doyle correctly notes, "In a hierarchical system, overladen with the trappings and values of monarchy, accountability is painfully difficult."[39] Failed accountability is painfully evident in the cover-up of sexual abuse by bishops who failed to believe accusations against clerics, moved priests to other parishes when accusations were credible, required nondisclosure agreements in lawsuits, and failed to recognize the structurally sinful church reality that perpetuated such cover-ups.[40] The Second Vatican Council attempted to return the church to its earlier historical communion ecclesiological model and Pope Francis has made efforts to shift to a synodal, dialogical model, but the limited success of those efforts is demonstrated by the limited inclusion of laywomen and -men on sexual abuse review boards and the continued episcopal stonewalling that prevents transparency and episcopal accountability.[41]

Richard Sipe judges that its structures are at the foundation of sexual violence in the church.[42] Susan Ross summarizes the connection between patriarchy, hierarchy, and ecclesiology, which allows for the ongoing sexual abuse of women, men, adolescents, and children, the church structures that enable it, and the church leadership that covers it up. "A patriarchal theology of God, priesthood, and church serves to socialize both clergy and laity into a pattern of thinking and acting that supports masculine [hierarchical] power and feminine (lay) subordination."[43] Patriarchy and hierarchy have solid roots in scripture and have been perpetuated and institutionalized throughout the history of the Catholic Church.

The First Letter to Timothy, written around the year 100, issues a standard Jewish command: "Let a woman learn in silence with full submission. I permit no woman to teach or to have authority over a man; she is to keep silent" (1 Tim 2:11–12; 1 Cor 14:34). This hierarchical stratification of power and authority between women and men in the early church has been perpetuated in the Catholic Church up to our day. Unjust already in the first century, though in line with the cultural values of the time, it continues to be unjust in the twenty-first century and at least out of line with contemporary Western cultural values. The ecclesiological and ethical cues that church teaching on priestly ordination promotes is that clerics are powerful and dominant and that laity, both women and men, are weak and submissive to them. This hierarchical stratification of power was officially written into ecclesiology by Pope Pius X in 1906. The church, Pius taught, is

> essentially an unequal society, that is, a society comprising two categories of persons, the pastors and the flock…with the pastoral body only rests the necessary right and authority for promoting the end of the society and directing all its members towards that end; the one duty of the multitude is to allow themselves to be led and, like a docile flock, to follow the pastors.[44]

If we are ever to understand fully the sexual abuse and cover-up that bedevil the Catholic Church, the first step is to understand them in the context of this hierarchical stratification of power.

This hierarchical power is rooted in a pervasive image of God as a powerful male/father and ordained clerics as his sacramental representations. Almost fifty years ago, feminist theologian Mary Daly pointed out the obvious and dangerous equation: "If God is male, then the male is God."[45] Another early feminist theologian, Rosemary Radford Ruether, argued that patriarchal rule was established and is daily reinforced by the metaphor of male monotheism literally interpreted.[46] This interpretation is reinforced by a Christology that emphasizes Jesus's maleness as ontologically decisive and to be imaged in the church's sacramental theology. Based on this ontology, all leadership and authority must be invested only in ordained men. Since laity, both women and men, do not share in ordination and the ontological change it creates, they are relegated to the role of a docile and obedient flock.[47] The hierarchical church is justified by its grounding in a male God, his male son, and a male clergy instituted "by divine law."[48] Donald Palmer and Valerie Feldman argue that the belief in a divinely established, unequal community with designated power imbalances and exalted clergy, are obvious causes for the sex-abuse scandal.[49] We absolutely agree.

Ecclesiology has certainly contributed to the perpetuation of the sex-abuse crisis, but it can also contribute to its eradication. Ecclesiology has one commitment with two emphases: fidelity to "what was handed on by the apostles" and creative responses to reading the signs of the times.[50] What was handed on by the apostles has evolved historically in the twenty-first century church's understanding, from a hierarchical to a communion church, and Pope Francis's synodal ecclesiology, in dialogue with the signs of the times among the entire people of God, pope, bishops, priests, laity, and all people of good will. Although Francis's papacy has largely been defined in terms of synodality, a journeying together of people of faith, the sexual-abuse scandal and its cover-up and episcopal resistance to both him and his vision of a synodal church expose an entrenched hierarchical ecclesiology that betrays the gospel and abuses the vulnerable people whom the church is called to minister to and to serve.

The signs of the times indicate that the most difficult challenge the Catholic Church is facing since the Protestant Reformation is the clerical sex-abuse crisis. Theologian Massimo Faggioli describes this crisis as a "hermeneutic of systemic distrust," which is "the dominant hermeneutic of the church today." The church needs to reform "the episcopalist paradigm," including "the theology of the episcopate and the role of the episcopate in the government of the church" that is at the root of this crisis.[51] The episcopalist paradigm reflects a hierarchical ecclesiology and remains a foundational ecclesiological issue that enables clerical sex abuse and continues to promote the bishop's authority. It remains largely in place, despite Pope Francis's focus on a synodal ecclesiology. Anyone who doubts that hierarchical ecclesiology is a spiritually dangerous doctrine need only consider the Crusades, Inquisition, institutional corruption throughout history, and the present sex-abuse crisis and its cover-up by bishops. This latter event, we suggest, cries out for conversion and an ecclesiological paradigm shift. As the CDF notes in its statement on principles for collaboration between Catholic and non-Catholic health-care institutions.

"Institutions have an identity and character, but this is caused by decisions of natural persons."[52] This statement needs to be applied not only to Catholic health-care institutions and their administrators but also to the institutional church itself.

The decision of bishops like Cardinal McCarrick to commit and then cover up sexual abuse has fundamentally damaged their individual and collective authority and that of the church they represent. Australian theologian Neil Ormerod correctly notes that the abuse crisis has caused "a crisis of episcopal authority as lay Catholics [and society at large] have lost trust in the office of the Bishop."[53] Importantly, it is a loss of trust not only in individual bishops who committed or covered up sexual abuse but also in the bishop's office itself and in its ability to exercise credible authority on religious and ethical matters. The loss of trust and credibility profoundly impacts the bishops' authority and the Catholic perception of individual bishops and of the institutional church when it seeks to assert its authority. To understand this crisis of authority and authenticity Ormerod, drawing from Bernard Lonergan and Joseph Komonchak, explores the social nature of authority.[54]

Lonergan adopts Max Weber's concept of "legitimate authority," expanding that concept to include a normative dimension grounded in human authenticity. For Lonergan, the source of power in legitimate authority derives from the cooperation between communities that share values, meanings, and authenticity. This cooperation "confers on power the aura and prestige of authority. Unauthenticity leaves power naked; it reveals power as mere power. Similarly, authenticity legitimates authorities, and unauthenticity destroys their authority and reveals them as merely powerful."[55] Lonergan makes a further distinction between authority and authorities. Although authority is shared with the entire community, authorities are those who have been entrusted with particular offices and delegated with particular powers. External criteria, deduced from a community's shared meanings and values, legitimate and guide authorities. To be sufficient, as well as necessary, these criteria must include authenticity as well. Ethical authenticity requires God's grace and is grounded in personal holiness.[56] In the sex-abuse crisis, many bishops violated communal meanings, values, and personal holiness, all of which fundamentally damaged their authority and authenticity individually and collectively.

Komonchak embraces Weber's definition of authority and applies it to teaching authority. Legitimate teaching authority is "trustworthy power."[57] The trustworthiness of power associated with an office is contingent on the trustworthiness of the people holding that office. The authenticity of the office is dependent on the authenticity of the office holders. When the office holders violate trust, as many bishops did in the cover-up of clerical sex abuse, the office itself loses its trustworthiness and, therefore, its authenticity as a trustworthy power. This is where individual bishops' violation of trust has led the church. The lack of authenticity in individual bishops who covered up clerical sexual abuse has resulted in a lack of authenticity in the episcopal office in general. This lack of authenticity in individual bishops and in the episcopal offices they occupy, and its impact on the Catholic faithful, applies not only to how they have addressed the sex-abuse crisis but extends also to the entire church and all its ministries. The lack of authority, authenticity, trust, and credibility invite a fundamental paradigm shift in the church to restore authority and authenticity and to rebuild trust and credibility. Clericalism and hierarchicalism must both be eliminated and replaced with a communal, synodal ecclesiology.

HOMOSEXUALITY AND ORDINATION

Hierarchical ecclesiology manifests itself in the church's attempt to scapegoat homosexual priests for the sex-abuse crisis, rather than recognizing the guilt also of heterosexual abusers and the bishops who covered up their abuse and refused to hold them accountable. The church doubled down on its doctrinal language regarding homosexuality (see chapter 6) and targeted both homosexuality and "gay culture" as the source of clerical sexual abuse. In response to the sexual abuse crisis the Congregation for Catholic Education (CCE) issued an *Instruction* in 2005 to determine the suitability of candidates for seminary and ordination to the priesthood with homosexual tendencies. First, it does not explicitly state that the *Instruction* is in reference to the clerical sex-abuse crisis, but cryptically states that it is in response to "a specific question, made more urgent by the current situation."[58] The *Instruction* was issued relatively shortly after the news of the sex-abuse crisis broke in the United States in 2002, but its response distorts both experience and scientific findings on the relationship between homosexuality and clerical sex abuse. It calls for "affective maturity" of candidates for the priesthood. It then cites the *Catechism*'s teaching on homosexual acts and tendencies, and states emphatically that, although respecting all people, the church "cannot admit to the seminary or to holy orders those who practise homosexuality, present deep-seated homosexual tendencies, or support the so-called 'gay culture.'" "One must," it continues, "in no way overlook the negative consequences that can derive from the ordination of persons with deep-seated homosexual tendencies."[59] The *Instruction* reflects the church's conscious or unconscious distortion of the data of science with respect to the situation of clerical sexual abuse and the evidence of experience with respect to it.

First, Fred Berlin of John Hopkins University, an expert in sexual abuse and advisor to the USCCB, states emphatically that there is no evidence linking child abuse and homosexuality.[60] Robert Geffner, psychologist and editor of the *Journal of Child Sexual Abuse*, asserts that sexual abuse of minors is no more likely among homosexuals than heterosexuals.[61] Margaret Smith of the John Jay Report reported to the USCCB that "what we are suggesting is that the idea of sexual identity [or orientation] be separated from the problem of sexual abuse. At this point, we do not find a connection between homosexual identity and the increased likelihood of subsequent abuse from the data we have right now."[62] Michael Kimmel, professor of sociology at Stony Brook University, agrees and states that a perpetrator's selection of abuse victims often depends more on access than gender.[63]

The majority of abuse victims, as we saw in the statistics cited above, are young boys and male adolescents. Abusive priests would have easy access to altar boys and seminarians and could always be shielded under the auspices of mentoring a potential male victim, whereas it would be considered suspect for a priest to mentor a girl or female adolescent. It is important to note that both the Second Vatican Council and Pope John Paul II emphasize the importance of the sciences to inform theology and, we add, to formulate

Catholic doctrine. In church statements on the sex-abuse crisis and in responses to it, there is a clear lack of the abundant scientific data on the relationship, or more correctly the non-relationship, between sexual abuse and sexual orientation. Doctrinal teaching that homosexual orientation is "objectively disordered" also fails to consider extensive psychological, sociological, anthropological, and biological data that contradict such a claim.[64]

Interestingly, a more recent report on the USCCB's website cites Karen Terry, principal investigator of the John Jay Report on the sex-abuse crisis, that "neither celibacy nor homosexuality were causes of the abuse."[65] In spite of this reporting based on scientific evidence, the CCE has not revised its *Instruction* to match that evidence. In addition, Archbishop Broglio, who was elected president of the USCCB in November 2022, continues to defend the scientifically debunked claim he made in 2018 that "there is no question that the crisis of sexual abuse by priests in the USA is directly related to homosexuality." Asked whether he still defends that position after his election, he stated, "It's certainly an aspect of the sexual crisis that can't be denied" while claiming that it is "not to point a finger at anyone."[66] Not only is he denying the science, but he is directly pointing a finger at homosexuals en masse for being suspected sex abusers. Even though many heterosexual priests abused both children and adolescents, he does not make a general statement about heterosexual priests and sex abuse. In addition, the majority of bishops elected him as the new president of the USCCB despite his promotion of scientifically debunked claims and his opposition to Pope Francis's church reforms.[67]

Second, estimates suggest that between 28 percent and 56 percent of priests in the United States are homosexual.[68] Many speculate that the percentage has increased since the 1970s as many heterosexual priests left the priesthood to marry. Statistically, about 4 percent of priests have perpetrated sexual abuse crimes. Even if this statistic is a bit higher, due to underreporting of sexual abuse, there is a huge disparity between the number of priests who abuse, homosexual and heterosexual, and the number of ordained homosexuals. It is curious that there is not a similar *Instruction* by the CCE on heterosexual candidates for the priesthood regarding "heterosexual tendencies," since heterosexuals are as likely as homosexuals to abuse.

Third, the *Instruction* promotes closeted homosexuality among homosexual priests who are faithful, discerned their vocations, and truly want to live a celibate lifestyle in their ministry. The *Instruction* discourages honesty and transparency among homosexual seminarians who believe they have an authentic vocation but fear being rejected or dismissed because of the *Instruction*'s policy.[69] The interpretation and application of the *Instruction*'s criteria are very much dependent on the knowledge, understanding, and perspective of fallible vocation directors, seminary staff, spiritual directors, and bishops who may or may not have an ideology or agenda guiding their discernment process. Denying one's sexuality and sexual orientation is damaging emotionally and psychologically, and yet this is precisely what the *Instruction* promotes by putting men with a homosexual orientation under an inquisitorial microscope. In addition, the John Jay Report concludes "that priest candidates who would later abuse could not be distinguished by psychological test data, developmental and sexual history data, intelligence data, or experience in priesthood."[70] One may speculate that a policy that looks to homosexual tendencies to determine suitability or unsuitability for the priesthood may promote dishonesty in the screening process. Those who may be future abusers could be more susceptible to playing the system in order to move toward ordination, whereas those who are honest and transparent about their struggles could be dismissed.

SCANDAL?

A common justification for covering up clerical sex abuse is that to admit any sex abuse would cause "scandal" among the faithful and damage the church's ethical credibility and good name. The ethical obligation to avoid scandal is biblically based. Jesus warns anyone who would lead the "little ones" into sin that "it would be better for you if a great millstone were fastened round your neck and you were drowned in the depth of the sea" (Matt 18:6; cf. 1 Cor 8:10–13). He asserts that "temptations to sin are sure to come; but woe to him by whom they come!" (Luke 17:1). The *Catechism of the Catholic Church* defines *scandal* as an attitude or behavior that leads another to do evil; the one "who gives scandal becomes his neighbor's tempter....Scandal is a grave offense if by deed or omission another is deliberately led into a grave offense" (2284). It is clear, then, that in both scripture and church tradition scandal is a grave issue and something to be avoided. What is not clear, however, and what is not defined, is what precisely constitutes scandal and how claims of scandal are justified.

The assertion that an attitude or behavior would cause scandal is precisely that, an assertion, not an ethical argument, and like any assertion of right or wrong it needs to be justified by ethical argument. Scandal in the case of clerical sexual abuse is, we suggest, more likely to be caused by bishops' covering up the abuse than by openly exercising transparency and accountability. The bishops' claim of scandal, especially after the *Boston Globe* Spotlight story broke detailing the extent of the abuse and its cover-up by Cardinal Law, focused on the media's exaggeration of the abuse and its attempt to discredit the Catholic Church. This is summed up well by Archbishop Gabriel Montalvo, Pope John Paul II's representative to the United States: "We all know that we are going through difficult times and that some real problems within the church have been magnified to discredit the moral authority of the church." We believe it is true that sexual abuse has been magnified to discredit even the large number of nonabusing priests. More disturbing than this magnification, however, we suggest, is disgraced sexual abuser Cardinal McCarrick's disingenuous comment that "elements in our society who are very opposed to the church's stand on life, the church's stand on family, the church's stand on education...see in [the sexual abuse crisis] an opportunity to destroy the credibility of the church."[71] In protest of the *Boston Globe*'s criticism of the Catholic Church's handling of abuse cases, Cardinal Law, who did everything he could to cover up the abuse, excoriated the paper: "By all means we call down the power of God on the media, particularly the *Globe*." These and other comments by bishops highlight an attempt to use the principle of scandal to justify the claim that the media are leading people to sinful behaviors or attitudes that would call into question the church's ethical authority, credibility, and integrity.

In a homily we heard on John's bread of life discourse (ch. 6), a local priest went as far as to equate the disciples abandoning Jesus because they could not accept his invitation that, unless you eat my body and drink my blood, you will not have everlasting life, with people who have left the church due to the sex-abuse scandal. In his mind, the scandal of the sex-abuse crisis and its cover-up is that people would leave the church, not that priests sexually abused children and adolescents and bishops covered up the abuse. The ethical implications of all these statements is that the media and forces trying to undermine the church caused scandal by leading people to question the truth, holiness, and ethical credibility of the church and its leaders, who were themselves the scandal givers.

Our first point revolves around the definition of scandal and how assertions of scandal are to be justified. *Scandal,* to repeat, "is an attitude or behavior which leads another to do evil [or to sin]." This definition raises the question, Wherein lies the scandal in the case under discussion? Is it in the media's publicizing clerical sexual abuse and its cover-up, which, in fact, led people to question the authority, trustworthiness, and integrity of leaders in the Catholic Church and caused many to leave the church, or is it in the priests who sexually abused children and in the bishops who covered up that abuse and, in doing so, endangered scores of other children? The answer to that question, we believe, is obvious and introduces the distinction between scandal as an ethical principle and the dictionary definition of *scandal.*

The latter defines *scandal* as "an action or event regarded as morally or legally wrong and causing general public outrage." It is clear that the bishops who ignored complaints or shuffled abusing priests from place to place were following the dictionary definition of *scandal* and were in violation of the moral principle. Bishops who moved priests and covered up abuse were ethically and legally wrong. They were more concerned about the public outrage at the institutional church, and themselves, if the sexual abuse became public, rather than concerned with protecting potential future victims from sexual abuse. In fact, opting for the dictionary definition of *scandal,* bishops actually violated the ethical principle of scandal in at least two ways. They enabled abusive priests to continue to abuse and commit sinful acts and they led the institutional church into sin by covering up the abuse and damaging the church's ethical credibility.

CONCLUSION

This chapter focused on clerical sex abuse in the Catholic Church, on the priests and bishops who sexually abused children, on the bishops who covered up the abuse, and on the victims who suffered lifelong trauma from the abuse. We argued that doctrinal language on the ontological change effected by priestly ordination too often creates a culture of clericalism that enables the ordained to feel a sense of superiority. Clericalism is often cited as a cause of the sexual abuse crisis. The doctrinal language that bishops "vigilantly [ward] off any errors that threaten their flock…[and that they]…are to be respected by all as witnesses to divine and Catholic truth" creates a culture of hierarchicalism and enables a sense of power and unquestionable authority that led bishops to protect abusive priests and themselves at the expense of vulnerable children and adolescents. The doctrinal language of a hierarchical ecclesiology and episcopal paradigm enables a lack of personal and institutional transparency and accountability among many bishops. The episcopal language that, against all the scientific evidence, attempted to scapegoat homosexual priests for the sexual abuse traumatizes homosexual priests and enables bishops not to be accountable for their complicity in the scandal. A distorted understanding of the doctrinal ethical principle of scandal has been used to justify claims that the media was persecuting the church and leading people into sin by questioning the church's holiness, integrity, and authenticity. All of these doctrinal teachings enabled, and continue to enable, clerical sex abuse in the church and demand reform.

In the chapters that follow, we shift the focus from doctrinal language that *enables* sexual abuse and causes violence and trauma to the abused children and their families, to faithful Catholics in general, and to the church itself, and focus on doctrinal language that actually *causes* trauma. We begin with an explanation and critique of the theological and sexual anthropology that grounds Catholic sexual teaching, and then critically analyze the church's various sexual doctrines and how those doctrines can and do cause trauma to many of the faithful.

4

ANTHROPOLOGICAL DOCTRINAL LANGUAGE AND THEOLOGICAL ANTHROPOLOGY

Each and every marital act must of necessity retain its intrinsic relationship to the procreation of human life....This...doctrine...is based on the inseparable connection, established by God, which man on his own initiative may not break, between the unitive significance and the procreative significance which are both inherent to the marriage act. (*Humanae Vitae* 11–12)

Everyone, man and woman, should acknowledge and accept his sexual *identity*. Physical, moral, and spiritual *difference* and complementarity are oriented toward the goods of [heterosexual] marriage and the flourishing of family life. The harmony of the couple and of society depends in part on the way in which the complementarity, needs, and mutual support between the sexes are lived out. (*Catechism* 2333)

In this chapter, we seek to define the sexual person as foundational for Catholic doctrinal language that flows from that definition. That enterprise, of necessity, has to deal with the doctrinal definitions offered by the Catholic Church and we shall do that as the chapter unfolds. We note from the outset a tension, even a disconnect, between the church's theological understanding of the sexual person and the doctrines deduced from that understanding. The theological understanding emphasizes interpersonal relationship between a man and a woman whereas the doctrinal understanding emphasizes procreative acts. It is this doctrinal understanding, which we explain in the chapters that follow, that often causes sexual and spiritual violence and trauma among the faithful.

The Western world learned from Aristotle that the human being is a rational animal. It is important today that she or he learns educationally and experientially that the human is also a sexual being. We begin with defining and distinguishing three sexual realities that are related and are often confused: sex, gender, and sexuality.

SEX, GENDER, AND SEXUALITY

Sex is a biological reality. It refers to the physical genitals, to the biological aspects of being a sexual being, and to the physical expression of a sexual being. Sex determines the human being as either male or female. Pope John Paul II highlights the Catholic teaching that "man is created from the very beginning as male and female."[1] He insists both that "the light of all humanity is marked by this primordial reality" and that sex is not just an attribute of a person but a constitutive reality constituting the person as "he" or "she."[2] *Gender* is distinct from sex. It is a cultural not a biological reality, and determines whether a person is masculine or feminine. By sex, men and women are the same in every culture; by gender, they differ across cultures. Pope Francis asserts that sex and gender can be distinguished but not separated.[3] "Gender theory," pejoratively labeled "gender ideology," "intends to deny the greatest possible difference that exists between living beings: [biological] sexual difference."[4] Culture can influence gender but not define or construct it. Catholic anthropology asserts a strict sexual binary, male/female, and an intrinsic link between sex and gender; male is masculine and female is feminine. Many scientists, sociologists, philosophers, and theologians, however, challenge the strict sexual binary and the intrinsic relationship between sex and gender.[5] As we discuss in Chapter 6, intersex and transgender people fundamentally challenge these anthropological claims through their lived experiences.[6]

Sexuality is an essential component of human persons through which they experience themselves as lesbian, gay, bisexual, transgender, queer, or intersex, and are orientationally heterosexual, homosexual, or bisexual, and express themselves sexually to other sexual human beings according to their sexual orientation.

Human sexual activity has three distinct meanings: it is in the right circumstances procreative, it is unitive of the two persons engaging in it, and it is pleasurable. Historically, the Catholic Church has consistently taught that procreation is the primary, most important meaning of sexual activity and that the union of the two persons engaging in it very much the secondary, less important meaning. That teaching has shaped its sexual ethics. It has taught that, to be ethical, sexual intercourse must always be between a wife and a husband in heterosexual marriage for the purpose of procreating a child. All other sexual intercourse is ruled unethical, including all sex between gays and lesbians.

Up until the Second Vatican Council, the Catholic Church taught that procreation is the primary end of marriage, and that the union it effects between the spouses is a secondary end. We recall here Saint Augustine's statement that marriage "does not seem to me to be good only because of the procreation of children, but also because of the natural companionship of the sexes."[7] That idea gained support from Pope Pius XI, who, in his 1930 encyclical on Christian marriage, *Casti Connubii*, suggested that marriage could be seen "in a very real sense" beyond the procreative model "as the blending of life as a whole and the mutual interchange and sharing thereof."[8] That idea of marriage as a union between the spouses was taken up by Catholic theologians and eventually by the Second Vatican Council. In marriage, a woman and a man enter into a spousal relationship in which they initiate a mysterious union of their beings. This personal union of their beings, and not just the physical unions of their bodies, is what the oft-quoted "one body" of Genesis 2:24 intends. It is this interpersonal union that the physical union of their bodies in sexual intercourse both achieves and expresses, and it is this spousal union that is the primary end of both sexual activity and marriage.

The Second Vatican Council did not deal in detail with marriage, but its Constitution on the Church in the Modern World, *Gaudium et Spes*, offered theological material intimately related to our present discussion. Marriage, it taught, is a "communion of love... an intimate partnership of life and love."[9] In spite of insistent demands from a small, but vocal, minority led by Cardinal Ottaviani, head of the Vatican Holy Office, now the Congregation for the Doctrine of the Faith, to repeat the centuries-old tradition of marriage as primarily a procreative union, thus consigning spousal love to its traditional secondary place, the Council declared spousal love to be of the very essence of marriage. That spousal love is singularly expressed in sexual intercourse, which signifies and promotes "that mutual self-giving by which the spouses enrich one another" (GS 49). Marriage and the sexual intercourse of the spouses are still said to be "ordained for the procreation of children," but the Council insists that "does not make the other ends of marriage of less account" (GS 50). This teaching was enshrined in the revised *Code of Canon Law* in 1983, which states that marriage "is ordered to the well-being of the spouses and to the procreation and upbringing of children" (can. 1055, 1), with no suggestion that either end is superior to the other. In the contemporary Catholic Church, therefore, marriage and spousal sexual intercourse are held to have two ends: procreation and spousal union that is in no way secondary to procreation.

Having dealt with the first two meanings we assigned to marriage at the outset of this chapter, procreation and union of the spouses, we now deal with the third meaning, pleasure. The pleasure that accompanies sexual intercourse has always raised ethical concerns for the Christian churches, even though they acknowledge it as a good created by God. Those concerns have shaped their sexual ethics. Second- and third-century Christian thinkers were heavily influenced by the Stoic philosophers who, judging that sex was evil, restricted all sexual intercourse to marriage and to acts within marriage that were open to procreation. While combating these Stoic teachings, the nascent Christian Church was also infected by them, and they continue to be evident in Catholic teachings today.

MEANINGS OF PHYSICAL SEXUALITY: PLEASURE AND LOVEMAKING

There are two related meanings of the physical stages of sexual intercourse. The first is the physical and emotional pleasure associated with it; the second is the social interpretation of it as making love. Even though it is demonstrably an intrinsic dimension of just and loving sexual intercourse, sexual pleasure has always been morally suspect in the Christian tradition, and throughout history men have employed various strategies both to enhance their pleasure and to restrict the pleasure of their sexual partners. Sexual pleasure is a good created by God and gifted as grace to women and men. Like all gifts of God, it can be used for good and it can be used for evil, and the abuses of sexual pleasure and a hedonistic ethics based exclusively on pleasure and the objectification of the other are fully evident in the historical past and present. Such abuses, however, ought not and do not diminish the essential and valuable place of sexual pleasure as a natural component of human sexual ethics. For Plato, Aristotle, Augustine, and Aquinas, sexual activity and pleasure are "occupations with lower affairs which distract the soul and make it unworthy of being joined actually to God."[10] They are not, however, sinful at all times and in all circumstances. Augustine teaches that "evil does not follow because marriage and the sexual intercourse that characterizes it are good, but because in the good things of marriage there is also a use that is evil. Sexual intercourse was not created because of the concupiscence of the flesh, but because of good. That good would have remained without that evil if no one had sinned."[11] Indeed, Aquinas argues, within marriage sexual intercourse is meritorious,[12] and to forego the pleasure and thwart the end would be sinful.[13]

Ultimately, these judgments led Aquinas to the further unequivocal judgment that marriage is an uppercase Sacrament of the incomprehensible God,[14] which means that sexual activity, sexual pleasure, and sexual lovemaking, which are so important in marriage, are lowercase sacraments. Aquinas understood, at least inchoately, that the relationship between a husband and a wife should be a relationship of friendship and that sexual activity enhances that friendship.[15] His contemporary and theological rival, the Franciscan Bonaventure, is more explicit, calling friendship between the spouses the lowercase sacrament of the relationship between God and the soul.[16] Basil Hume, the saintly twentieth-century archbishop of Westminster, followed the line set by both. "When two persons love," he wrote after the death of a close friend, "whether of the same sex or of a different sex...

they experience in a limited manner in this world what will be their unending delight when one with God in the next."[17] Perhaps he was following his English compatriot, Aelred of Rievaulx, who in his classic treatise on friendship made the extraordinary, but defensible, claim *Deus amicitia est*, God is friendship.[18] Where there is just love, heterosexual, gay, or lesbian, there also is God. Therefore, we suggest that an essential component of any Christian sexual ethical principle must be a deeper understanding of sexual activity, sexual pleasure, and sexual lovemaking free of any necessary connection to biological procreation.

Catholic sexual teaching is grounded in an interpretation of natural law and the inseparability principle, which claims an intrinsic relationship between the unitive meaning and procreative meaning of sexual intercourse—the partners must be open to the biological transmission of life. We believe this is a weak, if not entirely false, principle since there is demonstrably no essentially procreative meaning to each and every sexual act. A woman is biologically infertile for a period every month and when she is postmenopausal. At those times her sexual acts, no matter how much she would desire otherwise, clearly do not have any essentially procreative meaning. We recognize, however, an interpersonal procreative meaning, namely, the partners procreate a life-in-communion with one another in imitation of God's inner life-in-communion. This interpersonal procreation of the life-in-communion of the partners happens in every just and loving reproductive and nonreproductive heterosexual and homosexual act.

We distinguish two types of pleasure in sexual intercourse: the pleasure of need and the pleasure of appreciation. The pleasure of need arises from satisfying the physical need a person has as the result of sexual desire. This pleasure is frequently taken rather than shared, and it brings sexual release, which can just as easily be achieved alone. The pleasure of appreciation results not from taking pleasure in the fulfillment of a personal need but in justly and lovingly sharing pleasure with a loved partner. This can never be achieved alone. The pleasure of appreciation is as much given as taken, and it brings not only physical relief but also personal, shared satisfaction and an enhanced sense of love, communion, and partnership. In sexual activity, both pleasures are available, but it is only when the pleasure of satisfaction is shared that the partners may truly be said to be "making love."[19]

The second meaning of sexual activity is *making love*, a term that demands explanation. I have needs, and so do others: needs for trust, for respect, for affection, for understanding, for acceptance as I am. Some people commit themselves to respond to my needs and I commit myself to respond to theirs. We say we are friends. We accompany one another on life's journey; we reveal ourselves mutually to one another; we assist one another and sustain one another when one or the other is weak; we provoke one another to realize our highest potential, to be the best we can be; we rejoice together when the best is achieved. In short, we will the good of each other; in an ancient understanding, we love one another.[20] It is then love that wills good to one another that we seek to clarify in this section.

As a freely willed act, love has two components. It is an evaluation of the good perceived in the partner and a commitment to actively seek and enhance that good. The action through which my commitment is expressed, whether it be a promise to love until death do us part or a just and loving sexual action, is the symbol of both my present love and my intention to love for the whole of my life. This symbol so relates and bonds me to the one I love that she or he can legitimately object ever after "you promised." In marriage, the spouses mutually commit to one another as lovers to make their love permanent and to live and communicate it as permanent. In reality, of course, because of the finiteness and sinfulness of human beings, although we can intend our love to be lifelong and indissoluble, we cannot make it lifelong and indissoluble at any given moment of our lives, for love, as life, stretches out into the unknown and uncontrollable future. What we can do, in Margaret Farley's wise words, is "initiate in the present a new form of relationship that will endure in the form of fidelity or betrayal." Commitment, to both the partner loved and to the loving relationship with her or him, she continues, "is love's way of being whole while it still grows into wholeness."[21]

The Greeks distinguished four kinds of love: *storge*, the love we call affection; *eros*, the love we call desire; *philia*, the mutual love we call friendship; *agape*, the love we call self-sacrificing love. Though all four kinds are legitimately called love, the good that is striven for in each is distinct. *Storge* is natural or instinctual love such as among family members; *eros* is love of another person for my good; *agape* is love for another person for that person's good; *philia* is love for the mutual good of both persons. We need to be careful here. In life these various loves are not as easily distinguished as they are on paper. Any just and loving relationship can have all four of them inseparably admixed, or one or more of them dominant at any particular time. Because *philia*, however, is mutual love, seeking the good of both persons, we suggest it as the best foundation for a stable relationship. That is what Judith Wallerstein found in her study of the "good marriage."

"My marriage depends on friendship," one man told her. "Sex you can have with anyone, I got married for companionship and respect and most of all for friendship."[22] A woman agreed. "Let me describe what makes our marriage work. We like each other. We have mutual respect. We trust each other." Love is important, she explained, but what gives love stability is "a basic sense of real trust, of really knowing where that other person is at and knowing that whatever they are going to do is going to be in your best interest as well as theirs."[23] In a marital relationship, when the mutuality of *philia* prepares the foundation on which the possible one-sidedness of both *eros* and *agape* are raised, spouses achieve mutual well-being through a love that is mutual (*philia*), unconditional (*agape*), and embodied (*eros*). When friendship is the foundation of a relationship, the friends or lovers recognize that the other's good is the primary way to reach both one's own good and the good of the other. When both those goods are achieved, so also is friendly and marital communion.

Because *eros* and the sexual pleasure it desires are so powerful and so easily misconstrued as the pleasure of need to the detriment of the pleasure of mutual satisfaction, there must be parameters for its responsible and ethical sexual expression. To be responsible, loving, and ethical, every sexual activity must be just. It must recognize and express the human freedom and equality of both partners, and it must be loving. It must will and actively seek the good of both partners. We conclude this section, then, by articulating a first thesis we believe to be sufficiently theologically established in it. Physical sexuality, including the sexual pleasure of satisfaction in every just and loving relationship, is part of the mystery of God's creation, and is a lowercase sacrament of the presence of the mysterious God in human history. It demands ongoing analysis to be better understood in its physical sense so that it can be better understood also in its theological sense as revelatory of the incomprehensible God.

THE PSYCHOLOGY OF SEXUALITY

Psychiatrist Jack Dominian presents an excellent synthesis of six psychological dimensions of human sexuality that further illuminate the sexual intercourse of a loving couple.[24] First, through sexual intercourse a couple affirms one another's personal and sexual identity. The sexual act is symbolic in that, when we become naked in front of another human person, we become totally and completely vulnerable. To make love in "a truly human manner"[25] is both a mutual affirmation and acceptance of the other with all her or his physical, emotional, psychological, and spiritual blessings and flaws. This affirmation and acceptance progresses through various stages.

As is well documented in human relationships, sexual activity is more frequent early in a stable sexual relationship,[26] and perhaps it is also more passionate. As a couple's relationship develops and deepens over the years, the routine of mutual affirmation and acceptance may lose its novelty and excitement, but this is not to be interpreted to mean that affirmation and acceptance cease. In reality, they increase as the couple comes to know and accept one another more profoundly and intimately over time. While the novelty and excitement of sexual activity may diminish with age, the affirmation and acceptance of the partner, a unique self created into the image and likeness of God and affirmed, accepted, and loved unconditionally, becomes more profound. Repetition may breed familiarity and a sense of routine, but it never breeds contempt. It deepens a person's striving toward unconditional affirmation and acceptance of the other as he or she is.

Second, sexual activity reflects, affirms, and creates gender identity, a fundamental dimension of sexual identity. Gender is concerned with the socially constructed meanings of femininity or masculinity. It is determined, as we have already affirmed, not by biology but by culture, ethnicity, and rearing experience, and is expressed in actions, interactions, and social roles. Dominian describes gender expression as a liturgy of exchange, a divine language,[27] in which a couple communicates with each other through sexual desire. In the formation and development of sexual identity through a recognition and embodiment of gender roles, it is crucial that sexual activity be a form of just, loving, open, and honest human communication. If it is, then the act is humanly communicative at the deepest level, transforming simple communication into interpersonal communion and functioning as what Martin Buber called "the [lowercase] sacrament of dialogue," in which "one tastes God."[28] The sparks of genuine dialogue between lovers, in which each turns toward the other, intends the other, receives the other, and affirms the other, illumines the presence of God who turns toward the human other, intends the other, receives the other, and affirms the other. If sexual activity is not just, loving, open, and honest communication, then the same act can stagnate, or even block, future possibilities for communication and formation of healthy sexual identity. This is an example of the essential ambiguity of human sexual activity.

When sexual encounters are abusive, violent, or exploitative, survivors of such experiences often suffer from lasting trauma that can damage their relationships with God and with others (including future sexual partners).[29] Theologian Jane Grovijahn argues that in sexual abuse "God is ripped out" of the survivor's body, "pummeling her into a visceral location of deicide."[30] Since our sexuality is a fundamental component of ourselves through which we both understand ourselves and relate to others, sexual violence harms the whole person. More than just the survivor's body is harmed: "Her very self—that root of whatever we like to think makes us persons—is attacked and violated."[31] Sexual violence—especially when it is committed against children—can communicate to the survivor that she is not worthy of the love of God or others.

As abuse survivor and anthropologist Cathy Winkler argues, "Rapists bury landmines in the bodies of their victims…confusion, nausea, nightmares, tremors, depression, shakiness" that explode later, converting the sexual desires and bodily sensitivities that can intimately unite us with another in love into opportunities for shame and terror.[32] The effect is that "[rape] is the experience of social death. Rapists want to socially exterminate us."[33] Survivors often struggle to accept love from others and, in some instances, to accept God's offer of unconditional love. Sexual violence and abuse can threaten survivors' access to religious faith and even salvation itself.[34] Our fundamentally relational nature makes us vulnerable to being "undone" by another.[35] Even in the absence of direct experiences of interpersonal violence, structural forms of violence against women and LGBTQI+ persons that generate "insidious trauma" can present barriers to authentic intimacy with God and everyone else.

Self-esteem is the third psychological dimension of human sexuality. Psychological studies indicate that one of the greatest threats to healthy human development, including sexual development, is poor self-esteem.[36] The Christian tradition has not always done a good job of emphasizing healthy self-love. Jesus's love commandment is well known: "You shall love your neighbor as yourself" (Mark 12:31; Matt 22:30; Luke 10:27). Not so well known is the fact that there are *three* commandments in this text: love God, love neighbor, and love self. Typically, the Christian tradition has interpreted neighbor love as altruistic and agapaic and self-love as egocentric and antithetical to the love of the gospel. This certainly can be the case, and modern cultures that emphasize radical individualism encourage egocentric love, but egocentric love is not the healthy self-love demanded by the gospel. Authentic self-love first affirms oneself as a self-in-God, good, valuable, and lovable, and then, in alliance with neighbor love, turns toward the loved other and offers this good, valuable, and lovable self-in-God fully to the other.

It is obvious that no one can give what he does not have. If a man does not have a dollar, he cannot give a dollar to a poor neighbor. If he does not truly and fully have himself, accept himself, in both his wholeness and his brokenness, he can neither give himself fully to another person nor fully accept the other person. So it is, too, with a woman. Structural forms of spiritual violence can significantly impact one's ability to love oneself and give oneself in love to another. Philosopher Theresa Tobin's case study of "Debbie" provides an apt example. Debbie is a white, middle-class Catholic woman who is not a direct survivor of clergy sexual abuse. But, following public attention to the clergy sexual abuse crisis in 2002, Debbie experienced an "overwhelming sense of betrayal by the church and a crisis of faith."[37] Tobin argues that Debbie's cumulative experience of misogyny in a church that prioritizes the moral imperative of female sexual purity at any cost produced "debilitating shame about being a woman."[38] This shame prohibited her from experiencing authentic intimacy with God and, we argue, presents barriers to giving herself freely in sexual intimacy to another human being.

Fourth, sexual activity is therapeutic and relieves distress. The human person is a psychosomatic unity, an intrinsic union of spirit and body. There is distinction between body and spirit but there is separation only when a person is dead, and there is ongoing and constant dialogue between them. When a couple makes love, each person brings to that experience all the psychological burdens that accompany daily life, including worries about the relationship, possible conception, work, finances, and children. Sexual activity makes possible the suspension of those anxieties and worries, at least for the moment, and has a healing effect on the individual. This relief of distress, however, depends on the nature of the relationship. If the relationship is just, loving, committed, and honest, relief of distress is often an intrinsic component of sexual activity. If, however, the relationship is promiscuous, inauthentic, or dishonest, while the physical act can suspend distress for the moment, the aftereffects of the experience can cause greater distress in the form of guilt, a sense of inauthentic or dishonest intimate communication, or objectification of the other.

Fifth, sexual activity is reconciling. There are no conflict-free relationships, not even in the most just and loving of relationships. Frictions, disagreements, misunderstandings are all inevitable aspects of any human relationship, and any and all of these experiences can create distress, trauma, and general distrust of the other in the relationship. One will find few couples who desire honest sexual intimacy at the peak of such quarrels, but intimacy returns after the resolution of the quarrel and may be an enhancement of it. Some couples claim that the best sex they have is after the resolution of an argument. This is because sexual intimacy heals the wounds caused by the quarrel and reestablishes the trust, commitment, and communion that may have been threatened by it. The sparks of this real-life, loving, and forgiving reconciliation illumine the presence in human life of the always reconciling and forgiving God. Again, just and loving sexual activity functions as a lowercase sacrament of the God present amid all the messiness of human and sexual life.

Finally, sexual activity is a profound act of thanksgiving. The embodied nature of the human person binds him or her to bodily expression, which is best exemplified, though by no means limited to, verbal language. Alongside, and indeed beyond, verbal language there is body language, and alongside and beyond body language there is ritual language, symbolic action with socially approved meanings. Couples can say to one another "I love you," or "I thank you," or "I forgive you," and in the spoken words they are reaching to meanings far beyond the sounds they make. They can say the same things in socially approved actions, by looks, by touches, by gifts, and in all of these actions they are similarly reaching far beyond the actions to express love, forgiveness, reconciliation, affirmation, thanksgiving. In the physical action of sexual intercourse, an action as symbolic as any spoken word, they express all these things in the most intimate, profound, and total way available to an embodied human being, namely, through the completely unmasked and, therefore, totally vulnerable body. They say to one another, in the words of the ancient Anglican wedding ritual, "with this body I thee worship."[39] They say, that is, in the etymological meaning of the word *worship*, I ascribe worth to you and to us, and for this worth I give thanks.

Couples who are Catholic cannot help but link this moment of sexual and mutual thanksgiving for human relationship with that liturgical thanksgiving for divine relationship they call Eucharist.[40] "This is my body which is given for you," Jesus says to his disciples at the Supper (Luke 22:19); "This is my body given for and to you," lovers say to one another in sexual intercourse. In both the Supper and in intercourse, the body and the person synonymous with it are vulnerable, even broken, but both body and person are given in love to the other, trusting that they will be received in love, handled with love, and healed. In the Supper, the body of Christ is given to be eaten; so, too, are the bodies of the truly human lovers in sexual activity. Theologian Adrian Thatcher points out legitimately that "many of the intimacies of lovemaking are fairly literally an eating of the body of the person one loves.

Kissing, especially deep kissing; the use of the tongue in caressing and stimulating; biting, sucking, and nibbling; these are all patently ways in which we eat the bodies of our lovers."[41]

The central theological point here is a very Catholic one. The God incarnate in the Christ who gives his body in the Supper for the salvation of all is also incarnate in the lovemaking of partners who give their bodies for the salvation of their relationship. The one ritual is as sacramental of the presence of God as the other, which is precisely why both Eucharist and marriage are listed among the Catholic uppercase Sacraments. We reemphasize that, though we are arguing here that heterosexual marriage is a Sacrament, what we argue about the stable, exclusive, just, and loving relationship applies also to same-sex relationships. They are also, at least, lowercase sacraments of, in Cardinal Hume's felicitous phrase, the "unending delight when one with God in the next."[42]

Any psychological-theological treatment of human sexuality and marital union must include their emotional dimensions. Emotions, strong, generalized feelings with both physical and psychological manifestations, are forms of evaluative judgments, apprehending value and disvalue for men and women. Martha Nussbaum argues that emotions "ascribe to certain things and persons outside a person's own control great importance for the person's own flourishing."[43] We caution that the evaluative judgment carried out by an emotion is not yet the rational judgment that affirms truth and goodness or the judgment of conscience that affirms ethical action. We prefer to say, therefore, in partial agreement with Nussbaum, that emotions are proto-judgments, preliminary apprehensions of value or disvalue leading to personal flourishing, which become part of the experiential data that precedes judgment of truth or conscience.

Emotions may be either positive or negative. Positive emotions include love, joy, hope, humor, trust, happiness, satisfaction; negative emotions include hatred, sadness, despair, anxiety, distrust, unhappiness, and dissatisfaction. Beyond the obvious physical union of bodies, there is in play in the act of just and loving sexual intercourse a complex combination of emotions that unites two individuals into one partnered person, the one body of Genesis. That act, on one occasion, can express mutual love, openness, healing, comfort, reconciliation and, on another occasion, heal trauma, woundedness, neediness, anxiety, or brokenness. Either way, the sexual act entails and reveals on discernment a wide spectrum of both positive and negative emotions. The revelation of these God-created emotions and their interpersonal outcomes in just and loving sexual intercourse also reveals their nature as lowercase sacraments, in and through which the God who creates, loves, heals, comforts, reconciles, and saves humans is incarnated and can be discerned. Emotional sexuality, we suggest, is part of the mystery of both divinity and humanity and demands, therefore, ongoing analysis to be better understood in an emotional sense so that it can be better understood also in a theological sense revelatory of the mysterious God.

SPIRITUAL/RELATIONAL SEXUALITY

The theological understanding of the communion between the three persons of the Trinity provides the model for, and is socially constructed from, genuine human communion, and divine grace is offered to each and every believer to share this communion with a loved partner through a multitude of actions, including sexual actions. To illustrate this theological claim, a group commissioned by the USCCB boldly asserts that mutually pleasurable sexual acts are possibly the human experiences that most fully symbolize the loving communication within the divine Trinity.[44] *The* characteristic of a stable sexual relationship, which distinguishes it from all other forms of friendship, is that it is expected to be an exclusive relationship. From what we have already explained in this chapter, it is not difficult to conclude that the communion between the partners expressed in sexual activity is a lowercase sacrament of the divine communion. That is precisely what the Catholic Church intends when it teaches that marriage is an uppercase Sacrament, an efficacious sign in human history of the God who *is* communion.

Sexual intercourse allows women and men a unique insight into the love and relationship shared within the Trinity. In that activity there is both a striving for the unconditional gift of self to the other and the unconditional reciprocation of the gift in return. Such mutuality, reciprocity, and unconditional acceptance reflect and reveal to careful discernment the total surrender of the persons in God. "It is our capacity to love and be loved," Charles Gallagher notes, "that makes us most God-like."[45] The love, including the sexual love, shared by a couple in relationship draws them more and more into communion, and this human communion reflects and reveals the divine communion, draws them closer not only to one another but also to God, and overflows into all their other relationships. Most profoundly, this sexual communion always procreates new life, just as the loving communion between the Father and Son always leads to the procession of the Spirit. Even in cases where the biological procreation of a child is neither possible nor desired for "serious reasons,"[46] their sexual union procreates and enhances the partners' life-in-communion in imitation, and as lowercase sacrament, of God and God's inner life-in-communion.

This is not to suggest that, in the moment of orgasm when the partners are momentarily isolated in each individual self, the divine communion is immediately revealed. It is to suggest, with the Catholic tradition, that the intimate communion achieved in just and loving intercourse, on reflection, reveals both the communion within the Godhead and the communion yet to be achieved between God and God's human creatures in glory. The God who is always mysterious to humans is sacramentally revealed to them on careful meditation on exclusive, just, and loving spousal sexual activity. The economic God is in very deed, as theologian Karl Rahner so consistently insisted, the immanent God.[47]

Spirituality is all about relationship. So, too, is human sexuality, from which "the human person receives the characteristics which, on the biological, psychological, and spiritual levels, make that person a man or a woman, and thereby largely condition his or her progress toward maturity and insertion into society."[48] Human sexuality, heterosexuality, lesbian and gay sexuality, bisexuality, intersexuality, and transgendered sexuality, is a gift from God that draws persons toward interpersonal relationship and communion. It is an intrinsic, mysterious dimension of human beings that draws an individual out of herself or himself and toward another. "Sexuality is a dimension of one's restless heart, which continually yearns for interpersonal communion, glimpsed and experienced to varying degrees in this life, ultimately finding full oneness only in God, here and hereafter."[49] In and through their sexuality and relationships humans seek to become both personally whole and holy. This relational gift is at the core of human identity and allows women and men to enter into communion with one another and with God. Our fundamentally relational nature, which makes us so vulnerable to harm from another, is also what gives us the opportunity to experience authentic union within ourselves, with others, and with God.

Relationship with the gospel "neighbor" takes several forms. First, and primarily, neighbor is the partner or intimate other with who I am in sexual relationship. Sexual acts are the most intimate communion between two people; in them two individuals become physically and personally a coupled one. Catholic tradition refers to this coupled relationship in terms of a covenant and a communion of persons and limits it, unreasonably we believe in light of the contemporary scientific evidence, to marriage between a man and a woman.[50] Neighbor also extends out into the human community beyond a person's family of support. Too often in Catholic history theology has focused on an individual's sexual acts and their impact on the individual's relationship with God, while neglecting the broader neighborly and societal implications of those acts. A shift in focus from only individuals to also broader community is especially relevant in sexual ethics. Too often, sexual and social ethics are seen in isolation from each other, each utilizing its own methodology and having its own point of reference. Whereas traditional Catholic sexual ethics tends to focus on physical acts and absolute norms that guide individuals and related couples, Catholic social ethics tends to focus on the network of human interrelationships that constitute a community and on general principles to guide these interrelationships towards the common good. Sexuality is a relational reality that challenges us to more fully integrate not only its individual but also its communal ethical dimensions.

NATURAL VERSUS HOLISTIC COMPLEMENTARITY

In the preceding, we draw heavily from the best of the Catholic tradition and its theological understanding of the goodness of human sexuality as an essential component of human dignity.

Unfortunately, there is a disconnect between this theological understanding of sexual human dignity and many of the sexual ethical doctrines, formulated as absolute norms. Pope Paul VI's encyclical *Humanae Vitae* reflects the theological understanding of the goodness of human sexuality but deduces from it an unjustified doctrine, the absolute prohibition of artificial contraception in the marital relationship, based on an unjustified principle, the inseparable link between the unitive and procreative meanings of the sexual act. The disconnect between theology and norms, we believe, resides in a fundamental anthropological (mis)understanding of the nature of the sexual person defined by "natural complementarity." This phrase was introduced into Catholic theological discourse by Pope John Paul II and justifies the absolute doctrines the Church teaches on human sexuality. In this final section, we present both that understanding and an alternative view of complementarity. In the following chapters, we present and critique the doctrines that the church deduces from its sexual anthropology and the spiritual and sexual trauma those doctrines cause among many of the faithful.

The phrase "natural complementarity" has appeared only relatively recently in church sexual teaching, in Pope John Paul II's *Familiaris Consortio* (1981).[51] Even though man and woman are conceded to be each "complete" in themselves, John Paul argues that "for forming a couple they are incomplete."[52] He further notes that "woman complements man, just as man complements woman....Womanhood expresses the 'human' as much as manhood does, but in a different and complementary way."[53] There are two general types of natural complementarity, biological and personal, explained elsewhere in church documents, with subtypes within each.

TYPES OF SEXUAL COMPLEMENTARITY IN MAGISTERIAL TEACHING	
I. Biological Complementarity	
Title	**Definition**
Heterogenital Complementarity	The physically functioning male and female sexual organs (penis and vagina)

Reproductive Complementarity	The physically functioning male and female reproductive organs used in sexual acts to biologically reproduce
II. Personal Complementarity	
Title	**Definition**
Communion Complementarity	The two-in-oneness within a heterogenital complementary marital relationship that is created and sustained by reproductive-type sexual acts
Affective Complementarity	The integrated psycho-affective, social, relational, and spiritual elements of the human person grounded in heterogenital complementarity
Parental Complementarity	Heterogenitally complementary parents who fulfill the second dimension of reproductive complementarity, namely, the education of children

According to the church's understanding of complementarity, since reproductive complementarity is not essential within a marital relationship, the foundation for any ethical sexual act is grounded in heterogenital complementarity, the physical genitals, penis and vagina. These are the sine qua non for an ethical sexual act. Reproductive complementarity limits ethical sexual acts to reproductive-type sexual acts. Any nonreproductive sexual acts, anal or oral sex for example when procreation is impossible, violate heterosexual complementarity and frustrate human sexual dignity. Personal complementarity flows from biological complementarity; the physical is foundational and primary; the relational is secondary.

While the church consistently condemns homosexual acts on the grounds that they violate heterogenital and reproductive complementarity (that is the so-called natural law argument), it does not explain why they also violate personal complementarity other than to assert that homosexual acts "do not proceed from a genuine affective and sexual complementarity."[54] This statement, however, begs the question whether or not such acts can ever be ethical on the level of sexual and personal complementarity. Though the church has not officially confronted this question, monogamous, loving, committed, same-sex couples have confronted it experientially and testify that they do experience affective and communion complementarity in and through their homosexual acts, a claim amply supported by scientific research.[55] They add that these acts also facilitate the integration of their human sexuality and bring them closer to self, to neighbor, and to God.

We suggest that the needed complementarity for an ethical sexual act is *holistic* complementarity that unites people bodily, affectively, spiritually, and personally in light of a person's sexual orientation. Heterogenital complementarity is needed for reproduction, but it is not needed for the sexual, affective, spiritual, and personal connection between two people that the recent Catholic tradition acknowledges as an end of marriage equal to procreation.[56] Though they cannot exhibit genital or reproductive complementarity, lesbian and gay individuals can exhibit this holistic complementarity. In light of the various types of complementarities listed above, an ethical sexual act must be an authentic integration and expression of holistic complementarity as set forth in the following diagram.

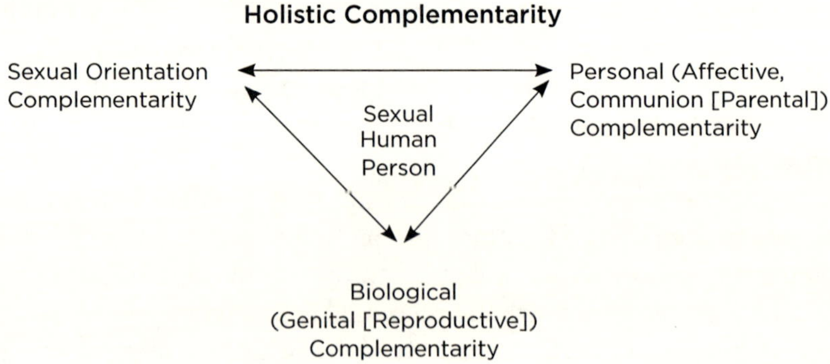

Holistic complementarity includes orientation, personal, and biological complementarity, and the integration and manifestation of all three in honest, loving, committed sexual acts that facilitate a person's ability to love God, neighbor, and self in a more profound and holy way.

Two immediate implications for Catholic sexual ethics follow if we espouse holistic complementarity as our foundational anthropology for ethical sexual acts. The first is that the church's absolute ethical norm prohibiting all homosexual acts and nonreproductive heterosexual acts must, at least, be reexamined. Without prior consideration of a person's sexual orientation, a sexual act that violates heterogenital complementarity can no longer be considered ipso facto intrinsically disordered. Genital complementarity is relevant in determining the ethics of sexual acts, but it is not the primary factor. The ethics of the use of the genitals in sexual acts must be determined primarily in light of orientation and personal complementarity.

The second implication for Catholic sexual ethics follows from the first, the foundation for doctrines on sexuality needs to be redefined. Current church teaching posits, for lesbians, gays, and heterosexuals, an intrinsic relationship between biological and personal complementarity in which heterogenital complementarity is primary and foundational. On this foundation, homosexual acts are ipso facto unethical because they violate heterogenital complementarity, regardless of sexual orientation and the relational meaning of the act for personal complementarity. In holistic complementarity, there is an integrated relationship among orientation, personal, and biological complementarity that serves as the foundation for sexual doctrines. In this relationship, for heterosexuals, lesbians, and gays, orientation and personal complementarity are primary, and they determine what constitutes authentic genital complementarity in a particular sexual act. If orientation complementarity indicates that two persons are of heterosexual orientation, then personal complementarity between them would indicate that authentic and ethical genital complementarity would be male-female. If orientation complementarity indicates that two persons are of homosexual orientation, then personal complementarity between them would indicate that authentic genital and ethical complementarity would be male-male or female-female. In current church teaching, heterogenital complementarity is the primary foundational dimension for the essential relationship between biological and personal complementarity. In our holistic complementarity anthropology, orientation and personal complementarity are the foundational dimensions for the integrated relationship among orientation, personal, and biological complementarity.

In light of these two considerations, we advance the following regarding sexual doctrines and ethical sexual acts. Sexual doctrines must be formulated, and ethical sexual acts must be defined, in light of a revised theological anthropology grounded in holistic, not heterogenital, complementarity. A person's sexual orientation is a fundamental dimension of her or his humanity, and sexual doctrines that prescribe or proscribe specific sexual acts must be formulated and applied in light of that orientation. Sexual doctrines must seek to facilitate the integration of holistic complementarity, orientation, personal, and biological complementarity. This integration does not allow for the absolute condemnation of particular sexual acts without due consideration of a person's sexual orientation and the meaning of this sexual act for persons in relationship—that is, in personal complementarity—which is expressed in and through genital (not necessarily heterogenital) complementarity. Whereas the church's model posits absolute doctrines forbidding homosexual acts and nonreproductive sexual acts for heterosexual married couples, our model cannot justify these absolute doctrines.

Instead, based on holistic complementarity, we propose the following doctrine. An abusive, dishonest, uncommitted, unloving, unjust sexual act, heterosexual or homosexual, is ethically wrong; a caring, honest, committed, loving, just sexual act, heterosexual or homosexual, is ethically right. The realization of holistic complementarity, that is, the integration of orientation, personal, and biological complementarity, determines whether or not a sexual act is ethical or unethical. In the case of a person with a homosexual orientation, an ethical, caring, honest, committed, loving, just, sexual act will be expressed with male-male or female-female genitalia. In the case of a person with a heterosexual orientation, an ethical, caring, honest, committed, loving, just, sexual act will be expressed with male-female genitalia.

CONCLUSION

Our understanding of holistic complementarity posits a primarily relational anthropology to justify just and loving sexual acts between people with a heterosexual, homosexual, or bisexual orientation. The church's understanding of complementarity posits a primarily physicalist, heterogenital, procreative anthropology to justify doctrines that prohibit all nonreproductive sexual acts, heterosexual or homosexual. This understanding has caused, and continues to cause, unnecessary sexual and spiritual trauma for both heterosexual and same-sex couples. The following chapters explore and critique the Catholic Church's specific doctrines on human sexuality.

5

ANTHROPOLOGICAL DOCTRINAL LANGUAGE AND MARITAL SEXUAL ISSUES IN THE CHURCH

(Part 1)

Every action which, whether in anticipation of the conjugal act, or in its accomplishment, or in the development of its natural "consequences," proposes, whether as an end or as a means, to render procreation impossible is intrinsically evil. (*Catechism* 2370)

If the divorced are remarried civilly, they find themselves in a situation that objectively contravenes God's law. Consequently, they cannot receive Holy Communion as long as this situation persists. (CDF, "Letter to the Bishops of the Catholic Church Concerning the Reception of Holy Communion by the Divorced and Remarried Members of the Faithful" 4)

The Church has consistently taught that human love "demands a total and definitive gift of persons to one another" that can only be made in marriage. (USCCB, "Marriage Preparation and Cohabiting Couples" 1)

Techniques that entail the dissociation of husband and wife, by the intrusion of a person other than the couple...are gravely immoral. (*Catechism* 2376)

In contemporary Catholic teaching, there are two major models of marriage: marriage as a procreative institution in which procreation is the primary end of marriage and marriage as an interpersonal communion in which the mutual love and communion of the spouses is the primary end. The latter model fully blossomed at the

Second Vatican Council,[1] but continuing confusion between the two models has led the Catholic Church to language and actions that cause spiritual trauma to both the spousal communion that is marriage and the spouses who attempt to live it. In this chapter, we examine the ethics of four common experiences related to marriage in our world that are the occasions of such language, actions, and trauma.

CONTRACEPTION

Several years ago, in a discussion with church officials on Paul VI's *Humanae Vitae*, we cited examples from human experience that could justify a married couple choosing to use artificial contraception. That choice, of course, violates *Humanae Vitae*'s assertion that "each and every marital act must of necessity retain its intrinsic relationship to the procreation of human life"[2] and its prohibition of every type of artificial contraception. A diocesan official responded that human experience has nothing to do with church teaching. That statement is simply wrong. It demonstrates a lack of understanding of the Catholic ethical tradition and the role and function of human experience as a source of ethical knowledge. On the twenty-fifth anniversary of *Humanae Vitae*, Richard McCormick noted the importance of "the place of experience and human reflection"[3] in any analysis of the encyclical's teaching, and that importance continues today.

Catholic ethics generally accepts four sources of ethical knowledge: scripture, tradition, reason, and experience.[4] Any Catholic ethic seeking to be normative will, of necessity, have to interpret and prioritize these four sources into a comprehensive theological ethics. Here, we focus on only one of those sources, human experience, which *Gaudium et Spes* lauds as opening "new roads to truth."[5] We note here that in contemporary Catholic theological ethics there are two schools of thought with respect to church doctrines. One school, sometimes labeled "traditionalist," defends absolute church doctrines; the other, sometimes labeled "revisionist," defends a critical approach to absolute magisterial norms.[6] The former argues *deductively* from past church teachings that human experience is to be judged by ethical norms derived from those teachings; the latter argues *inductively* from human experience itself that experience must be consulted in the formulation of ethical norms that contextualize ethical principles.

The Catholic natural law tradition teaches[7] and Pope John Paul II affirms[8] the relevance of experience for formulating ethical norms and criteria to judge the rightness or wrongness of an action. For example, how do we know that adultery is intrinsically wrong? Is it because the Church says so? No. It is because human experience has demonstrated that committing adultery damages relationships to one's spouse and family, to the spouse and family of the other person, and ultimately to God. To deny the ethical relevance of human experience for assisting in the formulation of norms for judging the rightness or wrongness of an action reflects a reductionist methodology where the only legitimate human experience is that which conforms to and confirms established norms. For instance, such a methodology allowed the church's approbation of slavery until Pope Leo XIII's rejection of it in 1890 and the denial of religious freedom until the Second Vatican Council's approbation of it in 1965.

We argue that a deeper reflection on human experience leads to the revision of the prohibition of artificial contraception and could alleviate sexual trauma caused by that doctrinal teaching. We must first define what we mean by human experience. We concur with George Schner's definition. *Human experience* is "the conscious apprehension of inner or outer reality through senses and mind…active participation in specific events and the knowledge gained by such participation."[9] We emphasize two things: experience is never a standalone source of theological ethics and "my experience" alone is never a source at all. Experience that is a source for theological ethics is communal experience, and only when it is in constructive conversation with the three other sources—scripture, tradition, and reason. Such experience, as consciously apprehended by and actively participated in by women and men, is never neutral experience. It is always socially interpreted by both individuals and communities in a specific sociohistorical context. It is differently construed, perhaps, by "me," by "us," and by "them," traditionalist and revisionist theologians, for instance. In a synodal church that is a communion of believers,[10] some of whom are laity and some of whom are celibate clerics with no experience of marriage, including the Bishop of Rome, the resolution of different interpretations of experience to arrive at ethical truth requires an open and respectful dialogue, such as that lauded and embraced by Pope John Paul II[11] and being integrated into the church by Pope Francis's process of synodality. Francis offers good advice for that dialogue. "Keep an open mind. Don't get bogged down in your own limited ideas and opinions but be prepared to change or expand them. The combination of two different ways of thinking can lead to a synthesis that enriches both" (*AL* 139).

Cultural experience provides a basis of reflection for the formulation of ethical norms. *Gaudium et Spes* teaches that "thanks to the experience of past ages, the progress of the sciences, and the treasures hidden in the various forms of human culture, the nature of man himself is more clearly revealed and new roads to truth are opened" (44). There is a serious disconnect between the universal teaching prohibiting artificial contraception and particular contextual issues that the teaching does not consider. We briefly explore two of those issues.

First, the bishops of Canada note the following in their statement preceding the 1994 U.N. Conference on Population and Development in Cairo: "We are convinced that unchecked growth in population is a function of poverty."[12] There is substantial evidence indicating a strong correlation in developing countries between high birth rates and extreme poverty leading to disease and early death.[13] Couples who do not have access to contraception and who live in dire poverty have to live with the reality of giving birth to children they cannot support and, too often, experience the death of those children. Such experiences are a source of trauma induced, in whole or in part, by Catholic doctrine that absolutely prohibits contraception.

There is also evidence that family planning policies that use contraceptives have reduced both fertility rates and death rates in many developing countries by more than half.[14] The populations in these countries are least able to provide adequate nutrition, care, and basic needs for children born into poverty as a result of, among other factors, failed "natural" attempts to regulate reproduction. Given the strong correlation between fertility and poverty, the Canadian Bishops' proposal is eminently reasonable and reflects the principle of responsible parenthood: "We recognize that a couple's responsibility to decide the number and spacing of their children must take into account a number of factors: the family's own limits in regards to health as well as their material resources."[15] In spite of this recognition, experience, and scientific evidence, the church has failed to change its teaching on contraception.

A second disconnect in the exceptionless norm prohibiting artificial contraception is that the church's only approved method of birth regulation, natural family planning, presumes mutual decision-making between the spouses in a marriage. While this may be the ideal of a marital relationship, it is not the cultural reality of the vast majority of married couples throughout the world, whose relationships are controlled by patriarchal cultures.[16] In these cultures, the husband is the authority in the home and in the marital relationship, and the fundamental equality required to freely practice natural family planning is absent. In this existential context, it is oppressive for the church to prescribe an approach to regulating birth that is countercultural and creates an undue burden and trauma for women. Given the varied existential contexts of lived marriages across the world, sexual norms cannot be a "one size fits all" ethic. Just as justice and fairness are general principles that must be adapted to specific cultural contexts, so too responsible parenthood must be adapted to specific cultural contexts. To teach and act otherwise is irresponsible, causes trauma, and can actually damage spousal relationships within a marriage.

Another type of experience is contemporary scientific experience. New discoveries challenge traditional ethical answers based on incomplete scientific knowledge and raise new questions that demand new answers. Some new answers will be drawn from traditional ethical principles, but in a more nuanced way that may lead to the revision of a norm. While the church has emphasized the need to integrate the discoveries of the human sciences in formulating ethical truth,[17] it has been very selective in doing so. This selectivity is evidenced in three distinct ways: first, when it ignores what the sciences have to contribute to the discernment of ethical truth when such a contribution would challenge a preestablished norm; second, when it allows science, defined in a narrowly biological sense, to disproportionately inform the normative; and third, when it misrepresents scientific evidence.

Experience indicates at least two realities about Catholic doctrinal teaching on artificial contraception. First, experience fundamentally challenges the doctrinal teaching and foundational principle on which it is based. The so-called inseparability principle claims an "inseparable connection, established by God, which man on his own initiative may not break, between the unitive meaning and the procreative meaning which are both inherent to the marriage act."[18] Basing itself on this inseparability principle, the church absolutely prohibits any artificial contraception to regulate fertility, since it prevents the procreative meaning and is claimed to disrupt the unitive meaning of the sexual act. The procreative meaning means that the couple has to be open to the transmission of life, but not that they actually have to biologically procreate. Pope Pius XII taught that a couple could choose not to procreate for the duration of the marriage for "serious reasons," but could only do so by using the rhythm method.[19] One major problem with the inseparability principle is that the procreative meaning of the sexual act is not present for most days during a woman's fertility cycle and is never present for infertile couples or postmenopausal women. It is morally meaningless to claim a biologically procreative meaning for every sexual act when the act lacks that meaning most of the time for fertile couples, and always for infertile couples. In such cases, there exists only a unitive meaning of the sexual act, an interpersonally, not biologically, procreative act. Sexual intercourse may be said to be biologically procreative only when actual reproduction is possible. That is why many theologians choose to discuss the unitive and procreative meanings of not every sexual act but of the overall marital relationship and prioritize the unitive meaning over the procreative meaning.[20]

Second, many women and married couples indicate that the Catholic teaching that allows only natural family planning as the method for fertility regulation within marriage puts incredible stress on the couple, especially on the wife, emotionally, psychologically, and spiritually, especially on poor couples who cannot afford another child. It does extensive, and demonstratively sometimes irreparable, damage to their marital relationship. The "rhythm method," as it was called before the technology of natural family planning, "failed over and over again while the necessity of denying themselves sex caused rifts in couples already stressed by the care of large families."[21] It is basic physiology that women desire sex most when ovulating, the time during which they may likely become pregnant and must abstain if they want to prevent pregnancy.

Patty Crowley, an American married woman and member of Pope John XXIII's Papal Birth Control Commission, comments that "any simple psychology book tells us that people who are in a constant state of stricture in an area that should be open and free and loving are damaging themselves and consequently others." Besides being unreliable, "rhythm is psychologically harmful, does not foster married love or unity and, moreover, is unnatural. To me and many Catholics rhythm is a manifestation of an attitude of many clergymen looking down from their pedestals, offering us glib platitudes and the letter of the law, without seeing our [experiences and] real problems." Crowley continues, "It just struck me as ridiculous....How could they be talking about marriage and birth control of all things without a lot more input from the persons involved?"[22] Her critique applies similarly to natural family planning. Crowley sums up well the frustration felt by married couples and the importance of experience to inform doctrinal teaching.

In addition, the doctrinal language that contraception is "intrinsically evil," and its use may constitute a mortal sin caused extensive trauma, again especially to women. They had to choose between honoring their or their husband's desire to have sex during a potentially fertile period and the possibility of an unwanted pregnancy, or eternal damnation if they chose to use a contraceptive. The teaching and its impact on marital relationships and, for many, relationship with God caused direct, indirect, or complex trauma. The experience of married couples both challenges the inseparability principle and indicates its traumatic impact.

Another issue that the church's ban on artificial contraception does not adequately consider is the reality of HIV/AIDS, especially in developing countries. It continues to condemn the use of condoms to prevent HIV, even in the case of serodiscordant married couples where one spouse is HIV+ and the other spouse is not. Cardinal Trujillo, then president of the Pontifical Council for the Family, claimed publicly that the HIV virus can penetrate through a latex condom. He also claimed that promoting condom use leads to sexual promiscuity.[23] The first claim is false; latex condoms, when used properly, *do* prevent the spread of the HIV virus. The second claim raises a merely correlational relationship to the level of a causal relationship, though there is no scientifically demonstrated causal connection between contraception and sexual promiscuity. There are two distinct issues regarding HIV and the use of condoms: protecting life and contraception. Given the socioeconomic context of people in developing countries where HIV medications are unaffordable for many, the principles of human dignity, marital love, and responsible parenthood would certainly justify the use of condoms where one spouse is HIV positive.[24]

The Second Vatican Council declared that the teaching of the Catholic Church is preserved by the Holy Spirit in all the faithful, laity and clerics together.

> The body of the faithful as a whole, anointed as they are by the Holy One (cf. 1 John 2:20; 2:27), cannot err in matters of belief [they are infallible]. Thanks to a supernatural sense of the faith which characterizes the people *as a whole*, it manifests this unerring quality when, "from the bishops to the last of the faithful," it manifests universal agreement in matters of faith and morals.[25]

The social sciences provide substantial evidence that the Catholic teaching on contraception is not believed by a vast majority of laity and clerics, including many bishops.[26] Some 85 percent of Catholic couples use a form of contraception prohibited by their church. In 1963, over 50 percent of American Catholics accepted church teaching on contraception; in 1987, that number dropped to 18 percent; in 2016, only 13 percent affirmed that teaching.[27] These statistics, combined with countless Catholic theological arguments challenging the teaching on contraception, warrant a revision of the doctrine. We align with German theologian Dietmar Mieth's statement: "[Fifty] years of non-acceptance that goes into very considerable detail should suffice to consider a revision"[28] of the Catholic doctrine on contraception.

DIVORCE AND REMARRIAGE

On October 14, 1994, the CDF made public a Letter on divorced and civilly remarried couples without an annulment, reaffirming Catholic doctrine prohibiting communion for the divorced and remarried without an annulment. "If the divorced are remarried civilly, they find themselves in a situation that objectively contravenes God's law. Consequently, they cannot receive Holy Communion as long as this situation persists."[29] It goes on to quote Pope John Paul II and his statement on this issue in *Familiaris Consortio*.[30] In our response to this doctrinal teaching, we explore first the trauma-inducing impact of this doctrine on civilly remarried couples, then the problematic theology behind the doctrine, and finally Pope Francis's proposal for a change in the doctrine that is pastoral, healing, and reflects God's unconditional love and mercy.

Doctrine on Divorce and Trauma

In and of itself, divorce is frequently a seriously trauma-inducing reality. Divorce can occur for a variety of reasons and its impact can cause emotional, psychological, relational, and spiritual trauma to the spouses, their children, and their extended family. This is the case for both Catholic sacramental marriages and nonsacramental marriages. In the United States, 34 percent of Catholics have experienced a divorce.[31] If an individual divorces and does not receive a church annulment, an official declaration that the marriage was always invalid, and remarries civilly, Catholic doctrine teaches that the remarried couple must live celibate, as brother and sister. If they do not do so, then they are considered to be in an adulterous relationship and prohibited from receiving communion.

This doctrine is another example where the church takes a deductive approach to ethical norms and takes little or no account of the particular circumstances of a person's lived experience that may have led to marital breakdown. There are many reasons why an individual would not seek an annulment, an uncooperative former spouse, personal trauma and anger, sexual abuse that led to the divorce, or treatment by the church that alienated a divorced spouse. Although the annulment process is meant to be merciful, healing, and reconciling to the church, that is not always the experience of those who seek to go through the annulment process. Prohibiting participation in communion if an individual remarried without an annulment may cause further trauma and alienation relationally, emotionally, psychologically, and spiritually. The one-size-fits-all approach to divorce and remarriage ignores the various lived experiences that brought people to divorce in the first place and functions as a form of banishment from the church, perceived as also banishment from God, which can be alienating, humiliating, oppressive, and detrimental to human dignity and well-being. When people are most vulnerable in their lives and trying to rebuild a meaningful, committed relationship, the doctrinal language imposes religious sanctions regardless of the individual circumstances that led to divorce and the failure to seek or receive an annulment. It communicates judgment and condemnation ("living in sin") rather than merciful accompaniment, compassion, and love. Statistics show that 62 percent of Catholics support a change in the doctrine on the denial of communion to the divorced and remarried.[32] The experience of divorced and remarried couples challenges the doctrine and the theological principle behind it.

Theological Defense of Doctrine on Divorce

The CDF's Letter purports to articulate the doctrine of the Catholic Church concerning marriage, divorce, and remarriage, a doctrine it claims to trace back to "fidelity to the words of Jesus Christ," citing Mark 10:11–12. It declares that a new marriage cannot be recognized as valid if a preceding marriage was valid and its spouses are still alive. That way of articulating the doctrine of the church is, we suggest, too loose to be true. The traditional teaching of the church is enshrined in the Code of Canon Law: "The essential properties of marriage are unity and indissolubility" (can. 1056). The words are important: "the essential properties of *marriage*," every valid marriage, not just Christian marriage, includes indissolubility and that by the will of God from the beginning. Since it teaches that God created marriage indissoluble, one would then expect the Catholic Church to hold all valid marriages as indissoluble. It never has and still does not.

From its earliest history, the church has always nuanced its teaching about divorce in light of some circumstance or other, and it continues to so nuance it today. Marriages of unbaptized persons, for instance, which the church regards as valid and indissoluble by God's will, are regularly dissolved "in favor of the faith of the party who received baptism" (can. 1143). This practice is known as the Pauline Privilege, from a nuance given to the words of Jesus by the Apostle Paul (1 Cor 7:12–16). At different times and for different reasons popes have added other nuances, all lumped together under the heading Petrine Privilege.[33] The church also enshrines in her law that in a Christian marriage indissolubility "acquire(s) a distinctive firmness by reason of the sacrament" (can. 1056). Valid sacramental marriages, therefore, one could expect, are immune to dissolution, but not so. Valid sacramental marriages which have not been sexually consummated are dissolved "by the Roman Pontiff for a just reason, at the request of both parties or of either party" (can. 1142).

Despite its claim, then, that indissolubility is an essential property of marriage, the Catholic Church dissolves some valid marriages of both baptized and unbaptized persons. The result of all this, canon lawyer James Provost judges, is that "the actual number of marriages to which the church's teaching on indissolubility actually applies is quite limited in practice."[34] When one takes due account of all the historical nuancing of the words of Jesus on marriage and divorce, it becomes clear that fidelity to the words of Jesus is far from the Catholic Church's absolute prohibition of divorce and remarriage.

Pope Francis: A Pastoral and Merciful Doctrine

Pope Francis seems to have taken due account of historical nuancing in his pastoral approach to the divorced and remarried and his nuancing of doctrinal teaching. He shows his grasp of Catholic theological ethics and practice when he confronts the "irregular situation" of those divorced and remarried without annulment. There are two ways, he declares, to deal with them, to cast them off from the church or to reintegrate them into the church. The church's way, he declares, "has always been the way of Jesus, the way of mercy and reinstatement [or reintegration]" (*AL*

296). He acknowledges that the divorced and remarried without annulment "can find themselves in a variety of situations, which should not be pigeonholed or fit into overly rigid classifications leaving no room for a suitable personal and pastoral discernment" (*AL* 298). In a footnote, he cites the Second Vatican Council's judgment that, even if they take the option the church offers them for participation in communion of living celibately as brother and sister, in this circumstance "it often happens that faithfulness is endangered and the good of the children suffers."[35]

Because the divorced and remarried are not all to be lumped into one circumstance but are in many different circumstances, some of which can lessen and even eliminate any ethical fault or sin, "a pastor cannot feel that it is enough simply to apply ethical laws to those living in 'irregular' situations, as if they were stones to throw at people's lives." This manner of acting would bespeak not the merciful heart of a minister of Christ but "the closed heart of one used to hiding behind the church's teachings…'judging at times with superiority and superficiality difficult cases and wounded families'" (*AL* 305). This manner of acting can cause further trauma for already traumatized divorced and remarried people. The divorced and remarried are in a variety of circumstances, which should not be pigeonholed into one rigid classification "leaving no room for a suitable personal and pastoral discernment," that is, for a suitable personal and pastoral decision of conscience.

Francis confesses that "no easy recipes exist" (*AL* 298), but "conversation with the priest, in the internal forum [confession] contributes to the formation [or discernment] of a correct judgment on what hinders the possibility of a fuller participation in the life of the church and what steps can be taken to re-establish it and make it grow." Fuller participation includes participating in the sacraments, including the Eucharist. To avoid any appearance of laxity, this internal forum discernment must include "humility, discretion, and love for the church and her teaching, in a sincere search for God's will and a desire to make a more perfect response to it" (*AL* 300). The outcome of this discernment process guided by a spiritual director is that personal conscience can recognize "with a certain moral security" that "a given situation does not correspond to the overall demands of the Gospel," that "what for now is the most generous response which can be given to God," and that "it is what God himself is asking amid the concrete complexity of one's limits, while not yet fully the objective ideal" (*AL* 303).

Discussion of a solution to the issue of communion for the divorced and remarried without annulment has caused much discussion among Catholics and has even given rise to the accusation that Francis is betraying the Catholic tradition. Francis's approach, however, is not a betrayal but a return to the authentic tradition that reflects Jesus's words and the merciful compassion of the gospel. The pope is simply restating clearly what is ancient Catholic doctrine and practice, though that doctrine and practice had been allowed to drift into the ethical shadows and in *Amoris Laetitia* is being mercifully and lovingly renewed. His restatement of Catholic doctrine and practice should be codified doctrinally and canonically to alleviate the trauma-inducing effects, of banning from communion the divorced and remarried without an annulment.

COHABITATION

Couples seeking to be married in the Catholic Church and not already living together are a rarity in the Western world today. Seventy percent of all first marriages in the United States are now preceded by cohabitation,[36] cohabitation more than doubled from 1996 to 2017,[37] and nearly 75 percent of Catholics approve of cohabitation.[38] Though it varies by country, the number of cohabiting couples in Europe has substantially increased as well.[39] Cohabitation, therefore, is an ever-increasing phenomenon in human experience, and human experience, as we have argued, is a long-established source of Catholic ethical reflection and judgment.[40] The reality of cohabitation that may or may not lead to marriage poses a challenge for Catholic ethical teaching that condemns premarital sex as intrinsically immoral. How do we navigate, from a Christian perspective, the disconnect between the reality of the lived experience of the majority of Catholic couples and this official Catholic teaching?

First, we define what we mean by the term *cohabitation*. It names the situation of a man and a woman who, though not married as husband and wife, live together and enjoy intimate sexual relations. Cohabitation so understood raises a crucial Catholic red flag, for it is contrary to traditional Catholic teaching that prescribes that, to be ethical, "any human genital act whatsoever may be placed only within the framework of marriage."[41] Second, we introduce an important distinction, for not all cohabitors or cohabitations are alike. Fifteen years ago, we submitted to the American church a twofold typology of cohabitors and their cohabitations: there are cohabitors who intend to marry one another in the future and cohabitors who do not intend to marry one another. The cohabitation of the former we named *nuptial cohabitation*, the cohabitation of the latter *nonnuptial cohabitation*.[42] We are happy to see Pope Francis embrace this distinction, if not our terminology, and we shall come to him in a moment. The two types of cohabitation have seriously different effects on any subsequent marriage.

A research datum about premarital cohabitation that has become beloved of anticohabitation commentators is that it tends to be associated with a heightened risk of divorce.[43] Their reliance on this datum leaves both them and their pastoral responses at risk of being outdated and inaccurate, for more recent studies report more nuanced data about the relationship of cohabitation and divorce. As early as 1992, Robert Schoen showed that the inverse relationship between premarital cohabitation and subsequent marital stability was minimal for recent birth cohorts, a result that he linked to the growing prevalence of cohabitation.[44] In 1997, Susan McRae demonstrated for her British sample that "younger generations do not show the same link between pre-marital cohabitation and marriage dissolution." She agreed with Schoen's conclusion that "as cohabitation becomes the majority pattern before marriage, this link will become progressively weaker."[45] That majority pattern has now arrived. In a sophisticated Australian study that controlled for age at cohabitation, educational level, importance of religion in the relationship, parental divorce, and having a child before marriage, all strong predictors of divorce, David de Vaus and his colleagues found that the link between cohabitation and marital instability was apparent only for earlier cohorts.[46] In 2017, Sheri Stritof reported the same datum from Europe.[47]

One of America's most respected marriage researchers, Linda Waite, endorses our thesis that not all cohabitors are alike. She explains that "those on their way to the altar," our nuptial cohabitors, "look and act like already-married couples in most ways, and those with no plans to marry," our nonnuptial cohabitors, "look and act very different. For many engaged cohabiting couples, living together is a step on the path to marriage, not a different road altogether."[48] Pope John Paul II teaches that conjugal love "aims at a deeply personal unity, a unity that, beyond union in one flesh, leads to forming one heart and soul; it demands indissolubility and faithfulness in definitive mutual giving; and it is open to fertility."[49] We submit that this describes the situation not only of married couples but also of nuptial cohabitors who have committed to such a loving relationship with one another and who, when their circumstances permit, will later come to the church to be married. They come to the church to publicly celebrate their love for each other and to give it stability through the public commitment of marital vows to each other, to the church, and to God.

The Final Report of the 2015 Synod on the Family condemned all cohabitation as unethical, guided by the Catholic tradition that, to be ethical, "any human genital act whatsoever may be placed only within the framework of marriage." In theory, Pope Francis ought also to condemn it for the same reason, but he does not. Instead, in *Amoris Laetitia,* he does three eminently Catholic things. First, he makes a distinction with respect to cohabitation; second, he invokes a long-established Catholic ethical tradition that teaches that circumstances can extenuate and even nullify ethical culpability; third, he invokes another long-established Catholic ethical tradition, the authority and inviolability of individual conscience.

First, Francis distinguishes between "cohabitation which totally excludes any intention to marry" (*AL* 53), or nonnuptial cohabitation, and cohabitation "not motivated by prejudice or resistance to a sacramental union, but by cultural or contingent situations" (*AL* 294), or nuptial cohabitation. Among contingent situations, he especially singles out material poverty that leads couples to judge that "celebrating a marriage is too expensive in the social circumstances…and drives people into *de facto* unions" (*AL* 294) like cohabitation. "*De facto* unions may not simply be equated with marriage" (*AL* 52), he argues, but they need a constructive pastoral response, rather than outright ethical condemnation that causes stress and trauma among those seeking to transform them into opportunities leading to the full reality of marriage. Cohabiting couples need to be welcomed and guided patiently; they need to be accompanied by church ministers, integrated into the church community, and pointed to the full reality of Christian marriage. The church, Francis argues, must "never desist from proposing the full ideal of marriage, God's plan in all its grandeur," but neither must it ever desist from accompanying "with mercy and patience the eventual stages of personal growth as these progressively appear" (*AL* 307).

Second, the pope sprinkles his exhortation with another firmly Catholic teaching. "Imputability and responsibility for an action," he explains, "can be diminished and even nullified by ignorance, inadvertence, duress, fear"; and "affective immaturity, force of acquired habit, conditions of anxiety or other psychological or social factors *lessen or even extenuate* moral culpability" and therefore grave sin.[50] Taking his stand firmly on that long-established Catholic tradition, Francis draws attention to the extenuating circumstances of "dire poverty and great limitations" (*AL* 50), as well as drug use and family and societal violence (*AL* 51). He complains, justly, of those who feel "it is enough to apply moral laws to those living in 'irregular situations' as if they were stones to throw at people's lives. This would bespeak the closed heart of one used to hiding behind the church's teachings, 'sitting on the chair of Moses and judging at times with superiority and superficiality difficult cases and wounded families'" (*AL* 305). Throwing stones at such people, especially the poor who have little control over their socioeconomic reality, and invoking God's judgment and condemnation is personal trauma inducing. It compounds the traumatic reality of living in poverty, for example, with a judgment of spiritual exclusion. Francis dismisses such a judgment as antithetical to the gospel. At times, "we put so many conditions on mercy that we empty it of its concrete meaning and real significance. That is the worst way of watering down [and abusing] the Gospel" (*AL* 311). "It can no longer be said," he argues, "that all those in any irregular situation are living in a state of mortal sin and are deprived of sanctifying grace" (*AL* 301). This all applies to nuptial cohabitors and to the challenging circumstances that may have forced them to begin their marital union before their ceremonial wedding.

Third, Francis acknowledges and employs throughout *Amoris Laetitia* the standard Catholic teaching on the authority and inviolability of individual conscience we discussed in chapter 1. "We find it hard," Francis declares, "to make room for the consciences of the faithful, who very often respond *as best they can* to the Gospel amid their limitations and are capable of carrying out their own discernment in complex situations." We have been called, he warns, "to form consciences, not to replace them" (*AL* 37, emphasis added). Cohabiting Catholics are not to be forced to act contrary to their consciences; nor are they to be restrained from acting in accordance with their consciences. Francis's pastoral approach to Catholic doctrine on cohabitation is good news indeed. It communicates hope, compassion, and mercy rather than trauma-inducing guilt, judgment, and alienation.

ARTIFICIAL REPRODUCTIVE TECHNOLOGY

There is another population of Catholic spouses, statistically less significant, but no less humanly important, than those we have considered. That population comprises spouses who need the help of artificial reproductive technology (ART) to conceive a child. The trauma experienced by such couples is twofold. The first trauma is a couple who realizes that, for whatever reason, they are unable to conceive naturally. The compounding second trauma is the judgment of Catholic doctrine that to use available technologies that could facilitate artificial conception are gravely unethical. In 1987, the CDF issued an *Instruction* prohibiting the use of ARTs. "The church's teaching on marriage and human procreation affirms the 'inseparable connection, willed by God and unable to be broken by man on his own initiative, between the two meanings of the conjugal act: the unitive meaning and the procreative meaning.'"[51] Basing itself on this inseparability principle, the church prohibits any "artificial fertilization." We reflect on that prohibition.

For the Catholic Church, artificial reproductive technologies (ARTs), defined as "non-coital methods of conception that involve manipulation of both eggs and sperm,"[52] interfere with the inseparability principle by separating the unitive and procreative meanings of sexual intercourse. Progressive theologians tend to think that, although ARTs often do not rely on direct sexual intercourse for reproduction, they still may indirectly fulfill both the unitive and procreative ends of marriage considered as an intimate interpersonal whole. When the marital relationship is seen, as it has been seen since Vatican II in contemporary Catholic theology, as an interpersonal whole, it seems reasonable to argue that at least some ARTs use modern science and technology to facilitate both the unitive and procreative meanings of the spousal relationship. *Gaudium et Spes* notes that "children really are the supreme gift of marriage" (*GS* 50) and, if they are and ARTs can help infertile couples realize this supreme gift, we may legitimately ask about the credibility of the church's prohibition of most ARTs.[53]

Since the integrity of marital intercourse and its direct relationship with reproduction is at the heart of the church's ethical analysis of ARTs, we next explore that analysis as it is articulated in the CDF's *Instruction*. The *Instruction* relies heavily on the personalist language of *Gaudium et Spes* to explain its perception of human dignity in relation to sexuality, marriage, and sexual intercourse. "The moral criteria for medical intervention in procreation," it argues, "are deduced from the dignity of human persons, of their sexuality and of their origin. Medicine which seeks to be ordered to the integral good of the person must respect the specifically human values of sexuality."[54] These foundational values are grounded in "the integral dignity of the human person"[55] reflected in the "conjugal union,"[56] which "must be actualized in marriage through the conjugal act."[57] These values, it is argued, establish the inseparable connection between the unitive and procreative meanings of every act of intercourse. Any technological separation of these meanings, either artificial contraception or artificial reproduction, violates the intrinsic dignity of spousal intercourse and renders the separation a violation and unethical. Medicine, the *Instruction* notes, must respect "the integral dignity of the human person first of all in the act [of intercourse] and at the moment in which the spouses transmit life to a new person."[58] There is, then, in the *Instruction* a clear no to ARTs, heavily based on the inseparability principle.

While the *Instruction* utilizes personalist language to explain the meanings of marriage and human sexuality, there is a tension between personalist and biological arguments in its different treatment of heterologous and homologous artificial insemination. In heterologous insemination the sperm or ovum is provided by someone other than a spouse; in homologous insemination both the sperm and ovum are provided by the spouses. The *Instruction* begins its consideration of heterologous insemination by answering in personalist terms the question, "Why must human procreation take place in marriage?" Fidelity in the marital relationship implies a "reciprocal respect of [the spouses'] right to become a father and a mother only through each other."[59] The *Instruction* grounds its moral assessment of heterologous insemination in the personalist dimension of marriage. Procreation must take place within marriage and within the marital relations of the spouses with one another and with their child, who is said to be "the living image of their love" and the "permanent sign of their conjugal union."[60]

The *Instruction* formulates its rejection of heterologous insemination by setting forth several ways in which it violates family relationships. First, it violates the marital relationship. Heterologous artificial fertilization "is contrary to the unity of marriage, to the dignity of the spouses, to the vocation proper to parents, and to the child's right to be conceived and brought into the world in marriage and from marriage."[61] Respect "for the unity of marriage and for conjugal fidelity demands that the child be conceived in marriage; the bond existing between husband and wife accords the spouses, in an objective and inalienable manner, the exclusive right to become father and mother solely through each other."[62] Second, the introduction of a third party into reproduction through the use of donor sperm or ovum "constitutes a violation of the reciprocal commitment of the spouses and a grave lack in regard to that essential property of marriage which is its unity." Third, heterologous insemination "violates the rights of the child; it deprives him of his filial relationship with his parental origins and can hinder the maturing of his personal identity."[63] The violation of all of these relationships leads "to a negative moral judgment concerning heterologous artificial fertilization."[64] We agree with these stated relational concerns and the prima facie negative ethical judgment on heterologous insemination.

When it addresses homologous artificial insemination the

Instruction shifts emphasis from personal relations to biological acts. The foundational principle for the *Instruction*'s ethical analysis of homologous artificial insemination is the inseparability principle.[65] Three questions emerge regarding the *Instruction*'s introduction of this inseparability principle. First, why does it make this methodological shift from a focus on relationships when ethically evaluating heterologous artificial insemination to a focus on the inseparability principle embedded in the act of spousal intercourse when ethically evaluating homologous artificial insemination? Second, what are the weaknesses of this inseparability principle with regard to homologous artificial insemination? Third, what would be the ethical implications for the latter if the *Instruction* was methodologically consistent?

First, while the arguments against heterologous artificial insemination in many relationships seem reasonable to us given the complications of donor sperm or ovum and their potential impact on spousal and family relationships, the same relational complications do not apply in homologous artificial insemination. When both sperm and ovum are provided by the parents, and a surrogate is not used to carry the embryo, no relational complication exists. All that can be claimed with certainty is that an act of sexual intercourse is not immediately responsible for procreation. While this fact gives us insight into the origin of reproduction, it gives us no insight into the ethical meaning of reproduction. Ethical meaning is discerned not in a fact, in this case the fact of technological assistance in the process of reproduction, but in the meaning of that fact for marital and family relationships. The application of the same personalist principle to both heterologous and homologous inseminations, we suggest, would lead to a different conclusion about the ethics of the latter.

Second, by introducing the inseparability principle in its discussion of homologous artificial insemination the *Instruction* clearly recognizes that there is a shift in the foundational principle in ethically evaluating both homologous and heterologous inseminations. The *Instruction*'s condemnation of homologous artificial insemination is "strictly dependent on the principles just mentioned."[66] In fact, there is a single principle, the inseparability principle, and this principle is nowhere to be found in church teaching prior to Pope Paul VI's encyclical *Humanae Vitae*.[67] It follows from the *Instruction*'s strict dependence on a particular principle to justify its argument against homologous artificial insemination that the argument is only as strong as the principle; if the principle is weak, so too is any ethical conclusion drawn from the principle.

The inseparability principle contains a "germ of truth" in what Richard McCormick calls an "aesthetic or ecological (bodily integrity) concern." He means that all artificial interventions into the sexual relationship, whether to prevent or procure reproduction, are a kind of "second best."[68] This is in line with the *Instruction*'s claim that conception realized through artificial insemination is "deprived of its proper function." To deprive a procedure of its "proper function," however, does not make the procedure ipso facto ethically wrong in every situation. It does not do so, McCormick legitimately insists, unless we "elevate an aesthetic-ecological concern into an absolute moral imperative";[69] and that is far from the experiential intentions of the vast majority of Catholic couples using ART.

The basis for the "aesthetic or ecological concern" is a product of the physicalism that has controlled the Catholic sexual tradition. In the tradition up to the Second Vatican Council, the primary end of marriage was always said to be procreation. This doctrine reflected a history that goes back to the time when the male was recognized as the sole source of life[70] and when procreation was recognized as the only legitimate meaning and end for sexual intercourse.[71] Our modern understanding of biology and human sexuality, however, teaches us that the male is far from the sole source of life and that procreation is not even possible in the vast majority of sexual acts. A couple can ethically justify their sexual intercourse when there is no possibility of procreation but they can never ethically justify it when there is no unitive meaning. It is reasonable, therefore, to argue that not only are the unitive and procreative meanings of the sexual act separable, and are often clearly separated, but also that the unitive meaning is now primary and the procreative meaning secondary.

Third, based on the foregoing, we draw what we believe is a reasonable conclusion about the ethics of homologous artificial insemination. If the premise on which an argument is based is weak, then any conclusion drawn from it will also be weak. We believe the inseparability principle is weak and far from demonstrated and cannot bear the weight of the *Instruction*'s conclusion absolutely prohibiting homologous artificial insemination. Given the desperation of an infertile couple to have a child and their intention, grounded in their mutual justice, love, and responsibility to have their marital relationship "crowned" (*GS* 48) by their child, and given the trauma caused to them by not being able to conceive through sexual intercourse, we believe the use of homologous artificial insemination can be ethical, facilitate both the unitive and procreative meanings of marriage, and reduce the trauma experienced by many infertile couples.

A Catholic woman of our acquaintance explained to us that, when she found out that she and her husband could not conceive, she was devastated and, blaming herself for the situation, angry with herself and severely depressed. She was encouraged when her obstetrician told her it still might be possible for her to conceive by harvesting her ova and having them fertilized by her husband's sperm in a petri dish and then implanted in her womb for development and, ultimately, the birth of their child. That encouragement was dampened by word from her local priest that such a procedure was judged unethical by the Catholic Church and was not permitted for Catholics. She and her husband were again angry, this time not with themselves but with the church that would deprive them of the joy of having a child. They decided to go ahead with the procedure and happily conceived two beautiful daughters. She herself continues to attend church services with her daughters, but her husband, still angry, refuses to have any thing to do with a church that had denied them such joy and had instead caused them such trauma. His reaction is, unfortunately, a common reaction to church doctrine existentially judged and experienced by infertile couples to be trauma inducing.

We are in complete agreement here with Lisa Cahill. Many Catholics, she notes, "perceive a difference larger than the Vatican allows between therapies used in marriage, even if they do temporarily circumvent sexual intercourse, and methods which bring donors into the marital procreative venture." She believes, and we agree, that "donor [heterologous] methods are more morally objectionable because they do not appreciate the unity as relationships of sexual expression, committed partnership, and parenthood."[72] While procreation in homologous artificial insemination is not the direct result of an act of sexual intercourse, it is the result of an overall marital relational act that expresses and facilitates the just love, commitment, care, concern, and dignity of the couple shared with a new human being, their child. Our argument defending the ethical acceptability of homologous artificial insemination is grounded not in the inseparability of the unitive and procreative meanings of a sexual act, but in the meaning and nature of a marital relationship. In the overall marital relationship, not in each and every sexual act, the unitive and procreative meanings may be legitimately inseparable.[73] With the *Instruction*, we affirm the connection of marriage, sexual love, and parenthood. We judge, however, that its claim that genuine marital love is incompatible with homologous artificial insemination to bring about a longed-for conception is unsupported and can be ethically ignored.

CONCLUSION

In this chapter, we explored four Catholic doctrines on four ethical issues relating to marriage and human sexuality, namely, contraception, divorce and remarriage, cohabitation, and ARTs. The doctrinal language teaches that all contravention of church teaching on these issues is gravely immoral and grounds for eternal damnation. Many individuals and couples experience direct, indirect, or complex trauma as a result of these doctrines and the church's portrayal of God's judgment as a result of these doctrines. Marital experience recognizes the complexity of these relational issues and the gospel, as presented by Pope Francis, emphasizes God's mercy, compassion, and unconditional love in irregular situations of human sexual relationships. God's healing balm of compassion, love, and mercy reduces or eliminates such trauma. We next explore LGBTQI+ issues and trauma-inducing doctrinal language with respect to them.

6

ANTHROPOLOGICAL DOCTRINAL LANGUAGE AND SEXUAL ISSUES IN THE CHURCH

(Part 2)

Although the particular inclination of the homosexual person is not a sin, it is a more or less strong *tendency ordered toward an intrinsic moral evil*; and thus the inclination itself must be seen as an *objective disorder*. (CDF, "Letter to the Bishops of the Catholic Church on the Pastoral Care of Homosexual Persons" 3; emphases added)

The context in which the mission of education is carried out is characterized by challenges emerging from varying forms of an ideology that is given the general name "gender theory," which "denies the difference and reciprocity in nature of a man and a woman and envisages a society without sexual differences, thereby eliminating the anthropological basis of the family." (Congregation for Catholic Education, *Male and Female He Created Them*, 2)

The process of identifying sexual identity is made more difficult by the fictitious construct known as "gender neuter" or "third gender," which has the effect of obscuring the fact that a person's sex is a structural determinant of male or female identity. Efforts to go beyond the constitutive male-female sexual difference, such as the ideas of "intersex" or "transgender," lead to a masculinity or femininity that is ambiguous. (Congregation for Catholic Education, *Male and Female He Created Them*, 25)

As Pope Francis's church-wide process on synodality continues, one point is common to many synodal reports coming from parishes and bishops' conferences, namely, that LGBTQI+ people feel marginalized "because circumstances in their own lives are experienced as impediments to full participation in the life of the church."[1] There is a call for the church to be more welcoming to the LGBTQI+ community and a desire among the faithful to accompany them and their families "with authenticity." Many people "who identify as LGBTQ+ believe they are condemned by Catholic teachings." Participants in the synod indicate that there is a crisis in the Catholic Church on how to minister to LGBTQ+ people and they "feel torn between remaining in the church and supporting their loved ones."[2] There are several important points from the USCCB's summary of diocesan synodal reports and its implications for members of the LGBTQI+ community. First, LGBTQI+ persons, their families, and friends feel marginalized from the Catholic Church and there is a consistent call to make them feel more welcome. Second, this marginalization can lead to trauma, alienation, and depression. Third, LGBTQI+ Catholics feel that church doctrine condemns them, and there is a call, both among laity and clergy, for a change in the church's sexual teaching and doctrinal language. We consider each of these points in turn.

CREATING A MORE WELCOMING COMMUNITY

Cardinal McElroy of San Diego recognizes the marginalization that LGBTQI+ people feel and calls for their "radical inclusion" in the church.[3] Numerous Bishop Conferences' synodal reports throughout the world also note this marginalization and the need for inclusion.[4] McElroy addresses the basis for marginalization and the way of radical inclusion. Marginalization occurs due to "structures and cultures of exclusion that alienate all too many from the church or make their journey in the Catholic faith tremendously burdensome." These structures and cultures have been shaped by Catholic sexual doctrine, which teaches that "all sexual acts outside of marriage constitute objectively grave sin." This blanket classification "has been to focus the Christian moral life disproportionately upon sexual activity." McElroy believes the question of inclusion is a pastoral question, not a doctrinal question. The question is how to treat LGBTQI+ people "in the life of the church, especially regarding questions of the Eucharist."[5] Pope Francis gives a traditional and merciful response to this question: "the Eucharist is not the reward of saints, but the bread of sinners."[6] Since all women and men are sinners, no particular group should be singled out and alienated from the community and its Eucharist. McElroy's pastoral question is also at the heart of Pope Francis's approach to marriage and family in *Amoris Laetitia*, where he proposes "new pastoral methods" to address questions of marital and sexual relationships within their existential context, especially as these are impacted by socioeconomic realities. These methods are pastoral but have doctrinal implications. McElroy also recognizes the doctrinal implications of a pastoral approach to LGBTQI+ people in his claim that "intrinsically disordered language [toward LGBTQI+ people] is a disservice."[7] Disorder "is a terrible word and it should be taken out of the *Catechism*."[8] McElroy's call for change in the *Catechism*'s language shifts the focus from a pastoral question to a doctrinal question regarding the church's language about LGBTQI+ people and their sexual identities, and about the condemnation of their sexual acts that flow from those identities. Before considering the doctrinal question, however, we consider trauma, depression, and anxiety related to marginalization from the Catholic community.

EXCLUSION AND TRAUMA

Cardinal McElroy correctly asserts that "it is a demonic mystery of the human soul why so many men and women have a profound and visceral animus toward members of the LGBT communities." This animus is also evident in the Catholic Church. One person comments on McElroy's article on inclusion, "The empirical data tells us that heterosexuals, especially families, are not interested in sharing the pew with gay couples on Sundays."[9] Exclusion from a religious community that teaches God's unconditional love and mercy and yet labels a person's sexual orientation "disordered" and promotes "just discrimination" against that person has an existential impact with salvific implications. It is well documented in the scientific community that discrimination against sexual and gender minorities causes trauma, anxiety, and depression.[10] Even when sexual and gender minorities attempt to conceal their identities to protect themselves against overt discrimination, the concealment itself, staying "in the closet," is associated with greater depression and anxiety. These are compounded by religious perspectives where the isolation and alienation are experienced in a community that is supposed to reflect God's unconditional love, but instead threatens eternal punishment due to a person's sexual actions that flow from her or his particular sexual orientation. This is the religious trauma experienced by LGBTQI+ people discussed in chapter 2.

Part of the demonic mystery of animus can be explained by church doctrine that singles out sexual sins as the greatest sins (no parvity of matter) and identifies homosexual orientation with the most egregious sexual violation, the clerical sex-abuse scandal. The church seems to be unaware of the impact of its association of clerical sex abuse with homosexuality and how that association not only ethically taints all gay priests but also the broader LGBTQI+ community. It encourages priests and others to remain "in the closet" so their sexual identity will not rouse suspicion about relationships with others, especially those of the same sex. This closeting of their true identity often causes depression, anxiety, and trauma. It also makes the unjustified association that people with same-sex attraction, male or female, have a propensity toward intrinsically evil acts. Given the lack of transparency and accountability of bishops who covered up priestly sexual abuse, we wonder whether the association between gay priests and pedophilia is a result of ignorance or simply a strategy to shift the focus from systemic church problems to individual gay priests. Regardless, the impact of this association has broader religious and social implications for LGBTQI+ people, and it promotes unjust discrimination, damages human dignity, and can be a source of trauma, depression, and anxiety experienced by LGBTQI+ persons.

CALLS FOR A CHANGE IN SEXUAL DOCTRINE

The animus toward members of the LGBTQI+ community is supported by Catholic doctrine on sexual orientation and so-called gender ideology. Cardinal McElroy points out that although the *Catechism*'s use of this phrase is philosophical, it is often interpreted in the United States and throughout the world as a psychological term, with personal and ethical implications that indicate LGBTQI+ people are somehow humanly and ethically disordered. McElroy's call to remove this phrase from the *Catechism* shifts Catholic teaching on LGBTQI+ issues from the pastoral to the doctrinal realm. In essence, his assertion is not only about the church needing to be more pastoral in its approach to LGBTQI+ people but also about changing church doctrine on LGBTQI+ sexual ethical issues.

European church leaders have gone further in the call to change church doctrine. Cardinal Hollerich of Luxembourg frankly argues that "the sociological-scientific foundation of [Catholic teaching on lesbian and gay people and acts] is no longer correct." It is, he believes, "time for a fundamental revision of the doctrine" on lesbian and gay people and their acts.[11] Bishop Helmut Dieser of Aachen comments that "same-sex feelings and love are not an aberration, but a variant of human sexuality." He maintains that church thinking on human sexuality in general, and homosexuality in particular, is "too simple." "Homosexuality," he argues, is "as science shows—not a glitch, not an illness, not an expression of any kind of deficit."[12] Similar statements have been made by Cardinal Marx[13] and the majority of German bishops.[14] The church must stop speaking of homosexuality in negative terms, embrace scientific understandings of human sexuality into its theological anthropology, and formulate doctrines that reflect this understanding. The results of this process will call for a revision of the doctrines themselves. To a critique of those doctrines we now turn.

Catholic Doctrinal Language against Homosexual Acts

We already hinted in chapter 2 at the trauma inflicted on LGBTQI+ persons by Catholic language about them. We now examine and critique that teaching in detail. Catholic doctrine condemns homosexual acts as "intrinsically disordered" and gravely immoral and does so on the basis of three arguments: first, the teaching of scripture; second, "the constant teaching of the Magisterium"; third, "the moral sense of the Christian people."[15]

The broader theological tradition, however, following contemporary experiential and scientific insights, approaches this teaching critically, to clarify its nonmeaningfulness in the changed contemporary sociohistorical context. Our exploration will show that the teaching of the Catholic Church about homosexuality is mistaken and homosexual sexual acts are not necessarily unethical or sinful; *some* homosexual sexual acts, just as some heterosexual sexual acts, those that are free, just, and loving, are perfectly ethical.

Biblical Doctrine on Homosexual Sexual Acts

There are two broad ways to read biblical texts. The first one is literally, understanding the text in the language of the modern reader; the other is historically critically, understanding the text in the time, culture, and language of the original writers. The first approach is the approach of all fundamentalisms, the second is the official approach, since the Second Vatican Council, of the Catholic Church.[16] When read as contemporary Catholic biblical doctrine requires that they be read, that is, in the "literary forms" of the writer's "time and culture,"[17] the texts that are advanced as a solid foundation of the Catholic doctrine about homosexual acts are revealed as not providing such a foundation. They are, rather, historically and culturally conditioned literary forms that demand careful historical-critical analysis, and that analysis raises questions in the informed theological mind. Two questions are central to the biblical texts on same-sex activity. First, does the Bible say anything about homosexuality as we understand it today? Second, if it does say something, what does it say and what does it mean?

The first question, does the Bible say anything about homosexuality as we understand it today, is a question of definition. What do we mean today by *homosexuality* and *homosexual*? The answer to that question is embedded in what both the contemporary sciences and Christian churches now take for granted, namely, that the noun *homosexuality* and the adjective *homosexual* refer to a person's psychosexual condition, produced by a mix of genetic, psychological, and social "loading,"[18] not to a person's sexual acts. Sexual orientation, in general, is defined as "the sustained erotic attraction to members of one's own gender, the opposite gender, or both—homosexual, heterosexual, or bisexual respectively."[19] Homosexual orientation, in specific, is "a condition characterized by an emotional and psychosexual propensity towards others of the same sex,"[20] and a homosexual is "a person who feels a most urgent sexual desire which *in the main* is directed towards gratification with the same sex."[21] Stephen Donaldson was, therefore, correct in 1994 to challenge the *New York Times*'s characterization of male prison rape as "homosexual rape" and to point out that prison rape is predominantly rape committed by those with a heterosexual orientation.[22]

Neither the Bible nor the Christian tradition rooted in it prior to the twentieth century ever considered homosexual orientation; they took for granted that everyone was heterosexual.[23] To look for any mention in the biblical texts of what today is called "homosexual orientation" is anachronism. One might as well search the Bible for advice on what automobile or computer to buy. The biblical passages cited as condemning homosexuality actually condemn same-sex behaviors and, since they assume heterosexuality to be the condition of every human person, they condemn them specifically as acts of perverted heterosexuals. In its modern meaning, homosexuality is not and cannot be a perversion of the heterosexual condition because homosexuals, by natural and definitive sexual orientation, do not share the heterosexual condition. Homosexuality is, rather, an *inversion* of the heterosexual condition that homosexuals, by no choice of their own, do not naturally share. They cannot be held morally accountable for something they did not choose.[24]

The context in which both Old and New Testaments condemn same-sex acts is based on a false assumption that all human beings naturally share the heterosexual condition and that, therefore, any homosexual behavior is a perversion of nature and unethical. Since that biblical assumption is now scientifically proven to be incorrect, the Bible has little to contribute to the discussion of homosexuality and homosexuals as they are understood today. We note here that the Bible contains many questionable moral teachings, on sex during menstruation, stoning adulterers, women's roles, slavery, and a host of others, all of which have been rejected by modern Catholic ethicists.[25]

Interpreting the Bible on Homosexuality

The most influential biblical text leading to the condemnation of male homosexual acts is the modern *interpretation* given to the biblical story of Sodom. Christian churches have taught that the destruction of Sodom was caused by the unethical male homosexual behaviors practiced there, and biblically uninformed Christians have uncritically believed what their churches taught them. Two questions may be raised with respect to this widespread interpretation, the first about its accuracy, the second about its basis in the biblical text. Our contextual exegesis will show that the homosexual interpretation of the Sodom story is neither accurate nor supported by a reading of the text in its historical and cultural context.

"Two angels came to Sodom in the evening, and Lot was sitting in the gateway of Sodom" (Gen 19:1). Lot offered the two angels the required Jewish hospitality, bringing them to his house and feeding them, but before they retired for the night men of Sodom surrounded the house and called for Lot to bring the two men out "that we may know [*yadha*] them" (Gen 19:5). That word *yadha* is critical for understanding what the men of Sodom were asking for. *Yadha* is the Hebrew word for the English *know*, but it is also used on occasion to mean specifically sexual intercourse. Which meaning is intended in this text? The sexual meaning of the word seems to be insinuated by two facts. First, if all the men of Sodom wanted was to get to know the strangers, why would Lot beg them "do not act so wickedly" (Gen 19:7). Second, the same word *yadha* is used in a clearly sexual sense when Lot offers his two daughters to the crowd: "Look, I have two daughters who have not known a man [*yadha*]; let me bring them out to you...only do nothing to these men, *for they have come under the shelter of my roof*" (Gen 19:8). We believe there is clear insinuation of homosexual intent against the two strangers at Sodom, which does not mean that the sin of the men of Sodom was the sin of homosexual behavior.

The clearer sin in the Hebrew text and context is the sin of inhospitality. That Lot is concerned about hospitality is made evident in the phrase we have underscored above, "do nothing to these men, for they have come under the shelter of my roof," that is, under the shelter of my hospitality, which embraces protecting them against the wrongful designs of the crowd. The men of Sodom are as bound by the law of hospitality as is Lot, but they demonstrate their sinfulness by not living up to the law. If *yadha* is to be understood in its sexual connotation, and we insist it is, then the men of Sodom demonstrate the extent of their inhospitality by intending homosexual assault of the strangers. If any action is condemned in the text, it is the crime of same-sex rape carried out by perverted heterosexual men. If the act of same-sex rape perpetrated by perverted heterosexual men is condemned in this text, that is a long way from a condemnation of the free, just, and loving homosexual acts of people with a definitive homosexual orientation. For Christians, a prime argument in support of our interpretation that the sin of Sodom is inhospitality is Jesus's mention of Sodom in the context of the inhospitality accorded his disciples (Luke 10:10–12).

If the Sodom story is about the condemnation of inhospitality by heterosexual men, no such claim can be made about the prescription of the Holiness Code in Leviticus. "You shall not lie with a male as with a woman; it is an abomination" (Lev 18:22), and "If a man lies with a male as with a woman, both of them have committed an abomination; they shall be put to death" (Lev 20:13). What the Holiness Code says could not be clearer, *male* same-sex *behavior* is an abomination. It is important we realize it is *male* acts that are prohibited in these texts. Women are inferior persons in the Jewish culture of the time and the text has no interest in what women do. In English the word *you* can apply to both males and females; in Hebrew the word used is used only of males. It is male homosexual acts that Leviticus says are an abomination, and that restriction yields insight into both the historical and cultural context in which Leviticus says what it says and what it might mean when it says it.

The first thing to be noted about the Hebrew context of the texts is bad biology. The ancient world understood that the male provided seed that contained the whole of life; the female simply provided the "field" in which the seed was sown to develop into a fully-fledged human.[26] To spill that seed, regarded as a little man, anywhere it could not develop properly, in a male body, for instance, was judged to be murder,[27] and murder was always held as an abomination. Those guilty of murder suffered the same penalty as our text prescribes for male same-sex acts, namely, death.[28] Since they waste no life, also because women in that patriarchal society simply do not count, female same-sex acts are not considered worthy of consideration anywhere in the Old Testament. The fact that it is only male homosexual acts that are declared an abomination introduces an important cultural consideration, that of male honor and the actions appropriate to it.

Extended family was and is "the primary economic, religious, educational, and social network"[29] in Mediterranean society. Within that network, males were the guardians of family honor, particularly the patriarch who headed the family and, for all intents and purposes, owned his wives and daughters. For a male to "lie with" another male, that is to act sexually like a female and allow himself to be penetrated, changed the order of nature established by God and compromised male honor, not only that of the male being penetrated but also that of his whole family. In such a context, of course, male same-sex acts would be an abomination, not qua same-sex acts but qua passive and dishonorable acts that threatened the patriarchal sexual structure that pervaded the Old Testament.[30]

But what of an utterly different historical and cultural context, a context in which not every human being is assumed to be by nature heterosexual, and some are known to have a natural homosexual orientation, a context in which male honor is not a dominant concern, a context in which male and female are understood to contribute equally to the procreation of new life? In such a context, male homosexual behavior need not be judged as dishonorable and ipso facto unethical. Free, just, and loving homosexual behavior, in keeping with a person's natural homosexual orientation, cannot be regarded as a perversion of a heterosexual condition. In today's scientific understanding of the contributions of both male and female to the procreation of new life, the spilling of male seed can no longer be regarded as the spilling of life, murder, and an abomination. In short, when the interpreter considers what the Bible says about male same-sex behavior and the historical and cultural context in which it says it, it is difficult to consider the Bible as saying anything more instructive in the present historical and cultural context than what it says about *kosher* laws, flagrantly ignored by

Christians (Lev 11). As understood today, male same-sex acts may or may not be unethical, but a judgment of their ethics today cannot be based on what the Old Testament says about the same-sex homosexual acts of perverted heterosexuals.

Christians give more credence to what the New Testament says about same-sex acts, especially what Paul says in his Letter to the Romans. It is important, again, to understand the historical and cultural context, in what is a Pauline attack on idolatrous Gentile society, not on same-sex acts. Paul offers standard Jewish accusations about Gentile idolatry. "What can be known about God is plain to them [Gentiles], because God has shown it to them" (Rom 1:19). But however plain the existence of the true God of Israel might be and however much Gentiles ought to have known God from the things God made, they "did not honor him as God or give thanks to him." Rather, "they exchanged the glory of the immortal God for images resembling a mortal human being or birds or four-footed animals or reptiles" (Rom 1:21–23). What is radically wrong with Gentiles, Paul argues, is that they are idolaters, and because they are idolaters, "God gave them up in the lusts of their heart to impurity...to degrading passions [think of the Holiness Code]. Their women exchanged natural intercourse for unnatural, and in the same way also the men, giving up natural intercourse with women," male sexual activity for sexual passivity, and "were consumed with passion for one another" (Rom 1:24–27). By behaving in this perverted sexual way, they both dishonored God and threatened the presumed natural structure. It is Gentile idolatry that is directly at stake in the Pauline text, and the unnatural, and dishonorable same-sex acts of perverted *heterosexuals* to which it is said to lead.

Magisterial Teaching on Homosexual Acts and Same-Sex Relationships

Contemporary misinterpretation of biblical texts taught by the authority of church leaders reinforces and perpetuates adherence to claims of established "facts" about lesbians and gays and their sexual acts, which in turn reinforces negative ethical affects about them. Our analysis of the biblical texts points to the direction of ethical discernment we propose as a way to arrive at an informed judgment about the ethics of same-sex acts. This direction challenges these "facts" and the negative affects and effects they generate. Catholic language teaches that same-sex acts are intrinsically disordered for the following reasons: they "are contrary to the natural law," the principles of which are reflected in human nature itself; "they close the sexual act to the gift of life"; and "they do not proceed from a genuine affective and sexual complementarity."[31] We consider each of these reasons in turn.

Natural Law Argument

First, today we know from science that there is in every human being a natural sexual orientation, but "nature" is always an interpreted category and there may be different interpretations about what is and what is not "nature." Catholic teaching distinguishes between "a homosexual 'tendency,' which proves to be 'transitory,' and 'homosexuals who are definitively [or naturally] such because of some kind of innate instinct.'" It asserts that "it seems appropriate to understand sexual orientation as a deep-seated dimension of one's personality and to recognize its relative stability in a person."[32] This "natural," stable, and definitive reality may be obscured by the obvious statistical preponderance of persons of heterosexual orientation, but it is in no way negated by that statistical preponderance. We are in complete agreement with the CDF when it teaches that "there can be no true promotion of man's [and woman's] dignity unless the essential order of his [and her] nature is respected."[33] Instructed by the evidence of science and universal experience, two of the sources of Catholic moral theology,[34] we disagree with it, however, on its exclusively heterosexual interpretation of that "essential order of nature."

We have considered Paul's use of *nature* as ordinary, normal, Jewish behavior, but the Catholic Church adopted the more universal Stoic meaning of the "nature" ordered by God[35] and sexually interpreted in a heterosexual and procreational direction. Any sexual activity that is not open to the transmission of life is, therefore, rhetorically condemned as contrary to this natural law as unethical. The fundamental principles that dictate this ethical judgment are contained, the church argues, "in the divine law—eternal, objective, and universal—whereby God orders, directs, and governs the entire universe and all the ways of the human community....This divine law is accessible to our minds."[36] "Accessible to our minds" raises hermeneutical questions. Already in the thirteenth century, Thomas Aquinas taught that the natural law is "nothing other than the light of understanding placed in us by God"[37] and that although the principles of the natural law are universal and immutable, their application "will be found to fail, according as we descend further into detail."[38] Pope Francis offers this same interpretation of natural law in his Post-synodal Exhortation, *Amoris Laetitia*.[39] For both Aquinas and Francis, the devil of the natural law, and any other general principle, is always in the details.

Our sexual anthropology recognizes scientifically demonstrated and definitive sexual orientation as an intrinsic dimension of human nature. As such, what is natural in sexual activity will vary depending on whether the person's natural sexual orientation is heterosexual, homosexual, or bisexual. Homosexual acts are natural for people with a homosexual orientation just as heterosexual acts are natural for people with a heterosexual orientation, though that alone does not make them ethical or unethical. They are natural because they flow from the fundamental human nature of a person created by God. They are ethical, we argue, when they are not only natural but also free, just, and loving.

Procreation and Complementarity Argument

The CDF teaches that same-sex unions lack "the conjugal dimension which represents the human and ordered form of sexuality," and that "sexual relations are human when and insofar as they express and promote the mutual assistance of the sexes in marriage and *are open to the transmission of new life*."[40] This doctrine articulates the unitive-procreative principle that in the twentieth century became the foundational principle for all Catholic sexual teaching.[41] The CDF uses the term *complementarity* in relation to this principle, a term that intends that two realities belong together and produce something that neither can produce alone, as when a woman and a man together produce a child that neither can produce alone. Sexual complementarity completes a heterosexual woman and a heterosexual man in marriage by bringing together their female and male biological and personal dimensions to produce a new human being.

Pope John Paul II consistently condemns same-sex acts on the grounds that they violate this heterosexual and reproductive complementarity, as they obviously do, but he fails to explain why they also violate personal complementarity, other than to assert gratuitously that same-sex acts "do not proceed from a genuine affective and sexual complementarity."[42] This assertion begs the question whether or not such acts can ever be truly unitive on the level of sexual and personal complementarity. Though the Catholic Church has not confronted this question, monogamous, loving, and committed same-sex couples have confronted it experientially and testify that they do experience unitive complementarity in and through their same-sex acts. Margaret Farley notes that the testimony of these couples witnesses "to the role of such loves and relationships in sustaining human well-being and opening to human flourishing" and "extends to the contributions that individuals and partners make to families, the church, and society as a whole."[43] The role of both same-sex and heterosexual loves and relationships was well described by the Second Vatican Council. "Expressed in a manner which is truly human, these actions signify and promote that mutual self-giving by which spouses enrich each other with a joyful and a thankful will."[44] This is what both heterosexual and same-sex couples do, we suggest, in their free, just, and loving sexual intercourse. The doctrine of the Catholic Church with respect to lesbians and gays is a thoroughly traditional Western doctrine. It has much to learn, for instance, from the doctrine of the indigenous American Indian nations, which European Americans did their best to colonize and destroy but failed. The nations name gay and lesbian persons as "two-spirit persons, which denotes the existence of feminine and masculine qualities in a single person."[45] Rather than being regarded as disordered, two-spirit persons are regarded as sacred, and perform many sacred actions in their tribes. It would promote the "radical inclusion" of LGBTQI+ people if official church teaching would embrace that perspective and drop hurtful and traumatic doctrine and language regarding them.

The Moral Sense of the Christian People and Homosexual Acts

Social science data suggest that the church's argument against same-sex acts based on "the moral sense of the Christian people" is now no longer viable. In a 1997 study, James Davidson and his colleagues found, with respect to same-sex acts, that 41 percent of Catholic parishioners agree with the church that they are always wrong and that 49 percent believe that, in certain circumstances, the decision to engage in such acts is up to the conscience of the individual.[46] A 2001 study replicated that figure of 49 percent, believing the decision to engage in same-sex acts belongs to the individuals; only 20 percent believed it had anything to do with the church.[47] The authors comment that their data "depict a trend away from conformity and toward personal autonomy" with respect to sexual issues.[48] That trend was most marked in "Post-Vatican II Catholics," those aged thirty-eight and younger.[49] Dean Hoge and his colleagues at Catholic University of America also document this trend away from authority to personal conscience in matters of ethics. In his study, he found that 73 percent of Latino Catholics and 71 percent of non-Latino Catholics judged that, in ethical matters, the final authority is the individual's informed conscience.[50] The same trend is well documented in other Western countries.[51] Recent polls indicate 76 percent of Catholics in the United States support homosexuality and 61 percent support same-sex marriage.[52] A reasonable theological question then arises: Does sociological data of this sort tell us anything about the doctrine of the church?

We offer an immediate answer: sociological data does not tell us what the church ought to believe and teach, for 76 percent, and even 100 percent, of Catholics could be wrong. The empirical data reported above, however, does two important things. It tells us both what the beliefs of Catholics actually are with respect to the ethics of same-sex acts and that these beliefs are not in agreement with the doctrinal beliefs proposed by the Catholic Church. This data may not tell us anything about the truth of church doctrine with respect to the ethics of same-sex acts, but it does tell us something about its relevance to the life of the contemporary church. It ought not to be either accepted or dismissed uncritically as if it had no relevance to the life of the church. Pope John Paul II teaches that "the church values sociological and statistical research," but immediately adds the proviso that "such research is not to be considered in itself an expression of the *sensus fidei*."[53] The pope is correct: empirical research neither expresses nor creates the faith of the church. It does, however, manifest what the church, understood as the communion of all the Catholic faithful, does and does not believe, and that experiential reality is a basis for critical theological reflection on any claim about what the church believes or does not believe. That critical reflection is always required of the church's theologians.[54]

Same-Sex Relationships

Psychologist Lawrence Kurdek has done extensive research on gay and lesbian couples and notes their characteristics compared to those of heterosexual couples. He shows that gay and lesbian couples tend to have a more equitable distribution of household labor, demonstrate greater conflict resolution skills, have less support from members of their families but greater support from friends, and experience similar levels of relational satisfaction compared to heterosexual couples.[55] Kurdek's work provides sound scientific evidence refuting church claims that same-sex acts are detrimental to human persons and their human relationships.

The CDF argues not only against same-sex relationships but also against same-sex parenting based on the unsubstantiated claim that, "as experience has shown, the absence of sexual complementarity in these unions creates obstacles in the normal development of children who would be placed in the care of such persons."[56] Reputable contemporary scientific evidence contradicts that claim. We address same-sex parenting in detail in chapter 7. Suffice to say that "there is no evidence to suggest that lesbians and gay men are unfit to be parents or that psychosocial [including sexual] development among children of gay men or lesbians is compromised in any respect relative to that among offspring of heterosexual parents."[57] The preponderance of research evidence led the American Psychological Association (APA) in 2020 to approve and disseminate an important resolution. Since "research has shown that the children of lesbian and gay parents are as likely as those of heterosexual parents to flourish," the APA opposes any, including parental, discrimination based on sexual orientation or gender identity.[58] We point out with John Courtney Murray that practical intelligence is preserved from ideology by having "a close relation to concrete experience."[59] The church's claim that homosexual acts "do not proceed from a genuine affective and sexual complementarity" appears to be not only unsubstantiated by concrete experience but also contradicted by that experience and scientific data. When faced with this contradictory scientific data, church rhetoricians refuse to accept it. Homosexual orientation is in itself neither ethical nor unethical. The same-sex acts that flow from it, however, are either ethical or unethical dependent on their context and circumstances.

TRANSGENDER AND INTERSEX PERSONS

Transgender and intersex persons are included in the acronym LGBTQI+ but since they rightly insist that their human reality is different from the reality of lesbians and gays, we assign them to their own section. *Transgender* is a relatively new word in the English language, appearing only in the past several decades, and its precise meaning is still under discussion. Its general meaning refers to people who change (hence *trans-*) from their birth gender to another gender or to no gender. We have earlier distinguished gender from sex. Sex is something biological; it is determined at birth on the basis of whether a child has male or female genitals, and it determines whether the child is male or female. Gender is something cultural; it is culturally assigned to a child at birth and determines whether the child is masculine or feminine and the attitudes and behaviors culturally expected of those with feminine or masculine genders. A person can change her or his gender with or without any surgical or hormonal intervention, and the resulting person is a *transgender* person. A person can also change her or his sex via either surgical or hormonal intervention and the resulting person is a *transsexual*. Gender is culturally assumed to be a stable and unchanging reality, and its implications are everywhere in human lives.[60] Despite the experiences of transgender people, any effort on their part to change their gender is still met with suspicion and opposition, especially in official Catholic teaching that labels such experiences "gender ideology," which is the "worst danger" that "cancels out differences" between men and women.[61]

The official Catholic anthropology and dominant approach to sex in our contemporary world is heterosexist. It is generally believed that in practice there are only two sexes, male and female, that the sexes are opposites, and that opposite-sex attraction is the God-intended and, therefore, Catholic human and ethical norm. Heterosexism generates negative attitudes, biases, and discrimination against anyone or anything that is perceived to threaten it, and intersex, transgender, transexual, gay, and lesbian persons certainly threaten it and often experience extreme negativity in their lives. The discrimination they suffer is sometimes so severe that it ends in their death, sometimes by suicide, sometimes by being killed by heterosexuals. Some theorists believe that gender identity, the subjective sense of being feminine or masculine, is rooted in biology, though no biological cause has ever been demonstrated for either feminine or masculine characteristics. Others believe that, while we are not born with a predetermined gender, we are born with a predetermined sex that can be actualized as gender in a particular cultural system, just as we are not born to speak a particular language but learn the language spoken in the culture in which we live.

In answer to the question of how many sexes there are, the majority reply that obviously there are only two, female and male. Why, then, we ask, did the ancient world in which there were only women and men biologically like us not believe that? Why did Greeks, Romans, Jews, and Christians down to the end of the seventeenth century believe that there was only one sex, that male and female bodies shared a single sex on a continuum, with males at its perfect end, females at its imperfect end, and hermaphrodites (present day intersex) somewhere in between?[62] That one sex was named *man*, and still today *man* is a generic term that incudes in itself men and women. The one-sex theory is obvious in the Creed of the fourth century Council of Nicaea (325) that Catholics pray most Sundays: "We believe in one Lord Jesus Christ, who for us *men* [*homines*] and for our salvation came down from heaven, was incarnate, and was made *man* [*homo*]." It would be incorrect to argue that "men" and "man" refer to individual males, for that would require the Latin *vir* that designates the individual man, rather than the generic *homo*. No, early Christian belief is that the Lord Jesus came down from heaven for the salvation of two genders, men and women, which were believed at the time to be in one sex, man.

On February 2, 2019, the Congregation for Catholic Education (CCE) issued a document, *Male and Female He Created Them: For a Path of Dialogue on the Issue of Gender in Education* (hereafter MFC).[63] As an effort at dialogue, embracing the perspectives of all those involved in the issue of sex and gender, MFC is deeply flawed. There is dialogue in it, but dialogue only with past Catholic pronouncements and their restrictive male-female binary. That binary controls every discussion in the document and in every Catholic document that deals with sex and gender, even though it "dates only from the end of the 19th century when both terms were invented by the medical establishment."[64] There is no dialogue with gay, lesbian, transgender, or intersex persons, or with those who scientifically study them to learn about their human and sexual experience. Intersex persons are mentioned in quotation marks, "intersex," as if they were not real human beings with very real and painful experiences but, rather, biological aberrations to be resolved.

Noted intersex scholar Megan DeFranza demonstrates that intersex is a well-known reality in human history, including in Christian scripture. She complains that "while some 'welcoming and affirming' churches readily employ arguments from the existence of intersex persons to justify accepting bisexualities, transsexualities, and homosexualities, conservative Catholics and Evangelicals may be tempted to shore up traditional categories of sex and gender, further marginalizing and traumatizing the intersex." She shows that "these are not the only options."[65] We endorse here the judgment of another noted intersex scholar, Susannah Cornwall, that theological ethics for intersex persons "will endorse the goodness of different kinds of embodiment and critique interventions more concerned with upholding conservative social [and church] norms than respecting the agency and integrity of the bodies in question." They will allow transgender and intersex persons "to make decisions about their own bodies and bodily expressions without an automatic assumption that they are incapable of responsibly and reflectively doing so."[66]

Webster's Unabridged Dictionary defines an *intersex person* as "one having both male and female sexual characteristics and organs; at birth an unambiguous assignment of male or female cannot be made." The Intersex Society of North America (ISNA) points out that "intersex isn't a discrete or natural category,"[67] and Thea Hillman rightly adds that what is called the "intersex community is far from homogeneous."[68] It is, rather, an umbrella term that covers a variety of intersex conditions. These include "congenital development of ambiguous genitalia, congenital disjunction of internal and external sex anatomy, incomplete development of sex anatomy, sex chromosome anomalies, and disorders of gonadal development."[69] All these conditions can be categorized as disorders only when compared to the taken-for-granted sex binary of male-female, and it is this negative comparison that provokes trauma, depression, and anxiety in parents and intersex persons themselves.

The body-rooted anthropology of MFC, we submit, is misguided scientifically and theologically. Scientifically, MFC fails to recognize both the bodily reality of intersex persons in general and the contemporary understanding of sex/gender in specific. Based on a review of medical literature from 1955 onward, Melanie Blackless calculated an intersex frequency of 2 percent.[70] The United Nations estimates that up to 1.7 percent of people are born intersex.[71] The range of frequency reveals that intersex is more common than Down's Syndrome frequency (0.125–1 percent depending on a woman's age), and deserves to be as well accepted as Down's. It is theologically unthinkable that the God and Father of Jesus the Christ would love a heterosexual majority that God has created and discriminate against an intersex minority that God has equally created. Intersex bodies can be ambiguous and troubling to physicians, parents, and religious leaders, but only when judged against the majority heterosexual male-female binary. They are not ambiguous and troubling to persons acting out of the "third sex" perspective advanced by many intersex persons. Externally, intersex genitals may be ambiguously male or female, or they may appear to be female or male; internally, children may have male-typical or female-typical anatomy. They may also have what Alice Domurat Dreger calls "mosaic genetics," XXY, XYY, or other combinations of sex chromosomes.[72] This biological condition of intersex persons, externally and internally, makes it difficult to assign a particular gender/sex to a person through therapy or surgery.

David Reimer was born into a Jewish family as an identical male twin on August 22, 1965. He was not born intersex, but he lost his penis in a botched circumcision and, at eighteen months old, his parents agreed to his reassignment to a female sex and feminine gender recommended by psychologist John Money. David was surgically altered to fit his new feminine role, his testes were excised, and he was put on a regimen of female hormones. Reimer's post-reassignment experience is paradigmatic of the experience of many sex-reassigned individuals born intersex. In the controversy that followed Reimer's reassignment to a feminine gender, Money reported that Reimer had fully accepted her reassignment as female, showed an appropriate gender role, and was a happy little girl. Following a 1980 BBC documentary that reported that by age thirteen Reimer was not well adjusted and was rejecting the assigned feminine gender and female sex, his psychiatrist, Keith Sigmundson, revealed that Reimer had rejected reassignment to a female sex and feminine gender. She had her breasts removed, later got a reconstructed penis, and was married and living as the stepfather of his wife's children. Reimer's mother then came forward and revealed that Money's claim of a "successful" gender/sex reassignment was fabricated, and that she had kept silent on the fact that her son consistently rejected female sex and feminine gender and every attempt to socialize him as a girl.

Reimer described his yearly visits to the Johns Hopkins clinic, where an array of medical students handled and photographed his genitals, as "abusive,"[73] a judgment shared by many sex- reassigned intersex persons. Throughout his life, Reimer suffered from severe depression and eventually committed suicide in 2004 at age thirty-eight. That same year psychiatrist Cecilia Dhejne of Sweden's Karolinska Institute reported on a thirty-year study of intersex individuals who had sex reassignment surgery that revealed the frightening statistic that their suicide rate is twenty times higher than that of a comparable peer group.[74] Since the Reimer case, there have been many other reports of the rejection by intersex children of sex reassignment.[75] Given this overwhelming evidence, we recommend that the only ethical protocol for the treatment of intersex infants is a protocol that proscribes any reassignment surgery until the child has reached the age of consent, is in possession of all the relevant data, including the risks, the dangers, and the social outcomes, and can make her or his own choice. The same protocol is recommended for transgender persons and age-appropriate counseling should be provided to all the children as they grow.

CONCLUSION

This chapter highlighted the trauma and exclusion experienced by members of the LGBTQI+ community due to Catholic doctrinal teachings and the highly problematic theological, anthropological, scientific, and experiential foundations for, and justifications of, those teachings. In chapter 1, we highlighted the anthropological, ethical methodological, and ecclesiological tools that provide a "paradigm shift"[76] for Catholic theological ethics and justify revising Catholic sexual doctrines in general and doctrines on LGBTQI+ issues in specific.

We take to heart Pope Francis's call for theologians to be "open to the voice of the people, thus a 'popular' theology addressed mercifully toward the open wounds of humanity and of creation and within the wounds of human history."[77] This call includes, he continues, theologians' privileging experiential knowledge provided by the "common sense of people."[78] The wounds of LGBTQI+ people inflicted by the church and society are well documented. Discerning the "common sense of people" and the *sensus fidelium* of numerous cardinals, bishops, priests, and the vast majority of lay Catholics, whose consciences have concluded that doctrinal teachings on LGBTQI+ people alienate, cause trauma, and damage emotionally, psychologically, spiritually, and relationally, provide a clarion call for the revision of those teachings. So, too, does the doctrinal teaching that promotes so-called just discrimination against LGBTQI+ people. To a consideration of that doctrine we now turn.

7

DOCTRINAL LANGUAGE REGARDING LGBTQ+ PEOPLE AND THE CANONIZATION OF "NOT UNJUST" DISCRIMINATION

Every sign of unjust discrimination [toward people with deep-seated homosexual tendencies] should be avoided. (*Catechism* 2358)

Although the clerical sex-abuse scandal and its cover-up are the most well-known instances of sexual and spiritual violence in the church, there is another type of violence that is not as well known. It is the violence implicitly embedded in church documents that state that the church rejects "all unjust discrimination" against homosexual persons,[1] which implies, of course, that there can be "just discrimination" against them. The Catholic teachings that the "homosexual inclination is objectively disordered" and that "homosexual acts are intrinsically disordered"[2] enable and legitimate direct or indirect "just discrimination" against gay or lesbian persons, and the personal trauma that such "just discrimination" induces. These teachings suggest that homosexual orientation is such a departure from the heterosexual anthropology embraced by the church that gays and lesbians are less than fully human, less than real men and women, and mislead some to conclude that physical, psychological, and spiritual violence can be done to them without any moral blame.

Since the Supreme Court of the United States (SCOTUS) expanded the definition of *sex* in the Civil Rights Act of 1964 to include "sexual orientation" and "gender identity," the church has emphasized its doctrine of "just discrimination" to include all members of the LGBTQI+ community. We explored the trauma-inducing language against homosexual orientation in chapter 4 and against homosexual acts in chapter 6. In this chapter, we focus on the doctrinal language of so-called just discrimination. We explore several types of discrimination that the church enables and promotes that cause trauma and spiritual violence toward LGBTQI+ persons who suffer such discrimination. The unquestioned tolerance of such discrimination does violence also to the broader human community.

DISCRIMINATION AND EMPLOYMENT

The first type of discrimination is employment discrimination and the USCCB's opposition to any nondiscrimination legislation. We first examine the historical background of nondiscrimination legislation and then the USCCB's response to it.

Historical Background to the Employment Non-discrimination Act and Equality Act

In May 2012, President Obama became the first president to publicly support same-sex marriage. On June 26, 2015, in *Obergefell v. Hodges*, SCOTUS ruled that same-sex couples have a fundamental right to marry, and same-sex marriage was legalized throughout the nation. Since state sodomy laws were declared unconstitutional by SCOTUS only in 2003, this development in the law demonstrated a rapid evolution in social mores and cultural embrace of same-sex relationships. Given this cultural evolution, we could reasonably expect that laws prohibiting discrimination against LGBTQI+ persons in employment and housing would follow, but this has not been the case. Many who objected to the legalization of same-sex marriage for ethical or religious reasons have shifted cultural battle lines from marriage to employment nondiscrimination legislation. With its politics of division, the Trump administration promoted this shift by undoing many of the executive orders issued by President Obama to protect LGBTQI+ persons. That political action fueled the opposition of the religious right, including the USCCB, to the Equality Act, an offspring of the Employment Non-discrimination Act (ENDA).

ENDA, legislation to prevent employment discrimination based on sexual orientation, was first introduced in Congress in 1994, but at the time, it did not pass either in the House or the Senate. In 2013, the Senate passed ENDA legislation on a bipartisan vote (64–32), but the Republican-dominated House Rules Committee voted against it. In 2019, the House passed the Equality Act, expanding the protections of ENDA to include housing, credit, education, public spaces and services, and the jury system. This Act amends the 1964 Civil Rights Act and extends the prohibition against sex discrimination to include "sexual orientation, gender identity, or pregnancy, childbirth, or a related medical condition of an individual, as well as because of sex-based stereotypes."[3] As of 2024, twenty-three states and Washington, DC, have laws that prohibit discrimination in the public and private sectors on the basis of sexual orientation and gender identity, but there is still no federal law prohibiting such discrimination.

On October 8, 2019, SCOTUS heard three cases involving people who were fired from their place of employment because of sexual orientation (*Bostock v. Clayton County, Georgia*, and *Altitude Express v. Zarda*) or gender identity (*R. G. & G. R. Harris Funeral Homes v. Equal Opportunity Employment Commission*). The Court considered whether the 1964 federal employment discrimination laws that prohibit discrimination "because of sex" apply to sexual orientation and gender identity. SCOTUS ruled in June 2020 that the legal term *sex* is expanded to include sexual orientation and gender identity and that to discriminate in employment on that basis is unconstitutional. However, it remains up to each individual state to pass nondiscrimination legislation or to file a case with the courts that would challenge existing laws that do not prevent such discrimination.

Sociological surveys indicate that only one-third of respondents know that legal protections do not exist on the basis of transgender identity and only one-quarter know that they do not exist on the basis of lesbian, gay, and bisexual identity.[4] A 2018 survey reports that 69 percent of respondents support laws that protect

LGBT people from discrimination, 23 percent oppose such laws, and 8 percent have no opinion.[5] In April 2019, Quinnipiac University conducted a poll that found 92 percent of American voters surveyed believe that employers should not be able to fire a person based on that person's sexual orientation or sexual identity.[6] Although these statistical studies show a large majority national support for nondiscrimination legislation, there has also been shown to be a decline in support among Republicans since 2015. For young Republicans (ages 18–29), support declined from 74 percent to 63 percent; and among liberal Republicans, from 68 percent to 59 percent.[7] This decline correlates with the period of the Trump administration's legislative actions against the LGBT community, which could certainly account for the decline, but the data do not show a causal relationship between the two. Despite overall public support, even among Catholics, of nondiscrimination legislation, the USCCB continues to vehemently oppose such legislation.

USCCB's Opposition to Nondiscrimination Legislation

Catholic support for nondiscrimination laws is high—68 percent of Catholics support transgender rights;[8] 72 percent of Hispanic Catholics, 71 percent of white Catholics, and 68 percent of other nonwhite Catholics all support laws that protect LGBTQI+ people against discrimination in jobs, public accommodations, and housing.[9] There is, however, ongoing resistance to, and advocacy against, such legislation by the USCCB, which has written to Congress encouraging it not to pass ENDA or the Equality Act, commissioned lawyers to write an *amici curiae* brief to SCOTUS in support of employers in the three cases cited above, and encouraged Catholics to write their state and national legislators to vote against nondiscrimination legislation. The USCCB argues that the Equality Act and a ruling by SCOTUS in favor of the plaintiffs that would revise the term *sex* in the Civil Rights Act to include sexual orientation and gender identity would violate the common good and human dignity.[10]

In its letter to Congress opposing the Equality Act, the USCCB reaffirms its commitment to human dignity, stating that "each and every person should be treated with dignity and respect." That dignity surely demands a person's right to employment free from "unjust discrimination." "Rather than offering meaningful protections for individuals," however, the USCCB argues that "the Equality Act would impose sweeping [legislation] to the detriment of society [and the common good] as a whole."[11]

In its Backgrounder statement opposing the Equality Act, the USCCB explains why the Act is detrimental legislation. First, it claims that there is no widespread or systemic discrimination against the LGBTQI+ community like there was to warrant the Civil Rights Act protecting people on the basis of sex, religion, and race. "On the contrary," it states, LGBTQI+ "people today are often held in high regard in the market, as well as the academy, local governments, and media. Some studies suggest that people who identify as homosexual earn higher incomes than the national average."[12] Second, it claims the Equality Act would undo legal protections in Title IX for women and girls by allowing men who self-identify as women to compete for athletic scholarships. Proponents of the Equality Act argue that courts can decide individual cases of unfair claims to gender identity, which would occur only in isolated incidents that do not warrant legislative intervention. The Backgrounder responds that there is no basis for this assertion. "When opportunities for taking unfair advantage of a system exist, there will unfortunately be people who do so. Laws should function to curtail such behavior, not ignore it."[13] Third, "a consistent approach of dismissing individual instances and focusing on systemic problems supports the contention that the Equality Act is unnecessary."[14] We respond to the Backgrounder's claims.

The first claim on the widespread support of the LGBTQI+ community in certain segments of society ignores statistical data that details discrimination and harassment in the workplace that causes direct and indirect trauma. In a 2021 comprehensive study, UCLA's Williams Institute conducted a survey of LGBTQI+ employees and their experiences of employment discrimination over their lifetime, in the past five years, in the past year during the COVID-19 pandemic, and following SCOTUS's decision in *Bostock v. Clayton County*. This latter ruling expanded the term *sex* in the Civil Rights Act to include sexual orientation and gender identity. The findings are dramatic and disturbing: 46 percent of

LGBTQ workers experienced unfair treatment in employment at some point in their careers; 11 percent of LGBTQ employees of color were fired or not hired in the last year; 36 percent of employees of color and 26 percent of white employees experienced verbal harassment; 57 percent of LGBTQ employees reported that unfair treatment was motivated by religious beliefs; 38 percent of LGBTQ employees reported experiencing harassment at work; 26 percent of LGBTQ employees "cover," meaning they do not come out to coworkers out of fear of discrimination and harassment; and 34 percent of LGBTQ employees have left their job due to treatment by their employer.[15]

Such discrimination can cause direct trauma, when there is physical or psychological violence; indirect trauma, when an individual witnesses discrimination happening to another; or where there is a culture of homophobia, discrimination, and harassment in the workplace. The study notes that many LGBTQ employees suffer negative effects psychologically and physically, and experience reduced job satisfaction. Furthermore, it concludes that "employment discrimination against LGBTQ people continues to be persistent and widespread."[16]

Discriminatory behavior toward LGBTQ persons in the Catholic workplace is no better, and often worse. Firings of LGBTQI+ people who work for the church, Catholic schools, and Catholic institutions are well documented.[17] A 2014 study of the twelve countries with the largest Catholic populations in the world revealed that 78 percent of Catholics worldwide approved of and practiced artificial contraception in opposition to their church's teaching.[18] Many of that 78 percent are employed by the Catholic Church and suffer no consequences. Why, we ask, this inconsistent approach to violations of Catholic teaching on sexuality? The inconsistency among Catholic institutions that disproportionately fire LGBTQI+ employees for violating Catholic sexual teaching in comparison to other violations of church teaching is revealing. The many Catholics who use artificial birth control against the teaching of Pope Paul VI in *Humanae Vitae* without losing their Catholic jobs, and those who ignore Catholic social teaching that explicitly prohibits discrimination without any church repercussion, illustrate well the selectivity of the church that continues to propound discriminatory and traumatic doctrinal language against LGBTQI+ people.

The USCCB's claim that there is not widespread discrimination against members of the LGBTQI+ community, then, is contrary to the experiential evidence that documents widespread systemic discrimination and violence against that community. Its claim demonstrates the lengths to which the USCCB will go to ignore Pope John Paul II's call for science to inform theology and to deny reality in order to maintain the doctrinal status quo, reify traumatic doctrinal language, and promote discrimination, which too often results in physical violence and certainly includes spiritual violence against members of the LGBTQI+ community.[19] Discrimination and violence against the LGBTQI+ community is, and remains, an ongoing social and ecclesial issue that threatens human dignity, violates the common good, and requires legislation to protect a vulnerable population.

Second, it is unclear why the USCCB's assertion that postulates that people who take advantage of the system because laws are not in place to prevent them is applied only to transgender athletes and not also to landlords, employers, and educational institutions, including Catholic employers and educational institutions, who choose to discriminate based on sexual orientation or gender identity when nondiscrimination laws are not in place to protect against discrimination. Third, it is precisely the systemic problem or social sin of homophobia, discrimination, and violence against members of the LGBTQI+ community that requires such legislation. The USCCB seems to have a difficult time understanding the concept of social sin and its often-indirect impact on attitudes that shape people's perspectives on issues of race, sex, gender, and religion. This lack of understanding is evident in the USCCB's document against racism, *Open Wide Our Hearts*, which mentions social structures that underlie, create, and sustain racial inequality, but then ignores those structures and focuses only on the individual racist acts they provoke.[20] Most people are not consciously or deliberately racist, but they do participate in a society that has racist laws, structures, and institutions that perpetuate racism through white privilege, which is never mentioned in the document. Similarly, in its statements against nondiscrimination legislation, the USCCB fails to recognize the cultural reality of language and power structures, like Catholic hierarchy, and how these enable and promote attitudes and acts that directly or indirectly cause violence against and trauma to LGBTQI+ persons, and perpetuate the structural sins of homophobia and discrimination against them.

Secondary trauma is also evident in the USCCB's promotion of just discrimination and its teachings on homosexuality. Notably, according to a 2011 survey, 56 percent of Catholics who left the church cited its teaching on homosexuality as a primary reason for leaving.[21] More recently, the abusive treatment of gays and lesbians is cited by 39 percent of those raised Catholic who have left the church, compared to 29 percent of those raised in any other religion.[22] These statistics indicate at least two things. First, leaving the church seems to indicate the presence of religious trauma for those who experience or witness discrimination against LGBTQI+ people. Second, the higher numbers of those leaving the Catholic Church because of those teachings seems to indicate that it is one of the worst offenders in terms of its traumatic doctrinal language that translates into discriminatory treatment of LGBTQI+ people. Franciscan Daniel Horan surmises that history will not look kindly on how the Catholic Church has treated LGBTQI+ people, much as it does not look kindly on how it has treated slavery and antisemitism.[23] Yet many American dioceses are currently doubling down on discriminatory language and policies.

DISCRIMINATION, CONVERSION THERAPY, AND TRAUMA

In addition to federal legislation—ENDA and the Equality Act, which seek to codify nondiscrimination legislation—many individual states have either passed such legislation or have proposals to do so. In many so-called red states, there is often fierce opposition to passing nondiscrimination legislation, and that opposition is supported by the Catholic dioceses in those states. In the state of Nebraska, for example, there has been ongoing resistance to nondiscrimination legislation by the Nebraska Catholic Conference (NCC). Noteworthy, in all the USCCB's or state Catholic conference statements that discuss nondiscrimination legislation, no mention is made of Catholic social teaching, which absolutely opposes discrimination. Even the *Catechism of the Catholic Church*, in its statement about just discrimination against people with a homosexual condition, does not reference Catholic social teaching and its condemnation of such discrimination. This highlights a fundamental inconsistency and incoherency between Catholic social teaching, which opposes discrimination, and Catholic sexual teaching, which promotes discrimination.

In Nebraska, in the wake of SCOTUS's ruling expanding the word *sex* in the Civil Rights Act to include sexual orientation and gender identity, State Senator Megan Hunt of Omaha introduced bills LB120 and LB230 to prohibit discrimination in public accommodation, employment, and housing on the basis of sexual orientation or gender identity. The Nebraska Catholic Conference aggressively opposed such legislation, using false information and fear mongering to do so. First, the executive director of NCC claimed that the bills "offer no religious exemptions."[24] This is false, for the proposed law does provide religious exemptions for religious institutions, but not privately held businesses, corporations, or housing accommodations. The example the director cites, the case that became famous, Jack Phillips, the Colorado baker who refused to bake a wedding cake for a same-sex couple, is not grounds for a religious exemption since his company was a privately held business. Phillips would be in violation of both the recently passed Title VII that expands the term *sex* to include homosexual orientation and SCOTUS's ruling that legalized same-sex marriage. Second, the NCC claims that such legislative measures "pose a number of problems for individuals, families, and society as a whole" since they propose "a paradigm shift" of a traditional understanding of marriage and family that threatens the common good. "The practical implications are far-reaching," including "silencing and punishing those who hold to that traditional worldview."[25]

The NCC's position contradicts Pope Francis and his support for same-sex civil unions, which is not mentioned in any of the NCC's or USCCB's statements. Francis supports such civil unions precisely to insure legal protection for same-sex couples and to protect the Catholic teaching on the *sacrament* of marriage (*not* civil unions) between one man and one woman. It is disingenuous and false, then, to claim that such legislation would silence and punish those who hold a traditional, Catholic view of marriage.

Third, what the NCC and USCCB are seeking is not a religious exemption from a just, nondiscrimination law, but the prevention of what it perceives to be an unjust law. In a word, it is attempting to impose its doctrinal teaching and language on so-called just discrimination on the broader society. It is, of course, welcome to argue its case for why it believes nondiscrimination laws based on sexual orientation and gender identity are unjust, but it cannot impose its views on the broader society. Besides, as David Hollenbach and Thomas Shannon correctly assert, "the Church should not ask the state to do what it has not been able to convince its own members to do."[26] The church should not ask the state to enforce a teaching for discrimination against same-sex relationships and sexual acts that it cannot convince the majority of its own members to accept. The burden of proof is on the church to demonstrate that discrimination against LGBTQI+ persons protects the family and the common good and that same-sex acts are destructive of human dignity and cannot serve "the good of the person or society." So far neither the NCC nor the USCCB has offered a compelling argument for those claims. An unproven assertion should not be allowed as the basis to justify discrimination against LGBTQI+ people and impose the church's ethically questionable and trauma-inducing doctrine on the broader society.

The NCC has also opposed LB231, which would prohibit conversion therapy for homosexual youth. It believes that the bill would clearly be "unconstitutional, limiting free speech and religious freedom." The bill defines conversion therapy as follows: "a practice or treatment that seeks to change an individual's sexual orientation or gender identity, including efforts to change behaviors or gender expressions or to eliminate or reduce sexual or romantic attractions or feelings toward individuals of the same gender." Although the NCC recognizes the danger of therapies that rely on shaming or manipulation, it fears that such legislation would limit free speech between a client and a counselor and, since these techniques are already considered unethical under the professional licensing of mental health professionals, Nebraska does not need a law to ban that type of behavior. There are several responses to this line of reasoning. First and foremost, conversion therapy has been widely condemned by numerous professional organizations and those condemnations have been upheld legally in several Court rulings.[27] To claim that since it is unethical we do not need a law against it is simplistic and ridiculous. Racism is unethical, and yet we need laws in place to prevent white supremacists from racial discrimination and violence. There are many things that are unethical, including any type of discrimination, but without a law to ensure protections against discrimination we are dependent on the good will of people to act ethically, professional counselors in the case in question. If conversion therapy is ethically wrong, we would think that the NCC, which ostensibly stands for ethics and justice, would seek to codify it into law.

In addition, students in Catholic schools tell a different story about how teachers and priests approach LGBTQI+ people and issues. Reflecting on her experience at a Catholic grade school, Giuliana Weber recalls that "in our religion class every year, the teacher would bring up how homosexuality was a sin, and sometimes we'd have priests come in and talk about the same idea. We were told that we should pray for people not to be gay so that they could get into heaven." The priest's statement sounds remarkably similar to conversion therapy, what the NCC claims is clearly unethical. If some individual priests are not following ethical guidelines and asking students to pray for the conversion of gay people, it seems unreasonable and illogical to expect that others, such as therapists or the Catholic Church itself, might follow the ethical guideline not to shame or guilt people into compliance with church teaching.

Finally, in opposing nondiscrimination legislation, both the USCCB and the NCC rely upon the principle of "religious freedom" to justify discrimination. This is a recent principle derived from the Second Vatican Council's *Dignitatis Humanae*, its Decree on Religious Freedom. "In all his activity a man is bound to follow his conscience faithfully, in order that he may come to God for whom he was created. It follows that he is not to be forced to act contrary to his conscience. Nor, on the other hand, is he to be restrained from acting in accordance with his conscience, especially in matters religious" or, we add, ethical.[28] The USCCB asserts that the Equality Act's provisions clearly violate religious freedom and are a "radical denial of tolerance of people of faith who do not agree to the government's view of sexuality as established by the Act."[29] In this statement, the USCCB posits a generic "people of faith," which contradicts the individual consciences of the vast majority of people of faith who oppose the discrimination the USCCB is promoting and who support same-sex civil unions. While using religious freedom as an institutional principle to defend its discriminatory doctrinal language, the USCCB is suppressing the religious freedom and consciences of people of faith who disagree with its doctrinal language and teaching. As Daniel Horan correctly notes, within the USCCB and many conservative Catholic circles "'religious freedom' is only invoked by those who wish to suppress the rights and freedoms of others who may disagree with them."[30] Such a position is sadly ironic and a violation of individual consciences, human dignity, and the common good.

SAME-SEX PARENTING AND DISCRIMINATION

Church discrimination against LGBTQI+ persons extends to same-sex parenting as well. The USCCB's opposition to the Equality Act and same-sex parenting, adoption, or fostering, seeks justification from a CDF doctrinal teaching that "allowing children to be adopted [or fostered] by persons living in such [homosexual] unions *would actually mean doing violence to these children*, in the sense that their condition of dependency would be used to place them in an environment that is not conducive to their full human development."[31] The USCCB objection to the Equality Act, which would require federally funded adoption organizations, including Catholic organizations, to grant adoption or fostering rights to same-sex couples, is that it would threaten charitable organizations by forcing them either to violate their religious principles or to shut down due to the cessation of public funding. In a footnote to its letter of objection to Congress, the USCCB claims that "children raised by a married mother and father are statistically more likely to have positive social, economic, and health outcomes than those raised by same-sex couples."[32] This statement is consistent with the CDF's assertion, but unlike that assertion, which provided no scholarly references to support its claim, the USCCB statement provides three references, two from Paul Sullins, a Catholic priest who teaches sociology at the Catholic University of America, and one from Mark Regnerus, a sociologist at the University of Texas.

Sullins claims that children of same-sex parents are more likely than children of heterosexual parents to suffer from depression, suicidal thoughts, stigma, obesity, abuse, and parental distance. He concludes that households with gay or lesbian parents "may be problematic or dangerous" for the "dignity and security" of their offspring,[33] but he also advises that based on his limited evidence, his findings should be interpreted with caution and balance, and be "neither exaggerated nor dismissed out of hand on preconceived ideological grounds."[34] The USCCB ignores this caution and presents Sullins's evidence as if it were established scientific fact to substantiate part of its argument against the Equality Act that would "threaten charitable services."[35] Regnerus developed the New Family Structures Study (NFSS), which is an epidemiological study of lesbian, gay, bisexual parenting, surveying 15,000 people ages 18–39, to study the impact of LGB parents on children. His study concludes that people who had a parent in a same-sex relationship had a greater risk for negative outcomes such as being on public assistance, being unemployed, and having poorer education attainment.[36] The scholarship of both authors on same-sex parenting has been severely criticized by a majority of sociologists and professional organizations.

In a meta-analysis, Charlotte Patterson summarizes the evidence from more than one hundred scientific studies over twenty years. "There is no evidence to suggest," she concludes, "that lesbians and gay men are unfit to be parents....*Not a single study* has found children of gay or lesbian parents to be disadvantaged in any significant respect relative to children of heterosexual parents."[37] In her overview of the research, Joan Laird goes further to suggest that the scientific data indicate that same-sex parents are somewhat more nurturing and tolerant than heterosexual parents, and their children are, in turn, more tolerant and empathetic.[38] The preponderance of scientific evidence led the APA to approve and disseminate an important resolution. Since "research has indicated...that the children of sexual and gender minority parents are as likely as those of cisgender heterosexual parents to flourish," the APA opposes any discrimination based on sexual orientation or gender identity.[39] The thoroughly child-centered Child Welfare League of America (CWLA) is also convinced by the data that there are no significant differences between the parental attitudes and skills of heterosexual, gay, and lesbian parents.[40] In 1995, the League recommended that factual information about gays and lesbians should be provided "to dispel common myths about gays and lesbians."[41]

It is not the sexual orientation of gay and lesbian parents that produces negative outcomes in their children but the discrimination toward them generated by myths propagated by society and churches about their parents. Several recent studies have validated the claims for same-sex parents. In 2009, in Germany, Marina Rupp showed that same-sex parents are no less suitable to raise children than are opposite-sex parents.[42] In 2013, Ellen Perrin did the same for the United States.[43]

Nathaniel Frank, director of Cornell's What We Know Project,[44] which has collected and analyzed over seventy-five studies on same-sex parenting that all conclude that same-sex parenting is as effective and healthy emotionally, psychologically, and relationally as heterosexual couple parenting, judges that there are deep methodological flaws in Sullins's and Regnerus's studies.[45] The publisher of the journal in which Sullins's article appeared posted an online "Expression of Concern," stating that Sullins's article "has been cited to support arguments about same-sex marriage that Hindawi believes to be hateful and wrong."[46] The conclusion of numerous studies in several countries confirms these concerns.[47]

The fact that the USCCB statement cites two authors whose methods and study results are discredited by the scholarly and professional communities provides further evidence that the USCCB is grasping at straws to legitimize "just discrimination." Such discrimination causes trauma to and often violence against LGBTQI+ persons. The USCCB's discredited attempt is a clear violation of Catholic social teaching against discrimination, the *Catechism*'s teaching that homosexual people should be "accepted with respect, compassion, and sensitivity," and the USCCB's very own teaching. "It is deplorable that homosexual persons have been and are the object of *violent malice* in speech and action. Such treatment deserves condemnation from the Church's pastors wherever it occurs."[48] It is deplorable, indeed, and even more deplorable to see the USCCB consistently act contrary to its own teaching. Such actions damage the church's moral credibility, especially in the contemporary glare of the clerical sex-abuse crisis and its cover-up. The CDF provides no scientific evidence to substantiate its claim that "allowing children to be adopted [or fostered] by persons living in such [same-sex] unions *would actually mean doing violence to these children*," and the USCCB's "evidence" has been comprehensively discredited.[49]

DISCRIMINATION AND SEXUALITY POLICIES AT CATHOLIC SCHOOLS

Not only is employment, housing, access to public accommodations, and parental discrimination widespread both within public, private, and Catholic institutions, but discrimination and harassment are also widespread among our LGBTQI+ youth in public and Catholic schools. In 2016, Human Rights Watch documented widespread verbal and physical harassment and bullying of LGBTQI+ students in schools and the toleration by teachers of such discrimination and harassment because they see it as normal adolescent behavior.[50] Jesuit James Martin reports that the situation is similar in Catholic schools. Citing a University of California study, he reports that 85 percent of gay and lesbian youth between the ages of eight and eighteen have suffered the violence of verbal harassment at school, that 58 percent felt unsafe at school because of that violence, and that 27 percent have suffered actual physical violence at school.[51]

In a research project at a Catholic high school in Omaha, Nebraska, a student interviewed twenty-six LGBTQ students. Seventy percent of the students indicated they experienced discrimination at the school; over 50 percent considered skipping school because of harassment; 50 percent considered suicide; 26 percent reported attempting suicide because of severe discrimination. One student described his experience at the school: "If you come out at this school, they'll threaten to beat you, they'll threaten to rape you, they'll throw rocks at you. There's just a lot of bullying, slurs, physical harassment. I've never heard more slurs in my life before

I went to this school."[52] Students indicate that reports of harassment to school administrators were not taken seriously. This is at a Catholic school whose mission statement states that the school *forms and educates young men and women to become Christian leaders who empower others, promote justice and initiate change.*[53] The contradiction between the mission statement and the actual experience of LGBTQ students at this and other Catholic schools highlights the power of language we discussed in chapter 2.

In relation to LGBTQI+ people, Catholic doctrinal language on just discrimination and homosexual orientation as "objectively disordered" takes precedence over Catholic social teaching that promotes justice and the common good. Another student talks about her experience at a Catholic grade school:

> There wasn't any bullying or anything like that [against LGBTQI+ students], but just like a message of, "this is not okay" coming from the teachers. If such language is coming from other students at a public school, it can be brushed off. But when it's actually being taught in your classes that it's not okay to be trans, it's not okay to be gay, I think it's really despicable and I think it makes kids hate themselves [trauma]. If you wanna talk about indoctrination, that's indoctrination.[54]

This indoctrination, backed by religious teaching and authority, causes tremendous psychological and spiritual damage to children who are driven to hate themselves and to deny the fundamental Christian truth that they are created in the image and likeness of God. Rather than acknowledging the overwhelming scientific evidence about LGBTQI+ youth and their emotional, psychological, relational, and spiritual vulnerabilities, many dioceses throughout the United States are doubling down on their commitment to just discrimination in Catholic schools.

Multiple synodal reports and the USCCB's own summary of all the diocesan reports throughout the United States call for the church to welcome and "accompany with authenticity" our LBGTQ brothers and sisters and their families.[55] Yet two months after the Archdiocese of Omaha released its report, it issued a policy on human sexuality for students, parents and guardians, employees, and volunteers to be added to student/parent handbooks at Catholic schools and integrated into employee contracts. This policy ignores the message of welcome in the synodal report, alienates LGBTQI+ Catholics, and supports just discrimination against students, parents, employees, and volunteers at Catholic schools.

Several dioceses throughout the United States have issued similar policies.[56] The Omaha policy begins by stating a commitment to "spreading Gospel values and forming our faithful in Christ's teachings and in conformance with the magisterium." There are three specific directives in it for students, parents, guardians, employees, and volunteers. First, the school "shall not sponsor, endorse, facilitate, host, or provide any accommodation to any person, group, entity, event, or activity that would condone or promote a view of sexual identity that is contrary to the church's teachings, including views of gender and sexuality contrary to Catholic teachings." Second, schools "shall, at all times, act toward a person in accordance with his or her biological sex at birth. In all cases, the school must act in accord with Christian charity." Third, "at all times, students, children, and youth participating in...activities shall conduct themselves in accord with their biological sex at birth."[57] In specifying these directives, the policy notes students, employees, and volunteers at Catholic schools can be refused admission or hiring, and can be expelled, dismissed, or fired if they do not conform to them.

In addition, parents and guardians "must agree that the student will respect Catholic teaching concerning faith and morals, and particularly those addressing human sexuality as set forth in this policy." Regarding parents and guardians, "if serious concerns arise" regarding their "position or action with respect to the tenets of the Catholic faith," the principal or president should meet with the parent to discuss those concerns. If it is not resolved satisfactorily that a parent will "uphold Catholic principles" and will jeopardize a child's religious education, the child will not be admitted or will be dismissed if already attending the school. In relation to employees and volunteers, the policy specifies that all hold "ministerial positions" and must conform to this policy in their personal and professional lives.

We have several comments regarding the Omaha policy.

First and foremost, it ignores the archdiocese's and USCCB's synodal reports, issued just months earlier, on the need to welcome LGBTQI+ persons. Although the second directive specifies "the school must act in accord with Christian charity" in all cases, it is unclear how this policy reflects charity and welcomes this community with threats of expulsion, firing, and dismissal.

Second, the language is ambiguous, and it is left to administrators to attempt to interpret and apply the policy. It allows for students to have a "romantic date…only with a person of the opposite biological sex." Who defines what is and what is not a romantic date? What are the criteria for making this judgment between same-sex or heterosexual friends?

The policy notes that if an "expression of gender, sexual identity, or sexuality should cause confusion, disrupt the educational integrity of the Catholic education program, or cause scandal, the matter will be discussed with the student and his/her parent." If the matter cannot be resolved, the student may not be admitted to, or dismissed from, the school. All of these criteria are ambiguous and open to interpretation by any person who may be affected more by political/cultural/ecclesial bias than by an objective, correct interpretation of contemporary Catholic teaching. We ask what does "students will conduct themselves in accord with their biological sex at all times" mean? Pope Francis and the Congregation for Catholic Education in *Male and Female He Created Them* affirm that sex and gender are distinct though inseparable (6) and that scientific studies that attempt to discern how sexual difference is lived out in various cultures should inform our understanding of the interrelationship between sex and gender.[58] This acknowledges a plurality of cultural influences and understandings of how gender is expressed, which is nowhere acknowledged in the Omaha and other diocesan policies.

Third, the policy fails to distinguish between different, and even conflicting, magisterial teachings, to which all students, parents, school faculty, and archdiocesan administrators must conform. It gives unjustified emphasis to Catholic sexual teaching over Catholic social teaching. The *Catechism of the Catholic Church* calls for people with "deep-seated [or definitive] homosexual tendencies" to be "accepted with respect, compassion, and sensitivity," but it immediately goes on to state that "every sign of *unjust* discrimination in their regard should be avoided."[59] The condemnation of "unjust discrimination" against people with "deep-seated homosexual tendencies" leaves the door open for the promotion of so-called just discrimination against them. Yet Catholic social teaching is indisputably clear that such discrimination is unethical. The *Catechism* teaches that "the equality of men [and women] rests essentially on their dignity as persons and the rights that flow from it: 'Every form of social or cultural discrimination in fundamental personal rights on the grounds of sex, race, color, social conditions, language, or religion must be curbed and eradicated as incompatible with God's design.'"[60] The *Catechism*, it should be noted, does not include sexual orientation or gender identity in this list.

A statement to motivate Catholics to lobby state legislators against nondiscrimination legislation asserts that such legislation "would prevent a Catholic school from reprimanding a transgender male [*sic*] coach who insists on using the girls' shower and restroom facilities."[61] Such a statement is not only politically and legislatively motivated by the culture wars, but manifests the politics of fear that is driving polarization in both church and country. It also violates Popes John Paul II's and Francis's recommendation for a dialogue of charity when there are different opinions.[62] Notwithstanding the culture wars strategy behind any statement to promote unjust discrimination, if any coach is showering with students there are more fundamental institutional and personnel concerns than LGBTQI+ issues.

Pope Francis's distinction between same-sex *marriage* and same-sex *civil unions* sheds an entirely new light on ENDA and the Equality Act, and should be reflected in any Catholic policy. His support of legal protections for same-sex civil unions makes an important distinction between civil law and church doctrine, prioritizes Catholic social over sexual doctrine, recognizes that LGBTQI+ people are discriminated against and need legal protection, and calls the church to practice respect, compassion, and hospitality towards all people, including LGBTQI+ people. If respect, compassion, and hospitality should extend to civil and legal institutions, it should certainly extend to all Catholic institutions, including Catholic schools. Diocesan policies on sexuality for Catholic schools fail miserably here, especially when dealing with young people who are struggling to discern their sexual identities.

Fourth, one of the leading causes of young people leaving the church and of teen suicides or attempted suicides is discrimination and bullying on the basis of sexual identity.[63] In 2016, a Public Religion Research Institute (PRRI) international survey demonstrated that those raised Catholic were more likely than those raised in any other religion to cite negative treatment of LGBTQ+ persons as their primary reason for leaving the church.[64] The Trevor Project's 2022 Survey on LGBTQ Youth Mental Health found that 45 percent of those youth considered attempting suicide in the last year. Importantly, it also notes that "LGBTQ youth who found their school to be LGBTQ-affirming reported *lower rates of attempting suicide*."[65] LGBTQ-affirming, therefore, is a truly pro-life stance. Commenting on similar studies, Jesuit James Martin reports that 48 percent of LGBTQI+ youth reported engaging in self-harm in the past twelve months. This leads him to state the obvious: "Stigmatizing language, especially stigmatizing language from religion…can have [traumatic and] life-and-death consequences."[66] This is especially true in Catholic schools where sexuality policies use such stigmatizing language.

Although the diocesan policies speak out against bullying by individuals, they appear to be oblivious to the stigmatizing language and institutional bullying in the policies themselves. They appear oblivious also to the scientific data that indicate a strong correlation between mental health and negative stances on, and treatment of, LGBTQI+ persons, such as those reflected in the policies. The policies create a culture of fear for faculty, staff, and volunteers and cause the trauma of personal despair for LGBTQI+ students, parents, and families. According to David Palmieri, a theology teacher at a Catholic high school, "There is a disconnect between the legalism of many policies and the lived experiences of the human person. They are not creating schools of encounter [or accompaniment]. They help create a culture of fear."[67] This demonstrates Catholic institutional insensitivity to human dignity, ignorance of the sciences, and structural sin that perpetuates and supports discrimination and directly or indirectly promotes mental and even physical harm to students, faculty, staff, volunteers, and parents because of a student's sexual identity.

Fifth, the policies blatantly ignore and violate the Catholic doctrine on the authority and inviolability of personal conscience. Pope Francis states in *Amoris Laetitia* that the church is called "to form consciences, not to replace them" (37). In this statement, he has rediscovered and reinstituted the Catholic teaching on the authority and inviolability of a well-formed conscience. Such a well-formed conscience has the freedom to voice disagreement with the church's non-infallible teaching on sexual ethical issues without fear of punitive measures.

Finally, it is noteworthy and demonstrates the cynical legal calculation on the part of dioceses that the policies designate all employees and volunteers, whether they are involved in religious education or not, as ministerial. The "ministerial exception" is a specific legal designation that allows dioceses to dismiss anyone if a diocesan official judges they have violated the policy, regardless of their direct role or function in a specific ministerial capacity. In other words, it protects the diocese from discrimination lawsuits and promotes so-called just discrimination.

Few dioceses have ever formulated and circulated a policy to be implemented into the student-parent handbook for violating Catholic social teaching. One can be a climate change denier, a racist, a supporter of the death penalty, even a denier of the real presence of Jesus in the Eucharist, and suffer no penalty. This and other policies do not reflect a positive vision of synodality, and certainly not Pope Francis's vision of finding unity in diversity.[68] They more accurately reflect, rather, the divisive cultural and political perspectives poisoning the entire country and apparently shared by the leadership of many Catholic dioceses. They are sinful and are driving people from the church.[69]

Added to the violence LGBTQI+ students experience at Catholic schools is the violence they experience in some Catholic homes from parents who seek to bully them into the church's embraced female-male sexual binary, and banish them from their homes when this effort proves fruitless.[70] Banishment from their homes to the streets leaves children homeless, penniless, and prime candidates for sexual violence and exploitation. The California study reports that 40 percent of homeless youth served by social services are LGBTQI+ youth. The American Medical Association (AMA) acknowledges that there is an epidemic of violence in the United States against members of the transgender community, especially against transgender people of color.[71] Although it is difficult to establish a causal relationship between church teaching on just discrimination against members of the LGBTQI+ community and bullying or violence against them, the continued defense of such a stance and the failure of most bishops to speak out against it,[72] at the very least, sends a mixed message to people about the human dignity of LGBTQI+ people and the absolute prohibition of discrimination so clearly stated in Catholic social teaching.[73]

CONCLUSION

The synodal reports from dioceses throughout the United States and the USCCB confirm that the *sensus fidelium* of Catholic Church members largely opposes discrimination against LGBTQI+ people. In addition, many priests, bishops, cardinals, and laypeople are calling for changes in Catholic sexual teaching. There is an urgent need, we suggest, for a revision of Catholic sexual teaching that promotes "just" discrimination. There is an urgent need also for an evaluation of the church's role in defining the inalienable human dignity of all women and men and in discerning how this definition should influence its pursuit of the common good, universal human dignity, and Christian solidarity in a pluralist society.[74] We strongly recommend that, in the name of truth, justice, human dignity, the common good, and the gospel of Jesus, the Catholic magisterium eliminate the doctrinal language of just discrimination against LGBTQI+ people.

8

WOMEN AND TRAUMA IN THE CATHOLIC CHURCH

> Everyone, man and woman, should acknowledge and accept his sexual *identity*. Physical, moral, and spiritual *difference* and *complementarity* are oriented toward the goods of marriage and the flourishing of family life. The harmony of the couple and of society depends in part on the way in which the complementarity, needs, and mutual support between the sexes are lived out. (*Catechism* 2333)

> The unity of marriage, distinctly recognized by our Lord, is made clear in the equal personal dignity which must be accorded to man and wife in mutual and unreserved affection. (*Gaudium et Spes* 49)

> There exists a total equality [between men and women] with respect to the gifts of the Holy Spirit, with respect to the "mighty works of God" (Acts 2:11). (Pope John Paul II, *Mulieris Dignitatem* 22)

> I declare that the Church has no authority whatsoever to confer priestly ordination on women and that this judgment is to be definitively held by all the Church's faithful. (Pope John Paul II, *Ordinatio Sacerdotalis* 4)

In the preface, we noted the killing of LGBTQI+ people at the Pulse nightclub and considered the connection of that killing to the Catholic doctrinal language that degrades LGBTQI+ persons. We have also argued that the clerical sex-abuse crisis and its cover-up can be traced to the Catholic doctrinal language that elevates priests above laypeople. In this chapter, we consider the traumatic impact of the Catholic subordination of women to men despite the equality the church teaches between men and women and, following Pope Francis's mandate for theologians, argue to "demasculinize" the church, both theologically *and* ministerially.[1] We trace that trauma to Catholic doctrinal language and practice.

DOCTRINAL EQUALITY: GENDER AND ANTHROPOLOGY

Official Catholic doctrine teaches that all human beings are ontologically equal. Created in the image and likeness of God, there is one human nature that all males and females share. The further doctrinal claim, however, that women cannot image Christ in priestly ordination throws this ontological and anthropological claim into doubt. There are at least three possible responses to address this inconsistent claim. First, historically, the church recognized, and formulated doctrines according to, the subordination of women to men. Both share a single human nature, but within that nature, there was a male human nature that was superior and female human nature that was somehow inferior. This distinction is evident in church doctrines that designate women as inferior with corresponding inferior roles and functions in the church, society, and marriage. Such doctrines, in part, have been corrected, but the practical and relational consequences remain in varying degrees. The new wineskin of linguistic, anthropological, and ontological equality still holds the old wine of hierarchy, subordination, and the practical superiority of men to women.

Second, current church teaching recognizes the fundamental equality of all humans, male and female. However, as Phyllis Zagano notes, there continues to be a hierarchical subordination of women to men.[2] This subordination is evidenced in priestly ordination and, de facto, in heterosexual marriage. Popes John Paul II, Benedict XVI, and Francis have been explicit in emphasizing the fundamental equality between men and women, but in doing so they promote gender stereotypes that reinforce gender inequality and uphold the doctrine prohibiting women from priestly ordination. All three popes attach ontological meaning to male/female sex and masculine/feminine gender, with corresponding normative and sacramental implications for roles in the church. Genesis's second creation story reveals "the fundamental *truth…concerning man* created as man and woman in the image and likeness of God."[3] This fundamental truth reveals the dignity and fundamental equality between man and woman,[4] but their distinct physical natures entail distinct gender roles and functions in marriage and the sacraments.

Marriage, as we have seen, is defined in terms of male-female complementarity by which women are called to bring full dignity to motherhood and the conjugal life. Though John Paul II admits that women's roles have been defined too narrowly in terms of wife, mother, and family relationships without adequate access or representation in the public sphere, he also notes the following: "On the other hand, the true advancement of women requires that clear recognition be given to the value of their maternal and family role, by comparison with all other public roles and all other professions."[5] Pope Francis agrees:

> A mother who watches over her child with tenderness and compassion helps him or her to grow in confidence and to experience that the world is a good and welcoming place. This helps the child to grow in self-esteem and, in turn, to develop a capacity for intimacy and empathy. A father, for his part, helps the child to perceive the limits of life, to be open to the challenges of the wider world, and to see the need for hard work and strenuous effort. A father possessed of a clear and serene masculine identity who demonstrates affection and concern for his wife is just as necessary as a caring mother.[6]

For Pope John Paul II, men are never defined primarily in terms of their roles as husbands or fathers; more emphasis is given to their social roles. Pope Francis recognizes "a certain flexibility in roles and responsibilities," and more fluidity in the relationship between sex and gender. "Biological sex and the socio-cultural role of sex [gender] can be distinguished but not separated," he affirms along with the "reciprocity in nature of a man and a woman" (*AL* 56). Arguing from sexual complementarity to gender role complementarity, however, perpetuates imbalances in power and perpetuates social structures that limit women's creativity and contributions in the public and ecclesial realms. These distinctions between the feminine and the masculine in marriage and family life are determined more historically and culturally than ontologically.

Such definitions of complementarity have led many feminists to argue that complementarity, even under the guise of equality and dignity, always entails women's subordination.[7] Lisa Cahill proposes a more balanced approach to the interrelationship between sex and gender. It is the subordination and oppression found in traditionalist accounts of this relationship that leads her, at least in part, to consider gender as a foundational anthropological dimension in her ethical theory, and to refine it in light of critical social analysis. For Cahill, biological differentiation is an essential and universal component of human experience that affects the places of women and men in the world, but its overemphasis on biological differences to subordinate the feminine to the masculine is a situation that begs for redress. "Gender understood as moral project entails the social humanization of biological tendencies, capacities, and differences, including the social ties that they, by their very nature, are inclined to create."[8] This social humanization must take place in both marital and church contexts, and it takes place by the deconstruction and reconstruction of traditional gender roles and hierarchies in light of this humanization. Such reconstruction challenges many of the absolute magisterial norms on sexual ethics and allows for the ordination of women as deacons and priests.

Third, although Catholic doctrine officially recognizes the equality between men and women, the church continues to recognize two distinct male and female natures. Male human nature can reflect *persona Christi*; female human nature cannot. This church ontology is shaped by the image of Christ as bridegroom and his church as bride. Ecclesiologically, biological sexual differentiation and gender complementarity are used to defend the argument that only men can be priests. Jesus was a male, the apostles were males, and throughout its two-thousand-year history only males have been ordained to the priesthood in the Catholic Church.[9] Mary Daly's assertion remains true: "If God is male, then male is God."[10] A church metaphor presents Jesus as a bridegroom and the church as his bride, and drawing from this metaphor males represent Jesus as both bridegroom and priest who complements his female church-bride. Since only males can be bridegrooms, it is ontologically determined that only males can be priests. This perspective is reflected in Michael Novak's comment. "The priest's maleness is a reminder of the role played in our salvation by the sacramentality of human flesh—not flesh-in-general, but male flesh."[11] Catholic doctrine can defend the fundamental equality of men and women and still argue for their essential role differentiation in the church. There are clear social and church roles grounded in masculinity and femininity; true complementarity, John Paul II argues, must not entail a masculinization of the feminine or a feminization of the masculine.[12] Catholic teaching posits gender complementarity, grounded in biological differentiation, to justify clearly defined roles for men and women in both marriage and in the church.

CATHOLIC MARRIAGE

An obvious and culturally universal factor in marriage is the subordination of wives to husbands, which is simply the marital continuation of the general historical, cultural subordination of women to men. In the main, men are the stronger sex and women the weaker sex physically and economically, and this fact translates into the relationships of women to men in general and of wives to husbands in particular. Men are superior to women culturally and economically, a fact that is symbolized historically in sexual intercourse with the husband on top actively contributing seed and the wife on the bottom passively receiving his seed and safeguarding it for the birth of a new human being. The ancient Greek, Roman, and Hebrew understanding of conception was that the man's seed contained all that was necessary for new human life, and the wife merely provided a suitable "ground" or "field" for the man's seed, a true little man, to develop into a full-fledged human being, preferably male. To spill the seed anywhere it could not gestate properly, on the ground, in the mouth, or in an anal orifice, for instance, was regarded as murder.[13] The female ovum and its contribution to the development of a child was not discovered until the 1850s. Before its discovery, it was commonly held that the man was solely responsible for the generation of a new human being; the woman merely provided the fertile ground or field where the man's seed developed into a new human being.[14]

The worldwide and, sadly, Catholic tradition of marriage assumes the domination of men over women and, therefore, it is a tradition of patriarchy, male hierarchy, and inequality. We ask whether that is inevitably so, and historian of marriage John Gillis answers yes, it is inevitably so. He describes the conflict between the modern emphasis on the equality of the spouses and the still unequal burdens borne by wives in "the conjugal myth." This conjugal myth, he argues, "is so dominant today that many would deny there is anything fundamentally irreconcilable between the egalitarian dimension of conjugal roles and the roles women and men [actually] assume when they set up homes and have children."[15] He is speaking of British marriages, but they are not at all different from American marriages when it comes to the roles husbands and wives assume in marriage. There have been some improvements, but they are minimal. Lynn Jamieson reports that "large-scale studies show men taking up domestic work at a snail's pace. There are still significant numbers of couples trapped in deeply unequal relationships in which intimacy is at best the forced intimacy of a coercive and dominant figure."[16]

COMPLEMENTARITY, MARRIAGE, AND SEXUAL ETHICS

Many years ago, distinguished German theologian Karl Rahner emphasized the importance of anthropology for doing theology. "Today, dogmatic [and moral] theology must be anthropology and such an 'anthropological turn' is necessary and fruitful."[17] The Synthesis Report of the Synod of Bishops affirms the need for a critical and comprehensive anthropology: "Sometimes the anthropological categories we have developed are not able to grasp the complexity of the elements emerging from experience or knowledge in the sciences and require greater precision and further study."[18] These insights remain and are perhaps even more essential today with respect to sexual anthropology. Mary Ann Hinsdale notes correctly that, when considering Catholic theological anthropology, the concept of complementarity is "the issue under the issues" of that anthropology.[19] Pope John Paul II's introduction of complementarity into Catholic marital and sexual theology provided a justification for patriarchy on the basis of culturally and historically determined gender stereotypes. The idea of complementarity, if not the term itself, is used throughout John Paul's writings and applies to eschatological,[20] ecclesiological,[21] vocational,[22] and anthropological realities.

Basically, complementarity claims that certain realities belong together and produce a whole that neither produces alone. While space does not permit an exploration of how complementarity is applied to all these realities, we can note the following characteristics of its use. First, complementarity is nearly always classified along masculine and feminine lines,[23] and this classification is used biologically, metaphorically, or in combination of both. Commenting on the complementarity between man and woman and its relation to the "Role and Dignity of Women," Charles Curran notes two reasons that ground John Paul's theory of male and female complementarity: one practical, which we treat later in this chapter, and one theoretical. The practical reason is to defend the absolute prohibition of ordaining women to the priesthood. This focus on complementarity allows John Paul "to claim to accept the fundamental equality of man and woman and oppose discrimination and marginalization while still maintaining that women cannot be ordained priests."[24] The theoretical reason is reflected in his sexual anthropology in which man and woman complement each other in marriage and create a unity of the two. John Paul develops his theoretical notion of complementarity theologically, anthropologically, and scripturally, especially in reference to Genesis.[25] Genesis serves as the foundational text for his theology of the body as well. Unfortunately, as Curran notes, since "there are different theologies of the body"—single people, widows and widowers, celibates, and lesbians and gays—it "cannot serve as a theology for all bodies."[26]

The bodies it attempts to serve are male and female bodies in a heterosexual marriage which, John Paul II claims, have ontologically given qualities and characteristics. First, he claims, "though man and woman are made for each other, this does not mean that God created them incomplete."[27] Each individual has the potential to be complete by integrating the biological, psycho-affective, social, and spiritual elements of his or her identity. Claiming that men and women are complete in themselves seems to respond to the concerns expressed by some theologians that the idea of complementarity implies that celibate religious or single people are somehow not complete and lack something in their humanity.[28]

Second, when he moves from individual to couple, though man and woman are "complete" in themselves, John Paul II argues that "for forming a couple they are incomplete."[29] He further argues that "woman complements man, just as man complements woman....Womanhood expresses the 'human' as much as manhood does, but in a different and complementary way."[30] We may reasonably ask, however, where the incompleteness and the need for complementarity reside in an individual that is complete in himself or herself, but is incomplete for forming a couple. Where in the human person does this incompleteness exist that needs complementing by the opposite sex to complete it? John Paul II responds that "womanhood and manhood are complementary *not only from the physical and psychological points of view*, but also from the *ontological*. It is only through the duality of the 'masculine' and the 'feminine' that the 'human' finds full realization."[31] Kevin Kelly accurately notes that "ontological complementarity maintains that the distinction between men and women has been so designed by God that they complement each other, not just in their genital sexual faculties but also in their minds and hearts and in the particular qualities and skills they bring to life, and specifically to family life."[32] The masculine and feminine complement each other to create a "unity of the two,"[33] not only in sexual acts but also in marital life.

Several points need to be made regarding the claims that God created individuals complete in themselves but incomplete for forming a couple, and that this incompleteness is made complete through the affective complementarity of male and female. First, to claim that a person is complete in himself or herself indicates that the person is complete biologically, psycho-affectively, socially, and spiritually. Second, while it is clear that male and female complete one another biologically in terms of genitalia for reproduction, it is not clear how they are incomplete and complete each other psycho-affectively, socially, and spiritually. John Paul claims that "it is only in the union of two sexually different persons that the individual can achieve perfection in a synthesis of unity and mutual psychophysical completion."[34] Biological, psycho-affective, social, and spiritual elements of the human person are ontologically divided along masculine and feminine lines, however, without justification, save that these are God-given from the very beginning.[35]

We judge it reasonable to question, however, whether the psycho-affective, social, and spiritual elements are intrinsically divided along masculine and feminine lines and find completion only in male-female unity.[36] Besides genitalia, what are the "feminine" affective elements a man lacks and what are the "masculine" affective elements a woman lacks?

One finds certain gender stereotypes in church documents that promote a relational hierarchy and subordination of women to men where femaleness is defined primarily in terms of motherhood and nurturing, and maleness is defined in terms of fatherhood and activity.[37] With the exception of biological motherhood and fatherhood, the claim of gendered psychological traits does not seem to recognize the culturally conditioned and defined nature of gender, and does not adequately reflect the complexity of the human person and relationships. In her reflection on her own marriage and sexuality, Cristina Traina notes that "gender [complementarity] is the least relevant factor in the sustenance of a relationship." What are most significant for that sustenance in heterosexual marriage are "faith, friendship, generosity, communal support, the serendipity of personalities, sexual and verbal affection, and the hard work that goes into mutual formation of a working partnership."[38] The same may be said, we suggest, for same-sex relationships. For individuals in relationships, psycho-affective, social, and spiritual elements are not restricted to either gender, but may be found in both genders, may vary within relationships, and may express themselves differently depending on the relational contexts.[39] These traits also vary within relationships in which there may be two dominant people or two nurturing people. Do we want to claim that in these cases these two people do not complement each other? The masculinity and femininity of the nonbiological elements are largely conditioned and defined by culture and distinct individual personalities,[40] and are not essential components of masculine and feminine human nature mysteriously creating a "unity of the two."

Given that religious equality, nonpatriarchal, or "equal regard"[41] marriages are possible, theologian Adrian Thatcher argues that "in a nonpatriarchal marriage the husband has an equal partner in giving and receiving married love as Christ loves the Church. The love the husband has for his wife will be deeper because she will be his equal, not a dependent being capable only of obedience, submission, and reverence in relation to him."[42] So also, we add, the love of the wife for her husband will also be deeper because he will be her equal, not her lord and feared master. Historically, the theological anthropology of the domination of men and submission of women, and the theological perspective that morphed into complementarity, was used to justify hierarchy and too often kept women in sexually, physically, and emotionally abusive marital relationships. The hesitancy of Catholic Church authorities to grant annulments in the pre–Vatican II era perpetuated this hierarchy and engendered marital abuse.

The severe inequities in marriage just mentioned are experienced as much by Catholic as non-Catholic spouses. They are reinforced, indeed, by the doctrine of the Catholic Church. Two doctrines have dominated and controlled the church's approach to sexual ethics since Vatican II. The first doctrine is Pope Paul VI's declaration in 1968 that, to be ethical, "each and every marriage act must remain open to the transmission of life."[43] The phrase "marriage act" might intend a "Good morning" or "Good night" spousal kiss; it might even intend doing the dishes or vacuuming the living room, both frequently recurring marriage acts. It does not, of course, intend those simple marriage acts; it intends the marriage act of sexual intercourse. The second teaching is the declaration by the CDF in 1976 that, to be ethical, "any human genital act whatsoever may be placed only within the framework of marriage."[44] Michel Foucault accurately comments that "the communal family took custody of [sexuality] and absorbed it into the serious function of procreation."[45] In the teaching of the Catholic Church, every sexual act outside of marriage is sinful and every sexual act within marriage that is intentionally contraceptive is sinful.

The second of those teachings seriously impacts every Catholic spouse, especially every Catholic wife who suffers anxiety from the possibility of an unwanted, and frequently unaffordable, pregnancy, and who suffers ethical guilt with every intentionally contraceptive act. All that can be claimed with certainty in the church's understanding of complementarity is that heterosexual complementarity is necessary for reproduction. Even heterosexual complementarity is of only relative importance, however, for infertile couples where reproduction is biologically impossible, and will become increasingly insignificant as a fertile couple ages.[46] The further claim that there is an intrinsic difference between male and female whereby the male and female find psycho-affective, social, and spiritual completion in one another only in marriage is unsubstantiated experientially and scientifically. What is substantiated is the damage done to marital and familial relationships by gender inequality, a notion of complementarity that perpetuates gender inequality, and sexual norms that flow from that definition, especially when combined with economic poverty.

We believe that the church's account of complementarity relies primarily on heterosexual complementarity, entails an incomplete vision of gender, and neglects an adequate consideration of the experiential and relational dimensions of human sexuality.[47] It is this understanding of complementarity that perpetuates the superiority, hierarchy, and patriarchy of males and the subordination, inferiority, and subservience of females within marital and sexual relationships. It also perpetuates the doctrine of a male-only priesthood.

SEX AND ORDINATION

Several years ago, on an episode of *The Colbert Report*, Stephen Colbert, a committed and lifelong Catholic, interviewed former President Jimmy Carter, a committed Southern Baptist. During that interview, Colbert asked Carter if he would ever consider becoming Catholic. Carter responded that if a female priest asked him, he might consider it. The audience was enthusiastic about his response, but his response was essentially that this will never happen. The church has consistently affirmed that only males can be ordained priests. Pope Francis, however, is presently considering the possibility of ordaining women deacons.

The pain of this doctrinal stance for both women and men has led many to leave the Catholic Church due to what they see as clear gender discrimination grounded in a distorted anthropology and ecclesiology. As one Catholic woman comments, "After 33 years, I left the Catholic Church, something I never thought I would do....I left for various reasons, but the primary reason was the failure to accept the reality that some women are called to the priesthood, and the only obstacle for them is their [biological sex]. I know men who have [left] as well. One said to me, 'I'll go back if the Catholic Church ever values my daughter as much as it values my son.'"[48] In this section, we first consider and critically analyze the church's doctrine on priestly ordination. Second, we consider current church discussions on the ordination of women deacons. Third, we cite two recent major events in the church that challenge the church's anthropological complementarity and justify a reconsideration, if not a revision, of church sexual teaching and sacramental teaching on the ordination of women as priests and deacons.

Priestly Ordination and Complementarity

The greatest discrimination against believing Catholic women is probably their church's refusal to permit their ordination to the priesthood or diaconate. This refusal causes great pain and trauma to the women who feel called by God to these ministries. The debate about women's ordination came to the fore in the late twentieth century, when in 1976 the American Episcopal Church ruled that women could be ordained to the priesthood. On November 30, 1975, Pope Paul VI wrote to Donald Coggan, the archbishop of Canterbury, explaining the Catholic position. The Catholic Church

> holds that it is not admissible to ordain women to the priesthood, for very fundamental reasons. These reasons include: the example recorded in the Sacred Scriptures of Christ choosing his apostles only from among men; the constant practice of the Church, which has imitated Christ in choosing only men; and her living teaching authority, which has consistently held that the exclusion of women from the priesthood is in accordance with God's plan for his Church.[49]

In 1983, with the publication of its revised Code of Canon Law, the Catholic Church solemnly restated its inflexible position: "Only a baptized male validly receives sacred ordination" (can. 1024).

The theological objections to ordaining women have doubtful probative value, as we shall show, but they have a very ancient *anthropological* basis. Aristotle taught that "the female is a misbegotten male"[50] and should not, therefore, have any authority over males. Thomas Aquinas followed Aristotle, but with a careful distinction that those who accuse him of misogyny always ignore. He agrees with Aristotle, but only on the level of biology.

> As regards individual [biological] nature, woman is defective and misbegotten, for the active force in the male seed tends to the production of a perfect likeness in the masculine sex, while the production of woman comes from a defect in the active force....On the other hand, as regards human nature in general, woman is not misbegotten but included in nature's intention as directed to the work of generation.[51]

Woman is *biologically* inferior to and weaker than man, Aquinas agrees, but she is *naturally* equal to him. Lisa Sowle Cahill commends Pope John Paul II "for speaking out against injustice to women, and giving attention to biblical evidence for the equality of women and for the sinfulness of their subordination to men," but she adds that "the practical consequences of biblical and personalist themes are far from receiving full recognition."[52] Contemporary Catholic doctrine theoretically insists on the equality of women and men, but also regularly employs the fact of their biological differentiation and complementarity to support its doctrine of not ordaining women.

Mary Ann Hinsdale explores the church's theological anthropology, focusing on its teaching on gender complementarity as "the issue under the issues" in its theological anthropology and official Catholic doctrine that builds on it.[53] We have treated complementarity and sexual ethics above. Here, we focus on complementarity and the sacrament of ordination. Although church doctrine does not use the term *complementarity* in its statements limiting ordination to only men, it is, we agree, the issue under the issue. We consider those doctrines, how complementarity functions within them, and critique them.

Church Documents against Women's Ordination

Several major church documents prohibiting the ordination of women have been published in recent history: *Inter Insigniores* (*IS*) (1976),[54] *Ordinatio Sacerdotalis* (*OS*) (1994),[55] *Responsum ad Dubium* (*RD*) (1995),[56] and *Ad Tuendam Fidem* (*TF*) (1998).[57] *IS* was a response from the CDF to a petition by the first Catholic Women's Ordination Conference to "ordain women now," in 1975 and the "irregular" ordination of women priests in the U.S. Episcopal Church in 1976. The term *complementarity* was not introduced into official church doctrine until Pope John Paul II's 1981 apostolic exhortation, *Familiaris Consortio*, so it is not surprising that the term is not present in *IS*. However, gender complementarity is clearly evident in *IS* and functions as an anthropological justification for opposing women's ordination. Though *IS* quotes *Apostolicam Actuositatem*, which calls for women's greater participation in the church's apostolate, it maintains a strict patriarchal and hierarchal anthropology, grounded in gender differentiation, that constrains that participation. A central argument in *IS* is the metaphor in which Christ is presented as the bridegroom and the church is presented as his bride; a second is that Jesus established that the priest, who acts sacramentally *in persona Christi*, must be a man since there must be a "natural resemblance to Christ."[58] Jesus's maleness, of course, is a historical fact, and this fact is used to justify an exclusively male priesthood.

Pope John Paul II's main purpose in *OS* was to put an end to all discussion on the possibility of ordaining women. In it, he repeats many of the same arguments of *IS*, and declares "that the church has no authority whatsoever to confer priestly ordination on women and that this judgment is to be definitively held by all the Church's faithful."[59] Three points of this statement are noteworthy. First, John Paul emphasizes that the nonadmission of women to priestly ordination does not equate to women having lesser dignity than men. Second, like *IS*, he deems it important to emphasize that it is not discriminatory against women. Third, his declaration that this doctrine is to be definitively held shuts down the possibility of dialogue. In these three points, Pope John Paul invokes an anthropological justification, equal human dignity grounded in distinct roles, functions, and services dependent on biological sex, concerns with violations of Catholic social teaching and the perception that the church's stance constitutes discrimination, and a church perspective that suppresses any theological dialogue. The last point is a curious one. One would think that, if a statement was in fact true and part of divine revelation, that theological dialogue would be encouraged and supported since that obvious truth would be better revealed through the process of dialogue. The defensive, authoritarian reaction to the possibility of women's ordination betrays a patriarchal, authoritarian ecclesiology and undermines the equality that Pope John Paul emphasizes in his understanding of complementarity.

The CDF's *RD* and John Paul's *TF* emphasize this third point. The former declares *OS* to be "definitive," infallible, and irrevocable; the latter seeks to protect against "errors from certain members of the Christian faithful," especially theologians, to ensure that they uphold truths taught definitively by the magisterium. *TF* explains canonical sanctions on those who "obstinately" reject or question definitive teachings through their scholarship with a "just penalty."

John Paul's *Christifideles Laici* (*CL*) incorporates the term *complementarity* to highlight the anthropological and ecclesiological divisions in the Church. Anthropologically,

> the condition that will assure the rightful presence of woman in the Church and in society is a more penetrating and accurate consideration of the *anthropological foundation for masculinity and femininity* with the intent of clarifying woman's personal identity in relation to man, that is, a diversity yet mutual complementarity.[60]

John Paul discusses the vocation of the faithful in terms of complementarity. Church communion, he writes, "is characterized by a diversity and a complementarity of vocations and states in life, of ministries, of charisms and responsibilities" (*CL* 20). The diversity is between pastors, who "must always acknowledge that their ministry is fundamentally ordered to the service of the entire People of God," and the lay faithful, who "must acknowledge that the ministerial priesthood is totally necessary for their participation in the mission in the Church" (*CL* 22). There is a strict hierarchy of pastors over lay faithful and a specific limit to the Holy Spirit's gifting of charisms whereby "no charism dispenses a person from reference and submission to the *Pastors of the Church*" (*CL* 24). Pope Francis has affirmed Pope John Paul's statement in *OS*.[61] Pope John Paul II and contemporary Catholic teaching seek to meld complementarity, equality, holy orders, and the masculine into a seamless infallible doctrine of a male-only priesthood.

Critical Analysis of Complementarity and Ordination

There are several responses to the church's theological anthropology that attempts to justify its prohibition of ordaining female priests. First, Elizabeth Johnson states succinctly the problem of emphasizing Jesus's maleness as an essential foundation for a male-only priesthood:

> I do not think one can overestimate the seriousness of the charge brought against Christology, that of all the doctrines of the church it is the one most used to oppress women....The fundamental problem lies in androcentric interpretations of the maleness of the human Jesus, which lift his sex to the level of ontological necessity, and the incorporation of Jesus as male so interpreted into a divine Father-Son relationship, which totally excludes women from the most intimate of divine exchanges.[62]

Second, and following from Johnson's christological critique, there is a basic critique of biblical exegesis that highlights the subjugation of women to men that the contemporary church understanding of complementarity continues to substantiate. That Christ called men to be apostles is completely understandable in the historical and cultural context in which he lived, a context in which women were thoroughly subject to men and were not even permitted to speak in public. Vatican II's document on biblical exegesis and revelation, *Dei Verbum*, taught that "the biblical interpreter must investigate what meaning the sacred writer intended to express and actually expressed in particular circumstances as he used contemporary literary forms in accordance with the situation of his own time and culture."[63] In 1976, following this approach to biblical exegesis, the Pontifical Biblical Commission warned that "difficulties" are created by "a study of the biblical data from the perspective of a later conception of the eucharistic priesthood," a twenty-first century conception, for instance. It concluded that the New Testament could not settle the question of whether women could be ordained to the priesthood.[64] That warning has consistently been ignored in every discussion about the ordination of women. Also ignored is the fact that Jesus surprisingly surrounded himself with women in his ministry, that several women shared Paul's ministry, and that one of them, Junia, he explicitly calls *apostolos*, apostle (Rom 16:7). This latter fact was carefully editorialized out in the Revised Standard Version of 1971.

The claim that the consistent teaching of the church has always held the exclusion of the ordination of women has no probative value, for that teaching authority has regularly changed its teaching over the centuries, and it can certainly change again. Pope Francis's comment at the opening of the three-year synodal process is appropriate here: "That expression—'We have always done it that way'—is poison for the life of the church. Those who think this way, perhaps without even realizing it, make the mistake of not taking seriously the times in which we are living. The danger, in the end, is to apply old solutions to new problems."[65] We think of all the years that the church condoned slavery, only for Pope Leo XIII to teach in 1888 that slavery was against both divine and natural law. A pope could reverse the prohibition of the ordination of women to the priesthood in much the same way.

A third critique of Catholic teaching against women's ordination is the attempt to justify the claim that the doctrine, and the complementary anthropology defending the doctrine, are not discriminatory. It is interesting that the first paragraph of *IS* cites *Pacem in Terris* and *Gaudium et Spes*, two documents establishing Catholic social teaching, promoting the rights of women, and speaking out against discrimination. The claim that church teaching prohibiting the ordination of women is discriminatory is a common one, especially in light of Catholic social teaching.

"Every form of social or cultural discrimination in fundamental personal rights on the grounds of sex, race, color, social conditions, language, or religion must be curbed and eradicated as incompatible with God's design."[66] Church teaching prohibiting the ordination of women, denying that the prohibition is discriminatory and justifying the prohibition and discrimination on the basis of complementarity, is challenged anthropologically, theologically, and ecclesiologically. We consider those various challenges.

INTERSEX, SCIENCE, AND COMPLEMENTARITY

The Catholic definition of *complementarity* asserts that female-male biological differences are ontologically and anthropologically definitive, determine the "constitutive identity" of a person, and serve as the point of departure for defining what it means to be human biologically, psychologically, relationally, spiritually, and vocationally. This biologically based anthropology, we submit, is misguided scientifically, scripturally, and theologically.

Scientifically, it fails to recognize the bodily reality of intersex persons in general, as we discussed in chapter 6, and the contemporary scientific understanding of gender/sex in specific. The biological reality and "ambiguity" of intersex persons, externally and internally, fundamentally challenges a strict male-female binary and natural complementarity, and makes it difficult to assign a particular gender/sex to an intersex person through therapy or surgery. Contemporary scientific understandings of gender/sex compound this difficulty.

The sciences have established that gender is both biologically and culturally determined by genetics, hormones, brain chemistry, and cultural rearing experience. A child's gender/sex cannot be determined by a physician in infancy via an appropriate therapeutic surgical procedure, as the Congregation for Catholic Education's *Male and Female He Created Them* (*MFC*) suggests.[67] Gender/sex can be discerned by all persons, including intersex persons, only as they grow in experience, knowledge, and understanding of themselves in the cultural perspective in which they are immersed. The science surrounding sex, intersex, and gender challenges *MFC*'s simple claim on the ability to determine the constitutive identity of an individual merely by determining his or her biological sex as male or female. Furthermore, it highlights the understanding of gender shaped by history, culture, and a complex biochemical interaction between hormones, genetic make-up, neurology, and environment. Intersex does not allow for a clear biological determination and, therefore, constitutive identification of the person. Besides, too much emphasis has been, and continues to be, placed on biological differences in society, church, and employment to subordinate the feminine to the masculine. Gender/sex entails the social humanization of biological differences and capacities, and this social humanization takes place in both society and church via traditional roles and hierarchies. Ongoing reconstruction challenges many absolute Catholic norms in sexual ethics and the sacrament of ordination.

The Second Vatican Council abandoned the focus on *sexed bodies* and replaced it with a focus on *related persons*. In marriage, it teaches, a man and a woman enter into a personal covenant in which "the spouses mutually bestow and accept each other,"[68] not each other's bodies as was so biologically legislated in the 1917 Code of Canon Law.[69] This focus on interpersonal covenant, we insist, brings not only marriage but also all human friendship relationships into line with the rich biblical traditions of covenant between God and God's people and Christ and Christ's church.

Relation is constitutive of the identity of both God and humans created by God. DeFranza opts to call this approach "social"[70] but, though we have no great disagreement with the term *social*, we prefer the term *relational* as more clarifying of the intractable mysteries of both the hidden God and God's largely hidden human creatures. The church's use of complementarity, which prioritizes biology over personal relationship in its anthropology, and relies on an exclusive female-male biological binary, is theologically outdated and renders all of its teaching on gender/sex, at the very least, debatable if not downright wrong. Personal, covenantal relations between God, women, and men, not biology, is dominant in scripture. Females, males, and intersex persons can all enter into such covenantal relationships, imaging God in their own unique, God-created way.

SCRIPTURE, CREATION, AND COMPLEMENTARITY: RELATIONSHIP OVER BIOLOGY?

God's relationship with creation in general, and with God's human creation in specific, precedes the actual act of the creation of humans as female and male. Genesis begins with God in relationship to the possibility of creation and out of this relationship comes actual creation. "In the beginning when God created the heavens and the earth…the earth was a formless void" (Gen 1:1–2). Creation's form follows from God's relation to its possibility; it does not preexist that relation. Relation is primary and creation's materiality flows from that relation. Even in God's creation of *'adam*, humankind, not a male, "God created humankind [*'adam*] in his image, in the image of God he created them; male and female he created them" (Gen 1:27). God creates the sexed bodies of women and men out of relationship to their possibility, and sexed bodies are the actualization of that possibility.

The Gospel of John affirms this relational prioritization. It begins with the relation between God Creator and God Savior. "In the beginning was the Word [*Logos*], and the Word was with God, and the Word was God.…All things came into being through him, and without him not one thing came into being" (John 1:1, 3). The masculine pronoun *him* is used, as is common in male-dominated cultures when sex is unclear, to designate God as spiritual, relational being, not male-sexed, relational being. The relation between God and *Logos* is at the root of all creation, including the creation of male, female, and intersex. God's relation with humans creates their every form and sex. Just as Jesus's relation to God the Creator was established before Jesus's sexed humanity, so too humans' relation to God is established before their sexed humanity as male, female, or intersex. Relation is primary; biology very much secondary. In a wonderful way the reality of intersexed people, though statistically a created minority, confirms and privileges this relationality; it challenges the female-male binary and the inadequate biological anthropology on which it is based.

We propose, then, a holistic-relational anthropology that prioritizes personal relation over biology, though it includes biology as an essential and integral dimension.[71] We relate to God, self, neighbor, and the material world as embodied persons. Our holistic-relational anthropology views the human person as a holistic being, mind, soul, and body, where the relational is impacted by the psychological, spiritual, and biological. The biological functions not as *the* integrating dimension, but as *a* dimension *integrated* with the whole of human dimensions. Constitutive human identity is not defined by biology, as it is in much of the church's sexual and sacramental anthropology. It is defined by a holistic-relational anthropology that integrates all dimensions of the human and does not constrain God's gifting of charisms or ecclesial roles and functions in terms of biological sex. Real human diversity, including biological diversity, better images God's infinity than any humanly constructed unreal human uniformity.

ECCLESIOLOGY AND COMPLEMENTARITY

We agree with feminist theologian Mary Hines: "A massive transformation of the church's structures is needed to free them from the patriarchal, hierarchical, and clerical assumptions that prevent the church from becoming a prophetic community of equal disciples committed to the task of liberation for all people."[72] Hines highlights three models of the church that would promote and realize this transformation: the church as inclusive community, following Jesus's and the early church's example; authority grounded in subsidiarity or participatory justice that promotes consent and respect for all members; and the globalization of the church, which recognizes the church's universality while respecting and building upon the particularity of local churches and cultures.[73] In the words of Pope Francis, an inclusive community should not seek uniformity, "but a unity in diversity" (*AL* 139). This unity in diversity allows for pluralism in the church and respects divergent cultural practices in sexual ethics and sacramental theology.

Hines's three models incorporate Catholic social teaching into a holistic, relational understanding of complementarity. Jesus's ministry was inclusive, not exclusive, even for women. His encounters with women throughout the Gospels, especially after his resurrection, demonstrate this inclusivity, which is at the heart of Catholic teaching on human dignity. Catholic social teaching promotes participatory justice or subsidiarity. A church that does not include women in leadership roles, which includes decision-making capacity at the highest levels, is in direct denial of subsidiarity. Unity in the global church allows for plural incarnations of Catholic sexual doctrines, which are reflected more in Catholic social teaching's moral principles than in sexual norms and doctrines.[74] We add a fourth model that encapsulates and builds upon Hines's models and Pope Francis's commitment to synodality. This fourth ecclesiology, combined with Catholic social teaching, calls for a just church[75] and full inclusion of women vocationally as priests and deacons to exercise the charisms gifted to them by the Holy Spirit. We concur with Lisa Cahill's assessment that "in the divine image, human and ecclesial community is a communion of persons-in-relation whose genuine [sexual and gender] diversity or difference is essential and not inimical to their equality."[76]

RECONSTRUCTING COMPLEMENTARITY: EVOLVING UNDERSTANDINGS

Two recent events in the church provide fundamental challenges to its theological anthropology, and the gendered stereotypes that anthropology promotes, and can serve as a basis for reconstructing complementarity. Those events are Pope Francis's and the German bishops' approval and blessing, respectively, of same-sex civil unions and the synodal discussion to ordain women deacons.

Same-Sex Civil Unions

We have dealt elsewhere with civil unions and Pope Francis's support of their legalization.[77] "What we have to create," he declared, "is a civil-union law. That way they are protected. I stood up for that."[78] A civil union is a legally recognized social arrangement similar to marriage created primarily to provide legal recognition and protection to couples wishing to live together and to be recognized as a couple. Francis's call for legal justice for same-sex couples in civil unions prioritizes justice and Catholic sexual teaching over absolute Catholic doctrines based on any complementarity. The German bishops' approval of blessing same-sex civil unions[79] recognizes that affective complementarity can extend beyond natural complementarity between male and female in marriage and can be realized in same-sex civil unions as well.

The underlying issue of Pope Francis's support of same-sex civil unions, the German bishops' call to bless same-sex civil unions, and the call of many bishops for a revision of Catholic sexual teaching[80] is a call for a revised sexual anthropology and a revised understanding of natural complementarity. Pope Francis's promotion of dialogue on the ordination of women deacons also contributes to the call for a deconstruction and reconstruction of complementarity.

Ordination of Women Deacons

Shortly after becoming Pope, Francis called for the need for women to have "a more incisive presence…in the Church." He has repeated that call on several occasions. In the preparatory document for the worldwide synod to be held in Rome in 2023–2024, he asks, "How can the Church of our time better fulfil its mission through greater recognition and promotion of the baptismal dignity of women?" The document clearly states,

> In baptism, the Christian enters into a new bond with Christ and, in Him and through Him, with all the baptized, with all humanity, and with the whole of creation. Sons and daughters of the one Father, anointed by the same Spirit, by virtue of sharing the same bond with Christ, the baptized are given to one another as members of a single body enjoying equal dignity (cf. Gal 3:26–28). The listening phase reaffirmed the awareness of this reality, indicating that it must find ever more concrete realization in the life of the church, including through relationships of mutuality, reciprocity and complementarity between men and women.[81]

If all people, through baptism, share the gifts of priest, prophet, and king as *Lumen Gentium* asserts (31), why do men share these gifts in greater capacity than women in terms of priestly and deacon ordination and leadership in the Church?

Pope Francis has taken concrete steps to realize "a more incisive presence" of women in the church, including positions in Vatican offices and members of Vatican Congregations, called for by *Praedicate Evangelium*.[82] In 2016, in response to a meeting of the International Union of Superiors General, Pope Francis agreed to institute a commission exploring the question of women deacons. He also acknowledged, however, two important points that needed addressing before discussing this issue, namely, the need to include more women in leadership roles in the church and the problem of clericalism. These points, as well as the question of female deacons, are intimately related to theological anthropology. Doctrinally excluding women from leadership roles, even though they carry out these roles daily in the church throughout the world, is a manifestation of the subordination of women to men. Pope Francis designates clericalism "a scourge" on the church but he has been slow to make the connection between this scourge and the patriarchy and hierarchy that flows from a complementary anthropology that enables and justifies a culture of clericalism and hierarchicalism.[83]

Synodal discussions on the possibility of women's roles and functions in the church, the ongoing discussion on the possibility of ordaining women deacons, and calls for changes in Catholic sexual ethics all give some hope for a revised anthropology that actually recognizes women's equal dignity with men and leads to sexual and sacramental doctrinal changes that reflect that dignity.

THE TERM *COMPLEMENTARITY*: TO RECONSTRUCT OR ABANDON?

We add one final comment on the term *complementarity*, which is foundational for Catholic sexual and sacramental doctrines. Many people, especially feminists, have argued that given the historical, anthropological, and ecclesiological baggage that comes with the term and promotes gender stereotypes, a patriarchal hierarchy, and continues to subordinate women to men, the term itself should be abandoned. Others, including ourselves, have attempted to reform the term to reflect ongoing historical, theological, scientific, and cultural knowledge and understanding. From our perspective, both options have strengths and weaknesses. To abandon the term given its use and abuse in church teaching, and to use a different term to explain a healthier sexual and sacramental anthropology, could serve to both deconstruct and reconstruct that anthropology and the doctrines formulated from it. On the other hand, changing the term can be similar to putting new wine into old wineskins and the anthropological and conceptual old wineskin of complementarity could define the new wine of a different term or phrase. This is certainly the case with "personalism," for instance. Reflecting on the theological evolution at the Second Vatican Council from a focus on a biological understanding of natural law to a personalist understanding of natural law illustrates this danger. Pope John Paul II is often labeled a personalist philosopher and theologian. John Paul's personalism, however, took the new wine of a term and placed it in the old wineskin of an ontologically prioritized biological and physicalist understanding of the human person contained in traditional sexual doctrine. Contrast this personalism with that of Louis Janssens's personalism, which fundamentally rejected that biological ontological prioritization and the traditional anthropology it reflected. Janssens ontologically prioritized relationship in natural law and a holistic understanding of the person in his formulation of the human person integrally and adequately considered.[84]

We have opted for continuity of the current language of church teaching, to retain the term *complementarity*, and to deconstruct and reconstruct it based on the incorporation and complementarity of the sources of ethical knowledge. Either option, abandoning the term and choosing another, or reforming the meaning of the term, have strengths and weaknesses and we do not definitively opt for one option over another. Both options, however, agree that the traditional and current use of the term in church teaching is incorrect, patriarchal, promotes gender and sexual discrimination against women, violates Catholic social teaching, and denies science and human experience. It also can cause trauma in women who are subjected to violations of human dignity in sexual and marital relationships, produce doctrines on human sexuality that fail to recognize explicit hierarchical anthropology, and make women feel like second-class citizens in a church that preaches human dignity and fundamental equality between men and women but hypocritically fails to recognize that dignity in church practice.

Pat Perriello judges that reforms and nuances of the concept of complementarity that include changes in thinking about doctrinal teaching on sexuality and sacraments might take one or two centuries.[85] Given the ongoing exodus of members from the Catholic Church due, in large part, to its teachings on sexual ethics and women's nonroles in the church, as well as the ongoing sexual abuse crisis, it is questionable whether that timeline is acceptable in terms of realizing social justice or sustaining Catholic affiliation and institutional stability in the long term.

CONCLUSION

Pope Francis recognizes that "one of the great sins we have had is 'masculinizing' the church," and invites theologians to help "de-masculinize" the church theologically.[86] In this chapter, we have attempted to respond to this invitation but have extended it to ministerial roles in the church. We see the failure to ordain women deacons and priests as a historical and ongoing masculinization of the church, and we hope that through the process of synodality and Pope Francis's invitation, we will move toward a more just and inclusive church in all doctrinal language and teaching, including the ministerial level of ordination and leadership within the church.

Recognizing the trauma and pain caused by the masculinization of the church as well as the broader traumatic impact of sexual ethical and sacramental doctrinal language among the faithful, we have responded in this book to Francis's broader invitation for theologians. In his 2023 *motu proprio, Ad Theologiam Promovendam,*[87] Pope Francis challenges theologians to open up to the world and to humanity, "with its problems, its wounds, its challenges, its potential." He affirms that theological reflection must make room for, and construct, "an epistemological and methodological rethinking," and that "good theologians, like good pastors, also smell of the people and the street and, by their reflection, pour oil and wine on the wounds of men [and women]."[88] Throughout this book, we have investigated the traumatic wounds of men and women induced by the church's doctrinal language and teaching and, drawing from Pope Francis, tradition, scripture, reason, and experience, have proposed epistemological, anthropological, and methodological rethinking to revise that language and teaching to heal those wounds and prevent future wounds by promoting human dignity and the common good.

NOTES

PREFACE

1. National Catholic Reporter Staff, "Statements by US Bishops on Orlando Shooting," *National Catholic Reporter*, June 22, 2016, https://www.ncronline.org/news/spirituality/statements-us-bishops-orlando-shooting.

2. Adrian Thatcher, *Vile Bodies: The Body in Christian Teaching, Faith and Practice* (London: SCM Press, 2023), 14.

3. Pope John Paul II, *Vita Consecrata* (March 25, 1996), 32, https://www.vatican.va/content/john-paul-ii/en/apost_exhortations/documents/hf_jp-ii_exh_25031996_vita-consecrata.html; *Familiaris Consortio* (November 22, 1981), 16, https://www.vatican.va/content/john-paul-ii/en/apost_exhortations/documents/hf_jp-ii_exh_19811122_familiaris-consortio.html.

4. *Catechism of the Catholic Church* (Vatican City: Libreria Editrice Vaticana, 2000), 2358, https://www.usccb.org/sites/default/files/flipbooks/catechism/568/#zoom=z.

CHAPTER 1

1. Pope Francis, *Ad Theologiam Promovendam*, https://www.vatican.va/content/francesco/la/motu_proprio/documents/20231101-motu-proprio-ad-theologiam-promovendam.html.

2. Francis, *Ad Theologiam Promovendam* 3.

3. Pope Francis, "Intervention of the Holy Father at the 18th General Congregation of the 16th Ordinary General Assembly of the Synod of Bishops, 25.10.2023," https://press.vatican.va/content/salastampa/en/bollettino/pubblico/2023/10/25/231025f.html.

4. Ashley McKinless and Zac Davis, "Cardinal McElroy: Sex and Sin Need a New Framework in the Church," *America*, February 3, 2023, https://www.americamagazine.org/faith/2023/02/03/cardinal-mcelroy

-inclusion-sexualty-244650. See also James F. Keenan, "LGBT Catholics and 'Disordered' Language: A Biblical Model for Change," *America*, March 12, 2024.

5. Catholic News Service, "Cardinal Hollerich Says Church Teaching on Gays 'No Longer Correct,'" *Angelus*, February 2, 2022, https://angelusnews.com/news/world/cardinal-hollerich-says-church-teaching-on-gays-no-longer-correct/.

6. Catholic News Agency, "German Bishops' Leader: Day of Same-Sex Blessings Not 'Helpful,'" *CNA* (April 29, 2021), https://www.catholicnewsagency.com/news/247452/german-bishops-leader-day-of-same-sex-blessings-not-helpful.

7. Catholic News Service, "German Cardinal Calls for Change in Church Teaching on Homosexuality," *National Catholic Reporter*, March 31, 2022, https://www.ncronline.org/news/theology/german-cardinal-calls-change-church-teaching-homosexuality.

8. Catholic News Agency, "German Catholic Bishops Welcome Initiative Seeking Change in Church Teaching on Sexuality," *Angelus*, January 25, 2022, https://angelusnews.com/news/world/german-catholic-bishops-welcome-initiative-seeking-change-in-church-teaching-on-sexuality/.

9. Karl Rahner, "Theology and Anthropology," *Theological Investigations*, vol. 9 (London: Darton, Longman, and Todd, 1972), 28.

10. See Dicastery for the Doctrine of the Faith, "Declaration *Dignitas Infinita: On Human Dignity*," April 8, 2024, https://press.vatican.va/content/salastampa/en/bollettino/pubblico/2024/04/08/240408c.html. For a critique of *Dignitas Infinita*'s understanding of sexual human dignity, see Salzman and Lawler, "*Dignitas Infinita*: Anthropologically and Methodologically Consistent?," *Marriage, Families, & Spirituality* 30, no. 1 (2024): 143–53.

11. See Pope Francis, *Amoris Laetitia* 56 (hereafter cited in text as *AL*).

12. Joseph A. Selling, "The 'Meanings' of Human Sexuality," *Louvain Studies* 23, no. 1 (1998): 32; see also Selling, *Embracing Sexuality: Authority and Experience in the Catholic Church* (Aldershot, UK: Ashgate, 2001), 149–62.

13. *Persona Humana* (1975), 1, https://www.vatican.va/roman_curia/congregations/cfaith/documents/rc_con_cfaith_doc_19751229_persona-humana_en.html.

14. Selling, "The 'Meanings' of Human Sexuality," 35.

15. This paragraph is adapted from Todd A. Salzman and Michael G. Lawler, *Virtue and Theological Ethics* (Maryknoll, NY: Orbis, 2018), 160–61.

16. John Paul II, "The Relationship of Science and Theology: A Letter to Jesuit Father George Coyne," *Origins* 18 (November 1988): 376.

17. See Ted Peters, *Science and Theology: The New Consonance* (Boulder, CO: Westview, 1999).

18. *Familiaris Consortio* (1981), 11, https://www.vatican.va/content/john-paul-ii/en/apost_exhortations/documents/hf_jp-ii_exh_19811122_familiaris-consortio.html.

19. John Paul II developed this position in a series of talks he gave from 1979 to 1981. These talks are now published as *The Theology of the Body: Human Love in the Divine Plan*, with a foreword by John S. Grabowski (Boston: Pauline Books and Media, 1997).

20. John Paul II, *Theology of the Body*, 48.

21. John Paul II, *Theology of the Body*, 49.

22. It is important to note that the distinction between biological sex (male/female) and socially constructed gender (masculine/feminine) is frequently absent in church discussions of complementarity. See Susan A. Ross, "The Bridegroom and the Bride: The Theological Anthropology of John Paul II and Its Relation to the Bible and Homosexuality," in *Sexual Diversity and Catholicism: Toward the Development of Moral Theology*, ed. Patricia Beattie Jung with Joseph A. Coray (Collegeville, MN: Liturgical, 2001), 56n5.

23. Ross, "Bridegroom and the Bride"; and David M. McCarthy, "The Relationship of Bodies: A Nuptial Hermeneutics of Same-sex Unions," in *Theology and Sexuality: Classic and Contemporary Readings*, ed. Eugene F. Rogers (Oxford: Blackwell, 2002), 206–10.

24. John Paul II, "Authentic Concept of Conjugal Love," *Origins* 28 (March 4, 1999): 655.

25. John Paul II, "Letter to Women" (July 27, 1995), 7, http://www.vatican.va/content/john-paul-ii/en/letters/1995/documents/hf_jp-ii_let_29061995_women.html.

26. See Ronald Modras, "Pope John Paul II's Theology of the Body," in *John Paul II and Moral Theology: Readings in Moral Theology No. 10*, ed. Charles Curran and Richard McCormick (Mahwah, NJ: Paulist Press, 1998), 149–56.

27. See Lisa Sowle Cahill, "Catholic Sexual Ethics and the Dignity of the Person: A Double Message," *Theological Studies* 50, no. 1 (1989): 145–46; Luke Timothy Johnson, "A Disembodied 'Theology of the Body': John Paul II on Love, Sex, and Pleasure," *Commonweal* 128, no. 2 (January 26, 2001): 11–17; Margaret Farley, *Just Love: A Framework for Christian Sexual Ethics* (New York: Continuum, 2006).

28. Karol Wojtyla, *Love and Responsibility* (Boston: Pauline Books and Media, 2013), 229–30.

29. Wojtyla, *Love and Responsibility*, 53.

30. See also The Pontifical Council for the Family, "Family, Marriage and 'De Facto' Unions," (January 11, 2001): "According to this ideology [of gender], being a man or a woman is not determined fundamentally by sex but by culture. Therefore, the very bases of the family and inter-personal relationships are attacked," 8, http://www.vatican.va/roman_curia/pontifical_councils/family/documents/rc_pc_family_doc_20001109_de-facto-unions_en.html. According to this statement, biological sex and not cultural gender is the foundation for interpersonal relationships.

31. Congregation for Catholic Education, "'Male and Female He Created Them': Towards a Path of Dialogue on the Question of Gender Theory in Education" (February 2, 2019), 31, emphasis added, https://www.vatican.va/roman_curia/congregations/ccatheduc/documents/rc_con_ccatheduc_doc_20190202_maschio-e-femmina_en.pdf.

32. *Gaudium et Spes* 48, https://www.vatican.va/archive/hist_councils/ii_vatican_council/documents/vat-ii_const_19651207_gaudium-et-spes_en.html.

33. Edward N. Peters, *The 1917 Pio-Benedictine Code of Canon Law* (San Francisco: Ignatius Press, 2001), can. 1081, 2.

34. See Michael G. Lawler, *Marriage and the Catholic Church: Disputed Questions* (Collegeville, MN: Liturgical Press, 2002), 77–85.

35. USCCB, *Ethical and Religious Directives for Catholic Health Care Services* (Washington, DC: USCCB, 2018), 8, https://www.usccb.org/about/doctrine/ethical-and-religious-directives/upload/ethical-religious-directives-catholic-health-service-sixth-edition-2016-06.pdf.

36. Charles E. Curran, *Catholic Social Teaching, 1891–Present: A Historical, Theological, and Ethical Analysis* (Washington, DC: Georgetown University Press, 2002), 131.

37. John A. Coleman, "The Future of Catholic Social Thought," in *Modern Catholic Social Teaching: Commentaries and Interpretations*, ed. Kenneth Himes (Washington, DC: Georgetown University Press, 2005), 527–29.

38. International Theological Commission, *In Search of a Universal Ethic: A New Look at Natural Law* (May 20, 2009), 55, http://www.vatican.va/roman_curia/congregations/cfaith/cti_documents/rc_con_cfaith_doc_20090520_legge-naturale_en.html.

39. *In Search of a Universal Ethic*, 85.

40. Brian Stiltner, *Religion and the Common Good* (Lanham, MD: Rowman and Littlefield, 1999), 178.

41. David Hollenbach, "The Catholic University and the Common Good," 2, https://www.bc.edu/content/dam/files/offices/mission/pdf1/cu22.pdf.

42. United States Conference of Catholic Bishops, Letter to Senate (Washington, DC: USCCB, 2022), https://www.usccb.org/resources/LetterSenateRFMA.pdf.

43. *Catechism* 1935.

44. *Gaudium et Spes* 16.

45. Pope Francis, "World Day of Peace: Overcome Indifference and Win Peace" (January 1, 2016), 5, https://www.vatican.va/content/francesco/en/messages/peace/documents/papa-francesco_20151208_messaggio-xlix-giornata-mondiale-pace-2016.html.

46. Pope Francis, "Message of His Holiness Pope Francis for Lent 2015: 'Make Your Hearts Firm' (Jas 5:8)," https://www.vatican.va/content/francesco/en/messages/lent/documents/papa-francesco_20141004_messaggio-quaresima2015.html.

47. Pope John Paul II, *Sollicitudo Rei Socialis* (1987), 38, https://www.vatican.va/content/john-paul-ii/en/encyclicals/documents/hf_jp-ii_enc_30121987_sollicitudo-rei-socialis.html.

48. *Sollicitudo Rei Socialis* 40.

49. Associated Press, "Germany's Catholic Bishops Vote to Approve Blessings for Same-Sex Couples," *National Catholic Reporter*, March 10, 2023, https://www.ncronline.org/news/germanys-catholic-bishops-vote-approve-blessings-same-sex-couples.

50. Dicastery for the Doctrine of the Faith, "*Fiducia Supplicans*: On the Pastoral Meaning of Blessings" (December 18, 2023), https://www.vatican.va/roman_curia/congregations/cfaith/documents/rc_ddf_doc_20231218_fiducia-supplicans_en.html.

51. USCCB, "A Compilation of Quotes and Texts of Pope Francis on Dialogue, Encounter, and Interreligious and Ecumenical Relations," https://www.usccb.org/resources/Quotes-of-Pope-Francis-on-dialogue.pdf.

52. Catholic News Agency, "German Bishops' Leader."

53. Catholic News Agency, "What Pope Francis Learned from Homeless Girl: 'Cry with the Suffering!'" (January 17, 2015), http://www.catholicnewsagency.com/news/what-pope-francis-learned-from-homeless-girl-cry-with-the-suffering-19592/.

54. Lawrence B. Finer and Rubina Hussain, "Unintended Pregnancy and Unsafe Abortion in the Philippines: Context and Consequences," *Guttmacher Institute*, August 2013, https://www.guttmacher.org/report/unintended-pregnancy-and-unsafe-abortion-philippines-context-and-consequences.

55. Stephen Vincent, "Filipino Church Vows Continued Opposition to 'Reproductive Health' Bill," *National Catholic Register*, December 20, 2012, http://www.ncregister.com/daily-news/filipino-church-vows-continued-opposition-to-reproductive-health-bill.

56. Louis Janssens, "Artificial Insemination: Ethical Considerations," *Louvain Studies* 8, no. 1 (1980): 3–29.

57. Cindy Wooden, "'*Amoris Laetitia*' at Three Months: Communion Question Still Debated," *National Catholic Reporter*, July 7, 2016, https://www.ncronline.org/news/parish/amoris-laetitia-three-months-communion-question-still-debated.

58. Edward Pentin, "Cardinal Parolin: *Amoris Laetitia* Represents New Paradigm, Spirit and Approach," *National Catholic Register*, January 11, 2018, http://www.ncregister.com/blog/edward-pentin/cardinal-parolin-amoris-represents-new-paradigm-new-spirit-new-approach. See also Pope Francis, *Ad Theologiam Promovendam* (November 1, 2023), 4, https://www.vatican.va/content/francesco/it/motu_proprio/documents/20231101-motu-proprio-ad-theologiam-promovendam.html.

59. See Richard B. Miller, *Casuistry and Modern Ethics: A Poetics of Practical Reasoning* (Chicago: University of Chicago Press, 1996).

60. *Amoris Laetitia* 304; Thomas Aquinas, *Summa Theologiae*, I–II, 94, 4.

61. John Paul II, *Familiaris Consortio* 34; Francis, *Amoris Laetitia* 295.

62. Michael G. Lawler and Gail S. Risch, "A Betrothal Proposal," *U. S. Catholic* 72 (June 2007): 18–22, http://www.uscatholic.org/life/2008/06/a-betrothal-proposal.

63. *Gaudium et Spes* 44.

64. Margaret A. Farley, "Moral Discourse in the Public Arena," in *Vatican Authority and American Catholic Dissent*, ed. William W. May (New York: Crossroad, 1987), 177.

65. Margaret Farley, "Moral Discourse," 177.

66. See Michael G. Lawler and Todd A. Salzman, "Catholic Doctrine on Divorce and Remarriage: A Practical Theology Analysis," *Theological Studies* 78, no. 3 (2017): 326–47.

67. John E. Thiel, *Senses of Tradition: Continuity and Development in Catholic Faith* (Oxford: Oxford University Press, 2000), 47.

68. Augustine, *De praed. sanct.* 14, 27, *Patrologia Latina* 44, 980.

69. *Lumen Gentium* (1964), 12, https://www.vatican.va/archive/hist_councils/ii_vatican_council/documents/vat-ii_const_19641121_lumen-gentium_en.html. Emphasis added.

70. Speech at the conclusion of the 2014 Synod on Marriage and the Family (October 18, 2014), https://w2.vatican.va/content/francesco/en/speeches/2014/october/documents/papa-francesco_20141018_conclusione-sinodo-dei-vescovi.html.

71. See Vatican Radio, "Papal Election Anniversary: Synodality a Key Change under Pope Francis" (December 3, 2017), http://en.radiovaticana.va/news/2017/03/12/papal_election_anniv_synodality_a_key_change_under_francis/1297800.

72. See Gerard O'Connell, "'*Amoris Laetitia*' Represents an Organic Development of Doctrine, 'Not a Rupture,'" *America* (April 8, 2016), https://www.americamagazine.org/faith/2016/04/08/amoris-laetitia-represents-organic-development-doctrine-not-rupture.

73. See Michael G. Lawler and Todd A. Salzman, "*Amoris Laetitia*: Has Anything Changed?," *Asian Horizons* 11, no. 1 (2017): 62–74.

CHAPTER 2

1. See Patrick J. Boyle, *Parvitas Materiae in Sexto in Contemporary Catholic Thought* (Lanham, MD: University of America Press, 1987), 31–44.

2. For a historical account of the evolution of the negative view of human sexuality in Christianity, see James F. Keenan, *A History of Catholic Theological Ethics* (Mahwah, NJ: Paulist Press, 2022), 102–10.

3. Bessel van der Kolk and Alexander McFarlane, "The Black Hole of Trauma," in *Traumatic Stress: The Effects of Overwhelming Experience on Mind, Body and Society*, ed. Bessel van der Kolk and Alexander McFarlane (New York: Guilford Press, 1996), 6–7; Maria Root, "Reconstructing the Impact of Trauma on Personality," in *Personality and Psychopathology: Feminist Reappraisals*, ed. L. S. Brown and M. Ballou (New York: Guilford Press, 1992), 237.

4. Root, "Reconstructing the Impact of Trauma on Personality," 229.

5. CDF, "Letter to the Bishops of the Catholic Church on the Pastoral Care of Homosexual Persons (October 1, 1986)," 3, https://www.vatican.va/roman_curia/congregations/cfaith/documents/rc_con_cfaith_doc_19861001_homosexual-persons_en.html.

6. Bessel van der Kolk explains, "People with PTSD have difficulty neutralizing stimuli in their environment in order to attend to relevant tasks. To compensate, they tend to shut down. However, the price for shutting down is decreased involvement in ordinary, everyday life." Bessel van der Kolk, "The Body Keeps the Score," in van der Kolk and McFarlane,

Traumatic Stress, 222. See also van der Kolk and Alexander McFarlane, "The Black Hole of Trauma," 4, 10, 14.

7. Bessel van der Kolk and M. S. Greenberg, "The Psychobiology of the Trauma Response: Hyperarousal, Constriction, and Addiction to Traumatic Reexposure," in *Psychological Trauma*, ed. Bessel van der Kolk (Washington, DC: American Psychiatric Press, 1987), 63–87.

8. van der Kolk, "Trauma and Memory," in van der Kolk and McFarlane, *Traumatic Stress*, 289.

9. Alexander McFarlane and Bessel van der Kolk, "Trauma and Its Challenge to Society," in van der Kolk and McFarlane, *Traumatic Stress*, 26.

10. Judith Lewis Herman, *Trauma and Recovery* (New York: Basic Books, 1992), 47, 49.

11. Herman, *Trauma and Recovery*, 52–66.

12. Shannon Sullivan, *The Physiology of Sexist and Racist Oppression* (New York: Oxford University Press, 2015).

13. Christopher Houck et al., "Sexual Abuse and Sexual Risk Behavior: Beyond the Impact of Psychiatric Problems," *Journal of Pediatric Psychology* 35, no. 5 (2010): 474.

14. Bronwyn Watson and W. Kim Halford, "Classes of Childhood Sexual Abuse and Women's Adult Couple Relationships," *Violence and Victims* 25, no. 4 (2010): 518.

15. Herman, *Trauma and Recovery*, 53.

16. Herman, *Trauma and Recovery*, 61.

17. Herman, *Trauma and Recovery*, 33.

18. Michelle Panchuk, "The Shattered Spiritual Self: A Philosophical Exploration of Religious Trauma," *Res Philosophica* 95, no. 3 (July 2018): 506.

19. Exposure to abuse at an early age is associated with the highest degrees of risk. Women tend to experience violence at younger ages than men do and, consequently, they are at greater risk for PTSD overall. See Vivia McCutcheon et al., "Age at Trauma Exposure and PTSD Risk in Young Adult Women," *Journal of Traumatic Stress* 23, no. 6 (2010): 811.

20. Strong emotional attachments forged *prior* to the traumatic violence can guard against development of PTSD: see Bessel van der Kolk et al., "A General Approach to Treatment of Posttraumatic Stress Disorder," in van der Kolk and McFarlane, *Traumatic Stress*, 432–33. *After* the traumatic event has occurred, positive responses to the disclosure of the trauma greatly improve one's chances of recovery: see Kate Walsh et al., "Adult Coping with Childhood Sexual Abuse: A Theoretical and Empirical Review," *Aggress Violent Behav.* 15, no. 1 (2010): 1–13, https://www.ncbi.nlm.nih.gov/pmc/articles/PMC2796830/. The authors summarize,

"For both male and female sexually abused youth, stronger perceived social support was related to increased self-worth and lower symptomatology."

21. Lisa Oakley and Justin Humphreys, *Escaping the Maze of Spiritual Abuse: Creating Healthy Christian Cultures* (London: SPCK, 2019), 31.

22. Menachem Ben-Ezra et al., "Losing My Religion: A Preliminary Study of Changes in Belief Pattern after Sexual Assault," *Traumatology* 16, no. 2 (2010): 7–13.

23. Catherine Cameron, *Resolving Childhood Trauma: A Long-Term Study of Abuse Survivors* (London: Sage Publications, 2000), 276–77. Cameron reports from her study that the majority of adult female victims of childhood sexual abuse who have not intentionally worked through their traumatic memories try to fill their days with many distracting activities. They do so, Cameron suggests, in order to intentionally avoid the opportunity for quiet reflection. Though some do turn to religious practices, it does not seem that these function as a tool for self-reflection but rather as another form of external engagement (276).

24. Root, "Reconstructing the Impact of Trauma on Personality," 239.

25. Root, "Reconstructing the Impact of Trauma on Personality," 239–40.

26. Rachel Yehuda, *Risk Factors for Posttraumatic Stress Disorder* (Washington, DC: American Psychiatric Press, 1999), xv.

27. Yehuda, *Risk Factors for Posttraumatic Stress*, xv.

28. Root, "Reconstructing the Impact of Trauma on Personality," 236. See the National Child Traumatic Stress Network, "Identifying the Intersection of Trauma and Sexual Orientation and Gender Identity: Part I: Key Considerations," https://www.nctsn.org/sites/default/files/resources/special-resource/identifying-the-intersection-of-trauma-and-sexual-orientation-and-gender-indentity-key-considerations.pdf.

29. Root, "Reconstructing the Impact of Trauma on Personality," 236–37. Theresa W. Tobin, "Religious Faith in the Unjust Meantime: The Spiritual Violence of Clergy Sexual Abuse," *Feminist Philosophy Quarterly* 5, no. 2 (2019): 6.

30. Root, "Reconstructing the Impact of Trauma on Personality," 240.

31. Tobin, "Religious Faith in the Unjust Meantime," 7–8.

32. Johanna Stiebert, "Abusive Theology and *LLF*," *Modern Believing* 64, no. 1 (2023): 9.

33. See Katie Collins Scott, "New Catholic Policies across US Create 'Culture of Fear' of LGBTQ Students, Advocates Say," *National Catholic Reporter* (September 15, 2022), https://www.ncronline.org/news/justice/omaha-archdioceses-new-school-policy-alienates-lgbtq-catholics; and Todd A. Salzman and Michael G. Lawler, "Omaha Archdiocese's New

School Policy Alienates LGBTQ+ Catholics," *National Catholic Reporter* (September 21, 2022), https://www.ncronline.org/news/guest-voices/omaha-archdioceses-new-school-policy-alienates-lgbtq-catholics.

34. Root, "Reconstructing the Impact of Trauma on Personality," 240.

35. Root, "Reconstructing the Impact of Trauma on Personality," 243–44.

36. Root, "Reconstructing the Impact of Trauma on Personality," 243–44.

37. Root, "Reconstructing the Impact of Trauma on Personality," 244.

38. Tobin, "Religious Faith in the Unjust Meantime," Article 5.

39. Erin Grace, "Breaking Faith: Growing Allegations about Ex-Creighton Prep Priest Cite Misconduct in Confession," *Omaha World Herald* (April 2, 2019), https://omaha.com/news/crime/breaking-faith-growing-allegations-about-ex-creighton-prep-priest-cite-misconduct-in-confession/article_3d813bec-b157-5523-9128-314492c6ad18.html.

40. CDF, "Letter to the Bishops," 3.

41. Tobin, "Religious Faith in the Unjust Meantime," 5.

42. Michelle Panchuk, "The Shattered Spiritual Self: A Philosophical Exploration of Religious Trauma," *Res Philosophica* 95, no. 3 (July 2018): 509.

43. Panchuk, "The Shattered Spiritual Self," 517.

44. Panchuk, "The Shattered Spiritual Self," 505. See also Tobin, "Religious Faith in the Unjust Meantime."

45. Thomas P. Doyle, "Sexual Abuse by Catholic Clergy: The Spiritual Damage," in *Sexual Abuse in the Catholic Church: A Decade of Crisis, 2002–2012*, ed. Thomas G. Plante and Kathleen L. McChesney (Santa Barbara, CA: Praeger, 2011), 176–77.

46. David Turnbloom et al., "Liturgy in the Shadow of Trauma," *Religions* 13, no. 7 (2022): 583.

47. Turnbloom et al., "Liturgy in the Shadow of Trauma," 583.

48. Marie Keenan, *Child Sexual Abuse and the Catholic Church: Gender, Power, and Organizational Culture* (New York: Oxford University Press, 2012), 96–97.

49. Keenan, *Child Sexual Abuse and the Catholic Church*, 25–34; 234–39. See also Bradford Hinze, *Confronting a Church in Controversy* (Mahwah, NJ: Paulist Press, 2022), 40; and Julie Hanlon Rubio and Paul Schutz, "Beyond 'Bad Apples': Understanding Clergy Perpetrated Sexual Abuse as a Structural Problem & Cultivating Strategies for Change," 2022, https://www.scu.edu/media/ignatian-center/bannan/Beyond-Bad-Apples-8-2-FINAL.pdf.

50. Gerald A. Arbuckle, *Abuse and Cover-Up: Refounding the Catholic Church in Trauma* (Maryknoll, NY: Orbis Books, 2019), 22.

51. Second Vatican Council, *Lumen Gentium* 8.

52. Pope John Paul II, "Homily of the Holy Father: 'Day of Pardon'" (March 12, 2000), https://www.vatican.va/content/john-paul-ii/en/homilies/2000/documents/hf_jp-ii_hom_20000312_pardon.html.

53. Congregation for Catholic Education, *Guidelines for the Use of Psychology in the Admission and Formation of Candidates for the Priesthood* (June 29, 2008), 5, https://www.vatican.va/roman_curia/congregations/ccatheduc/documents/rc_con_ccatheduc_doc_20080628_orientamenti_en.html.

54. Thomas C. Fox, "Study: No Link between Gay Priests and Sex Abuse Scandal," *National Catholic Reporter* (Nov. 19, 2009), https://www.ncronline.org/blogs/ncr-today/study-no-link-between-gay-priests-and-sex-abuse-scandal.

55. Pope Francis, *Laudato Si'* (2015), 4, https://www.vatican.va/content/francesco/en/encyclicals/documents/papa-francesco_20150524_enciclica-laudato-si.html.

56. Hinze, *Confronting a Church in Controversy*, 42–43.

57. Keenan, *Child Sexual Abuse and the Catholic Church*, 96.

58. Richard R. Gaillardetz, "Power and Authority in the Church: Emerging Issues," in *A Church with Open Doors: Catholic Ecclesiology for the Third Millennium*, ed. Richard R. Gaillardetz and Edward P. Hahnenberg (Collegeville, MN: Liturgical Press, 2015), 91.

59. See Rubio and Schutz, "Beyond 'Bad Apples.'"

60. Hinze, *Confronting a Church in Controversy*, 42.

61. Michel Foucault, *Discipline and Punish: The Birth of the Prison* (London: Allen Lane, 1979), 191.

62. Hinze, *Confronting a Church in Controversy*, 38.

63. Congregation for Catholic Education, "Instruction Concerning the Criteria for the Discernment of Vocations with Regard to Persons with Homosexual Tendencies in View of Their Admission to the Seminary and Holy Orders (2005)," 2, https://www.vatican.va/roman_curia/congregations/ccatheduc/documents/rc_con_ccatheduc_doc_20051104_istruzione_en.html.

64. Congregation for Catholic Education, *Guidelines for the Use of Psychology*, 10.

65. Richard Sipe, "Homosexuality and Catholic Culture," October 9, 2012, https://www.bishop-accountability.org/news2012/09_10/2012_10_09_Sipe_Homosexuality&.htm.

66. CDF, "Letter to the Bishops," 3.

67. Karen J. Terry et al., "The Causes and Context of Sexual Abuse of Minors by Catholic Priests in the United States, 1950–2020" (Washington DC: USCCB, 2011), 9–10, https://www.votf.org/wp-content/uploads/John_Jay_Causes_and_Context_Report.pdf.

68. See Peter Cimbolic and Pam Cartor, "Looking at Ephebophilia through the Lens of Cleric Sex Abuse," *Sexual Addictions & Compulsivity* 13 (2006): 347–59.

69. Lieven Boeve, "Conversion and Cognitive Dissonance: Evaluating the Theological-Ecclesial Program of Joseph Ratzinger/Pope Benedict XVI," *Horizons* 40, no. 2 (2013): 242–54.

70. See *Vos Estis Lux Mundi* (2019), https://www.vatican.va/content/francesco/en/motu_proprio/documents/papa-francesco-motu-proprio-20190507_vos-estis-lux-mundi.html.

71. See Austin Ivereigh, "The Anti-Francis Gatekeepers," *Commonweal* (January 27, 2023), https://www.commonwealmagazine.org/pell-Ganswein-Muller-francis-benedict-church-catholic-conservative.

72. See Foucault, *The History of Sexuality: An Introduction*, vol. 1 (New York: Knopf Doubleday Publishing Group, 1990).

73. Robert W. McElroy, "Cardinal McElroy on 'Radical Inclusion' for L.G.B.T. People, Women and Others in the Catholic Church," *America* (January 24, 2023), https://www.americamagazine.org/faith/2023/01/24/mcelroy-synodality-inclusion-244587.

74. Michael Stephen Patton, *Catholic Sexual Pathology and the Western Mind: The Ancient Era*, vol. 1 (New York: Peter Lang, 2020).

75. CDF, *Persona Humana*, n. VIII.

76. Keenan, *Child Sexual Abuse and the Catholic Church*, 235.

77. James Allison, "Yes, but Is It True?," https://jamesalison.com/yes-but-is-it-true/.

CHAPTER 3

1. See Linda Hogan, "Clerical and Religious Child Abuse: Ireland and Beyond," *Theological Studies* 72, no. 1 (2011): 170–186, and the bibliography cited therein.

2. See Gerald A. Arbuckle, *Abuse and Cover-Up: Refounding the Catholic Church in Trauma* (Maryknoll, NY: Orbis Books, 2019), 52–83.

3. Shaji George Kochuthara, "The Sexual Abuse Scandal and a New Ethical Horizon: A Perspective from India," *Theological Studies* 80, no. 4 (December 2019): 931–49.

4. Agbonkhianmeghe E. Orobator, SJ, "Between Ecclesiology and Ethics: Promoting a Culture of Protection and Care in Church and Society," *Theological Studies* 80, no. 4 (December 2019): 899.

5. Maria Clara Lucchetti Bingemer, "Concerning Victims, Sexuality, and Power: A Reflection on Sexual Abuse in Latin America," *Theological Studies* 80, no. 4 (December 2019): 921.

6. Donald Cozzens, *Sacred Silence: Denial and the Crisis in the Church* (Collegeville, MN: Liturgical Press, 2002), 8.

7. A. W. Richard Sipe, *Sex, Priests, and Power: Anatomy of a Crisis* (New York: Brunner-Mazel, 1995), 4, emphasis added; Cozzens, *Sacred Silence*, 8.

8. Bingemer, "Concerning Victims," 928.

9. John Jay College of Criminal Justice, *The Nature and Scope of Sexual Abuse of Minors by Catholic Priests and Deacons in the United States, 1950–2002* (Washington, DC: USCCB, 2004), 28, https://www.usccb.org/sites/default/files/issues-and-action/child-and-youth-protection/upload/The-Nature-and-Scope-of-Sexual-Abuse-of-Minors-by-Catholic-Priests-and-Deacons-in-the-United-States-1950-2002.pdf.

10. John Jay College, *The Nature and Scope of Sexual Abuse of Minors*, 69–70.

11. CARA, "Pain Never Disappears from Unhealed Wounds" (August 28, 2018), https://nineteensixty-four.blogspot.com/2018/08/pain-never-disappears-from-unhealed.html.

12. Brian Witte, "Maryland Probe Finds 158 Abusive Priests, over 600 Victims," *National Catholic Reporter* (November 18, 2022), https://www.ncronline.org/news/maryland-probe-finds-158-abusive-priests-over-600-victims.

13. Witte, "Maryland Probe."

14. Studies indicate that nearly one-third of female victims and a higher percentage of male victims never reveal their abuse to anyone. See Mary Gail Frawley-O'Dea, *Perversion of Power: Sexual Abuse in the Catholic Church* (Nashville: Vanderbilt University Press, 2007), 6.

15. Frawley-Odea, *Perversion of Power*, xiv.

16. Bradford Hinze, *Confronting a Church in Controversy* (Mahwah, NJ: Paulist Press, 2022).

17. Bessel A. van der Kolk, *The Body Keeps the Score: Brain, Mind, and Body in Healing Trauma* (New York: Penguin Books, 2014), 66.

18. Frawley-O'Dea, *Perversion of Power*, 23.

19. Bromberg, "On Knowing One's Patient Inside Out: The Aesthetics of Unconscious Communication," *Psychoanalytic Dialogues* 1, no. 4 (1991): 405–6.

20. See USCCB, *Promise to Protect and Pledge to Heal* (Washington, DC: USCCB, 2002; rev. 2018), https://www.usccb.org/resources/Charter-for-the-Protection-of-Children-and-Young-People-2018-final%281%29.pdf.

21. Office of the Attorney General: Commonwealth of Pennsylvania, Report I of the 40th Statewide Investigating Grand Jury (redacted, July 27, 2018), 300, https://www.attorneygeneral.gov/wp-content/uploads/2023/05/INVESTIGATING-GRAND-JURY-REPORT-NO.-1_FINAL_May-2023_Redacted.pdf.

22. Catholic News Agency, "U.S. Catholics Losing Trust in Clergy, Survey Finds," *CNA* (January 11, 2019), https://www.catholicnewsagency.com/news/40285/us-catholics-losing-trust-in-clergy-survey-finds.

23. Hinze, *Confronting a Church in Controversy*, 18.

24. Hinze, *Confronting a Church in Controversy*, 42.

25. Karen J. Terry et al., *The Causes and Context of Sexual Abuse of Minors by Catholic Priests in the United States, 1950–2010: A Report Presented to the United States Conference of Catholic Bishops by the John Jay College Research Team* (Washington, DC: USCCB, 2011), 124, http://votf.org/johnjay/John_Jay_Causes_and_Context_Report.pdf.

26. Julie Hanlon Rubio and Paul Schutz, "Beyond 'Bad Apples': Understanding Clergy Perpetrated Sexual Abuse as a Structural Problem & Cultivating Strategies for Change," 2022, https://www.scu.edu/media/ignatian-center/bannan/Beyond-Bad-Apples-8-2-FINAL.pdf.

27. Pope John Paul II, *Vita Consecrata* (1996), 32, https://www.vatican.va/content/john-paul-ii/en/apost_exhortations/documents/hf_jp-ii_exh_25031996_vita-consecrata.html.

28. Philip Murnion, "Priest: Beyond Employee, to Minister of the Sacred," *National Catholic Reporter* (September 27, 2002), http://natcath.org/NCR_Online/archives/092702/092702k.htm.

29. Orobator, "Between Ecclesiology and Ethics," 898.

30. Pope Francis, "Address by Pope Francis at the Opening of the Synod of Bishops on Young People, the Faith and Vocational Discernment (3 October 2018)," http://www.vatican.va/content/francesco/en/speeches/2018/october/documents/papa-francesco_20181003_apertura-sinodo.html.

31. Arbuckle, *Abuse and Cover-Up*, 80.

32. Terry et al., *The Causes and Context*, 5.

33. Royal Commission into Institutional Responses to Child Sexual Abuse, *Final Report: Preface and Executive Summary* (2017), 72, https://www.childabuseroyalcommission.gov.au/sites/default/files/final_report_-_preface_and_executive_summary.pdf.

34. Cited in Sipe, *Sex, Priests, and Power*, 56.

35. See Peter Feuerherd, "Pope Francis' Critics at Sacred Heart Seminary in Detroit Are Vocal Online," *National Catholic Reporter* (Jan 22, 2019), https://www.ncronline.org/news/people/pope-francis-critics-sacred-heart-seminary-detroit-are-vocal-online. See also Thomas Reese, "The Catholic Church's US Seminaries Need Reform," *National Catholic Reporter* (Feb. 13, 2019), https://www.ncronline.org/opinion/signs-times/catholic-churchs-us-seminaries-need-reform.

36. James F. Keenan, "Hierarchicalism," *Theological Studies* 83, no. 1 (2022): 95.

37. Pope Francis, *Vos Estis Lux Mundi* (2019), https://www.vatican.va/content/francesco/en/motu_proprio/documents/papa-francesco-motu-proprio-20190507_vos-estis-lux-mundi.html.

38. Rod Dreher, "Sins of the Fathers," *National Review*, August 15, 2018, https://www.nationalreview.com/2018/08/sins-of-the-fathers/. Cozzens, *Sacred Silence*, 114.

39. Thomas P. Doyle, "Canon Law and the Clergy Sex Abuse Crisis: The Failure from Above," in *Sin against the Innocents: Sexual Abuse by Priests and the Role of the Catholic Church*, ed. Thomas G. Plante (Westport, CN: Praeger, 2004), 31.

40. Government and independent commissions have noted the problematic role of hierarchical culture that covered up and perpetuated sexual abuse. See *Where from and Where To? The Truth, Justice and Healing Council, the Royal Commission and the Catholic Church in Australia* (The Truth, Justice and Healing Council, April 2018), 1:25, http://www.tjhcouncil.org.au/img/pdf/TJHC-Volume-1.pdf; and, John Jay College of Criminal Justice, *The Nature and Scope of Sexual Abuse*.

41. See, for example, Marie Collins, "Survivor Explains Decision to Leave the Vatican's Abuse Commission," *National Catholic Reporter* (March 1, 2017); Daniel J. Walkin, "Refusing to Recant, Keating Resigns as Church Panel Chief," *New York Times* (June 17, 2003).

42. See Sipe, *Sex, Priests, and Power*.

43. Susan Ross, "Feminist Theology and the Clergy Sexual Abuse Crisis," *Theological Studies* 80, no. 3 (2019): 639.

44. Pope Pius X, *Vehementer Nos* (1906), 8, http://www.vatican.va/content/pius-x/en/encyclicals/documents/hf_p-x_enc_11021906_vehementer-nos.html.

45. Mary Daly, *Beyond God the Father: Toward a Philosophy of Women's Liberation* (Boston: Beacon Press, 1993), 19.

46. Rosemary Radford Ruether, *Sexism and God-Talk: Toward a Feminist Theology* (Boston: Beacon Press, 1993).

47. See Neil Ormerod, "Sexual Abuse, a Royal Commission, and the Australian Church," *Theological Studies* 80, no. 4 (2019): 958–63.

48. James A. Coriden et al., eds., *The Code of Canon Law: A Text and Commentary* (Mahwah, NJ: Paulist Press, 1985), c. 207, 1.

49. Donald Palmer and Valerie Feldman, "Toward a More Comprehensive Analysis of the Role of Organizational Culture in Child Abuse in Institutional Contexts," *Child Abuse and Neglect* 74 (2017): 23–34; and Thomas P. Doyle, "Commentary: The Australian Royal Commission into Institutional Responses to Child Sexual Abuse and the Roman Catholic Church," *Child Abuse and Neglect* 74 (2017): 104.

50. *Dei Verbum* 8; see Richard Lennan, "Beyond Scandal and Shame? Ecclesiology and the Longing for a Transformed Church," *Theological Studies* 80, no. 3 (2019): 594.

51. Massimo Faggioli, "The Catholic Sexual Abuse Crisis as a Theological Crisis: Emerging Issues," *Theological Studies* 80, no. 3 (2019): 585.

52. Congregation for the Doctrine of the Faith, "CDF Principles for Collaboration with Non-Catholic Health Care Entities: Ministry Perspectives," *Catholic Health Association* (Summer 2014), https://www.chausa.org/publications/health-care-ethics-usa/article/summer-2014/cdf-principles-for-collaboration-with-non-catholic-health-care-entities-ministry-perspectives.

53. Ormerod, "Sexual Abuse," 963.

54. Bernard J. F. Lonergan, "Dialectic of Authority," in *A Third Collection*, ed. F. Crowe (Mahwah, NJ: Paulist Press, 1985), 3–9; Joseph Komonchak, "Authority and Magisterium," in *Vatican Authority and American Catholic Dissent*, ed. W. May (New York: Crossroad, 1987), 103–14.

55. Lonergan, "Dialectic of Authority," 7–8.

56. Lonergan, "Dialectic of Authority," 11; Ormerod, "Sexual Abuse," 963–64.

57. Komonchak, "Authority and Magisterium," 107.

58. CCE, *Instruction: Concerning Criteria for the Discernment of Vocations with Regard to Persons with Homosexual Tendencies in View of Their Admission to the Seminary and to Holy Orders* (November 4, 2005), Introduction, https://www.vatican.va/roman_curia/congregations/ccatheduc/documents/rc_con_ccatheduc_doc_20051104_istruzione_en.html.

59. CCE, *Instruction: Concerning Criteria*, 2.

60. Frawley-O'Dea, *Perversion of Power*, 125.

61. Frawley-O'Dea, *Perversion of Power*, 124.

62. Associated Press, "No Data Ties Sex Abuse to Gay Clergy," *Tampa Bay Times* (November 18, 2009), https://www.tampabay.com/archive/2009/11/18/no-data-ties-sex-abuse-to-gay-clergy/.

63. Michael Kimmel, "Focus on Pedophiles, Not Gays," *New York Newsday*, October 14, 2005.

64. See Frawley-O'Dea, *The Perversion of Power*, 237n11, for extensive references.

65. Public Affairs Office, "John Jay College Reports No Single Cause, Predictor of Clergy Abuse," USCCB (May 18, 2011), https://www.usccb.org/news/2011/john-jay-college-reports-no-single-cause-predictor-clergy-abuse.

66. Kevin Clarke, "Archbishop Broglio, Questioned on Abuse, Homosexuality and Whether He's a 'Pope Francis' Bishop in First Press Conference as USCCB Head," *America* (November 16, 2022), emphasis added, https://www.americamagazine.org/faith/2022/11/16/archbishop-broglio-president-usccb-244154.

67. See Michael Sean Winters, "Bishops Elect Anti-Francis Archbishop as New President," *National Catholic Reporter* (November 15, 2022), https://www.ncronline.org/opinion/ncr-voices/bishops-elect-anti-francis-archbishop-new-president.

68. Donald B. Cozzens, *The Changing Face of the Priesthood* (Collegeville, MN: Liturgical Press, 2000), 99.

69. See Frawley-O'Dea, *The Perversion of Power*, 120.

70. Public Affairs Office, "John Jay College Reports."

71. Joan Vennochi, "Shifting the Blame," *The Boston Globe* (April 23, 2002), https://archive.boston.com/globe/spotlight/abuse/stories/042302_vennochi.htm.

CHAPTER 4

1. Pope John Paul II, *Familiaris Consortio* 6.

2. Pope John Paul II, *Man and Woman He Created Them: A Theology of the Body* (Boston: Pauline Books, 2006), 10, 1.

3. Pope Francis, *Amoris Laetitia* 56.

4. Dicastery for the Doctrine of the Faith, "Declaration *Dignitas Infinita*: On Human Dignity" (April 8, 2024), 58, https://press.vatican.va/content/salastampa/en/bollettino/pubblico/2024/04/08/240408c.html.

5. There is pretty much universal agreement that gender *is* socially constructed, but how it is constructed is still debated among scholars. Scholars such as Luce Irigaray, Michel Foucault, Simone de Beauvoir, and Judith Butler have slightly different versions of how both sex and gender are socially constructed. For a conspectus, see Judith Butler, *Gender Trouble: Feminism and the Subversion of Identity* (New York: Routledge, Chapman and Hall, 1990).

6. See Susannah Cornwall, "Intersex and Transgender People," in *The Oxford Handbook of Theology, Sexuality, and Gender*, ed. Adrian Thatcher (Oxford: Oxford University Press, 2015), 671; *Sex and Uncertainty in the Body of Christ: Intersex Conditions and Christian Theology* (London: Routledge, 2016); and Megan DeFranza, *Sex Difference in Christian Theology: Male, Female, and Intersex in the Image of God* (Grand Rapids, MI: Eerdmans, 2015).

7. *Patrologia Latina* 40, 375.

8. Pius XI, *Casti Connubii* (1930), 24, https://www.vatican.va/content/pius-xi/en/encyclicals/documents/hf_p-xi_enc_19301231_casti-connubii.html.

9. *Gaudium et Spes* 47–48. Hereafter referred to in the text as *GS*.

10. Thomas Aquinas, *Summa Theologiae* (Suppl.), 41, 3.

11. Augustine, *Contra Julianum Pelag.*, 3, 23, 53, *PL* 44, 729–30.

12. *Summa Theologiae* III (Suppl.), 41, 4; 49, 5.

13. *Summa Theologiae* II–II, 142, 1.

14. *Contra Gentiles*, 4, 78.

15. *Summa Theologiae* II–II, 26, 11; see also *Contra Gentiles*, 3, II, 123, 6.

16. Bonaventure, *In Quart. Sent.*, 33, 1, 1.

17. Basil Hume, "Note" added after the death of a close friend to his "Observations on the Catholic Teaching Concerning Homosexual People," in his *Created Design*, 20–24. Cited in Alan Bray, *The Friend* (Chicago: University of Chicago Press, 2003), 298.

18. Aelred of Rievaulx, *Spiritual Friendship*, trans. Mark E. Williams (Scranton, PA: University of Scranton Press, 1994), 1:69.

19. See Evelyn Eaton Whitehead and James D. Whitehead, *A Sense of Sexuality: Christian Love and Intimacy* (New York: Doubleday, 1989), 103–5.

20. Aquinas, *Summa Theologiae*, I, 20, 1 ad 3. See also Plato, *The Symposium*, trans. Suzy Q. Groden (Boston: University of Massachusetts Press, 1970), 205D.

21. Margaret Farley, *Personal Commitments: Beginning, Keeping, Changing* (San Francisco: Harper and Row, 1990), 34. For a detailed analysis of commitment, see Scott M. Stanley, *The Power of Commitment: A Guide to Active, Lifelong Love* (San Francisco: Jossey-Bass, 2005).

22. Judith S. Wallerstein and Sandra Blakeslee, *The Good Marriage: How and Why Love Lasts* (Boston: Houghton Mifflin, 1995), 156.

23. Wallerstein, *The Good Marriage*, 169–70.

24. Jack Dominian, "Sexuality and Interpersonal Relationships," in *Embracing Sexuality: Authority and Experience in the Catholic Church*, ed. Joseph A. Selling (Burlington, VT: Ashgate, 2001), 12–15.

25. See *Gaudium et Spes* 49; *Code of Canon Law*, can. 1061.

26. Tom W. Smith, *American Sexual Behavior: Trends, Socio-demographic Differences, and Risk Behavior* (Chicago: University of Chicago Press, 2003), 74.

27. Dominian, "Sexuality and Interpersonal Relationships," 20.

28. Martin Buber, *Between Man and Man* (New York: Macmillan, 1948), 17.

29. We are grateful to our colleague Dr. Julia Feder for the formulations that immediately follow here.

30. Jane M. Grovijahn, "Theology as an Irruption into Embodiment: Our Need for God," *Theology and Sexuality* 9, no. 1 (1998): 31.

31. Grovijahn, "Theology as an Irruption into Embodiment," 32.

32. Cathy Winkler, "Rape as Social Murder," *Anthropology Today* 7, no. 3 (1991): 13.

33. Cathy Winkler, "Rape as Social Murder," 14.

34. Jennifer Erin Beste, *God and the Victim: Traumatic Intrusions on Grace and Freedom*, AAR Academy Series (New York: Oxford University Press, 2007). Michelle Panchuk, "The Shattered Spiritual Self: A Philosophical Exploration of Religious Trauma," *Res Philosophica* 95, no. 3 (July 2018): 505–30.

35. Susan J. Brison, "Outliving Oneself: Trauma, Memory and Personal Identity," in *Feminists Rethink the Self*, ed. Diana T. Meyers (Boulder, CO: Westview Press, 1996), 12–39.

36. Dominian, "Sexuality and Interpersonal Relationships," 14.

37. Theresa W. Tobin, "Religious Faith in the Unjust Meantime: The Spiritual Violence of Clergy Sexual Abuse," *Feminist Philosophy Quarterly* 5, no. 2 (2019): 14.

38. Tobin, "Religious Faith in the Unjust Meantime," 14.

39. Mark Searle and Kenneth W. Stevenson, eds., *Documents of the Marriage Ceremony* (Collegeville, MN: Liturgical Press, 1992), 151.

40. The connection of marriage and Eucharist is beautifully developed in Germain Martinez, *Worship: Wedding to Marriage* (Washington, DC: Pastoral Press, 1993).

41. Adrian Thatcher, *Liberating Sex: A Christian Sexual Theology* (London: SPCK, 1993), 89.

42. Cardinal George Basil Hume, "Note on Church Teaching Concerning Homosexual People," *Origins* 24, no. 45 (April 27, 1995): 767–68. See Salzman and Lawler, *Pope Francis, Marriage, and Same-Sex Civil Unions: Foundations for the Organic Development of Catholic Sexual Doctrine* (Lanham, MD: Rowman and Littlefield, 2024).

43. Martha C. Nussbaum, *The Upheavals of Thought: The Intelligence of Emotions* (New York: Cambridge University Press, 2003), 22.

44. See Charles A. Gallagher et al., *Embodied in Love: Sacramental Spirituality and Sexual Intimacy* (New York: Crossroad, 1985), 21–37.

45. Gallagher et al., *Embodied in Love*, 108.

46. Pope Pius XII, *Acta Apostolicae Sedis* 43 (1951): 846; Pope Paul VI, *Humanae Vitae* 10.

47. See Karl Rahner, *Foundations of Christian Faith: An Introduction to the Idea of Christianity* (New York: Seabury, 1978), 136–37; *The Trinity* (New York: Seabury, 1974), 22.

48. CDF, *Persona Humana* 1.

49. USCCB, *Human Sexuality: A Catholic Perspective for Education and Lifelong Learning* (Washington, DC: USCCB, 1991), 9.

50. See can. 1055, 1.

51. John Paul II, *Familiaris Consortio* 19.

52. Edward Collins Vacek, "Feminism and the Vatican," *Theological Studies* 66, no. 1 (2005): 173–74, referring to John Paul II, "Authentic Concept of Conjugal Love," *Origins* 28 (1999): 655.

53. John Paul II, "Letter to Women," *Origins* 25 (1995): 141.

54. *Catechism of the Catholic Church* 2357.

55. Lawrence A. Kurdek, "Differences between Partners from Heterosexual, Gay, and Lesbian Cohabiting Couples," *Journal of Marriage and Family* 68 (May 2006): 509–28; "What Do We Know about Gay and Lesbian Couples?" *Current Directions in Psychological Science* 14 (2005): 251–54; "Lesbian and Gay Couples," in *Lesbian, Gay and Bisexual Identities over the Lifespan*, ed. Anthony R. D'Augelli and Charlotte J. Patterson (New York: Oxford University, 1995), 243–61; "Are Gay and Lesbian Cohabiting Couples *Really* Different From Heterosexual Married Couples?," *Journal of Marriage and Family* 66 (2004): 880–900; Ritch C. Savin-Williams and Kristin G. Esterberg, "Lesbian, Gay, and Bisexual Families," in *Handbook of Family Diversity*, ed. David H. Demo, Katherine R. Allen, and Mark A. Fine (New York: Oxford University, 2000), 207–12; and Philip Blumstein and Pepper Schwartz, *American Couples: Money, Work, Sex* (New York: Morrow, 1983).

56. See *Gaudium et Spes* 48–50; *Code of Canon Law*, c. 1055, 1; Michael G. Lawler, *Marriage in the Catholic Church: Disputed Questions* (Collegeville, MN: Liturgical, 2002), 27–42.

CHAPTER 5

1. *Gaudium et Spes* 49–51.

2. Pope Paul VI, *Humanae Vitae* 11.

3. Richard A. McCormick, "'*Humanae Vitae*' 25 Years Later," *America* 169 (July 17, 1993): 10.

4. See Charles E. Curran, *The Catholic Moral Tradition Today: A Synthesis* (Washington, DC: Georgetown University Press, 1999), 48.

5. *Gaudium et Spes* 44.

6. See Todd A. Salzman and Michael G. Lawler, *The Sexual Person: Towards a Renewed Catholic Anthropology* (Washington, DC: Georgetown University Press, 2008), 48–123.

7. *Gaudium et Spes* 13, 21, 33, 37, 44, 46, 52; *Lumen Gentium* 37.

8. *Redemptor Hominis* (1979), 17, https://www.vatican.va/content/john-paul-ii/en/encyclicals/documents/hf_jp-ii_enc_04031979_redemptor-hominis.html; *Familiaris Consortio* 32, 73; and *Veritatis Splendor* (1993), 53, 86, 98, https://www.vatican.va/content/john-paul-ii/en/encyclicals/documents/hf_jp-ii_enc_06081993_veritatis-splendor.html.

9. George P. Schner, "The Appeal to Experience," in *Theology and Sexuality: Classic and Contemporary Readings*, ed. Eugene F. Rogers Jr. (Oxford: Blackwell, 2002), 31–32.

10. See Jerome Hamer, *The Church Is a Communion* (New York: Sheed & Ward, 1965); Michael G. Lawler and Thomas J. Shanahan, *Church: A Spirited Communion* (Collegeville, MN: Liturgical Press, 1995).

11. John Paul II, *Ut Unum Sint* (1995), 28–39, https://www.vatican.va/content/john-paul-ii/en/encyclicals/documents/hf_jp-ii_enc_25051995_ut-unum-sint.html.

12. Bishops of Canada, "Population and Poverty: The Cairo Conference," *Origins* 24, no. 14 (September 15, 1994): 249.

13. See Jeffrey D. Sachs, *The End of Poverty: Economic Possibilities for Our Time* (New York: Penguin Press, 2005), 64–66, 323–26; Population Reference Bureau, *Poverty Fuels Developing World's High Birth Rate* (Washington, DC, Aug. 2002).

14. See Warren C. Robinson and John A. Ross, "Family Planning: The Quiet Revolution," in *The Global Family Planning Revolution: Three Decades of Population Policies and Programs*, ed. Warren C. Robinson and John A. Ross (Washington, DC: World Bank, 2007), 421–49.

15. Bishops of Canada, "Population and Poverty," 249.

16. See Mary Stewart Van Leeuwen, "Teaching Equal Regard to the Abandoned Generation: Case Studies from a Psychology of Gender Class," in *The Equal-Regard Family and Its Friendly Critics*, ed. John Witte (Grand Rapids, MI: Eerdmans, 2007), 192–94.

17. See *Gaudium et Spes* 54.

18. *Humanae Vitae* 12.

19. See Pius XII, "Allocution to Italian Midwives," *Acta Apostolicae Sedis* 43 (1951): 835–54.

20. See, for example, McCormick, *The Critical Calling: Reflections on Moral Dilemmas since Vatican II* (Washington, DC: Georgetown University Press), 346–47; Joseph A. Selling, "The Development of Catholic Tradition and Sexual Morality," in *Embracing Sexuality: Authority and Experience in the Catholic Church*, ed. Joseph A. Selling (Burlington, VT: Ashgate, 2001), 149–62; Selling, "Magisterial Teaching on Marriage 1880–1986: Historical Constancy or Radical Development," in *Dialogue about Catholic Sexual Teaching*, Readings in Moral Theology, no. 8, ed. Charles Curran and Richard McCormick (Mahwah, NJ: Paulist Press, 1993), 93–97; Bernard Häring, "The Inseparability of the Unitive-Procreative Functions of the Marital Act," in Curran and McCormick, *Dialogue about Catholic Sexual Teaching*, 163–64; Lisa Sowle Cahill, "Sexuality: Personal, Communal, Responsible," in Selling, *Embracing Sexuality*, 165–72.

21. Mary J. Henold, "How Catholic Women Fought against Vatican's Prohibition on Contraceptives," *The Conversation* (June 25, 2018), https://theconversation.com/how-catholic-women-fought-against-vaticans-prohibition-on-contraceptives-94544.

22. Henold, "How Catholic Women Fought."

23. Human Rights Watch, "Access to Condoms and HIV/AIDS Information: A Global Health and Human Rights Concern: Part III: Condoms and the Vatican," http://www.hrw.org/backgrounder/hivaids/condoms1204/3.htm#_Toc89576907.

24. James F. Keenan, *Catholic Ethicists on HIV/AIDS Prevention* (New York: Continuum, 2000); Paul Farmer et al., eds., *Women, Poverty, and AIDS: Sex, Drugs, and Structural Violence* (Monroe, ME: Common Courage Press, 1996).

25. *Lumen Gentium* 12, emphasis added.

26. Robert McClory, *Turning Point: The Inside Story of the Papal Birth Control Commission, and How* Humanae Vitae *Changed the Life of Patty Crowley and the Future of the Church* (New York: Crossroad, 1995).

27. William V. D'Antonio et al., *American Catholics Today: New Realities of Their Faith and Their Church* (Lanham, MD: Rowman and Littlefield, 2007), 91; and Pew Research Center, "Very Few Americans See Contraception as Morally Wrong" (September 28, 2016), https://www.pewresearch.org/religion/2016/09/28/4-very-few-americans-see-contraception-as-morally-wrong/.

28. Dietmar Mieth, "*Humanae Vitae*: A Global Reassessment after Forty Years: Considerations beyond the Birth-Control Controversy," in *Homosexualities*, ed. Marcella Althaus-Reid (London: SCM Press, 2008), 128.

29. CDF, "Letter to the Bishops of the Catholic Church Concerning the Reception of Holy Communion by the Divorced and Remarried Members of the Faithful (September 14, 1994)," 4, https://www.vatican.va/roman_curia/congregations/cfaith/documents/rc_con_cfaith_doc_14091994_rec-holy-comm-by-divorced_en.html.

30. *Familiaris Consortio* 84.

31. Pew Research Center, "Family Matters" (September 2, 2015), https://www.pewresearch.org/religion/2015/09/02/chapter-3-family-matters/#:~:text=Among%20Catholics%20who%20have%20ever,%25)%20have%20experienced%20a%20divorce.

32. Michael Lipka, "Most U.S. Catholics Hope for Change in Church Rule on Divorce, Communion," *Pew Research Center* (October 26, 2015), https://www.pewresearch.org/fact-tank/2015/10/26/most-u-s-catholics-hope-for-change-in-church-rule-on-divorce-communion/.

33. See Michael G. Lawler, *Marriage and Sacrament: A Theology of Christian Marriage* (Collegeville, MN: Liturgical Press, 1993), 92–93.

34. James H. Provost, "Intolerable Marriage Situations: A Second Decade," *The Jurist* 50 (1990): 611.

35. *AL* 298, note 329; *Gaudium et Spes* 51.

36. Scott M. Stanley and Gelena K. Rhoades, "What's the Plan? Cohabitation, Engagement, and Divorce," *Institute for Family Studies* (April 2023), 3, https://ifstudies.org/ifs-admin/resources/reports/cohabitationreportapr2023-final.pdf.

37. Benjamin Gurrentz, "Cohabitation over the Last 20 Years: Measuring and Understanding the Changing Demographics of Unmarried Partners," *Census Bureau* (April 12, 2019), https://www.census.gov/library/working-papers/2019/demo/SEHSD-WP2019-10.html.

38. Christine Rousselle, "Survey Says: Most Catholics in US Reject Church Teaching on Cohabitation," *Angelus* (November 6, 2019), https://angelusnews.com/news/life-family/survey-says-most-catholics-in-us-reject-church-teaching-on-cohabitation/.

39. Jaap Dronkers, "Cohabitation, Marriage, and Union Instability in Europe," *Institute for Family Studies* (April 7, 2016), https://ifstudies.org/blog/cohabitation-marriage-and-union-instability-in-europe/.

40. Michael G. Lawler and Todd A. Salzman, "Human Experience and Catholic Moral Theology," *Irish Theological Quarterly* 76 (2011): 35–56.

41. CDF, *Persona Humana* 7.

42. Michael G. Lawler and Gail S. Risch, "A Betrothal Proposal," *U. S. Catholic* (June 2007): 18–22.

43. See, as an example replicated in diocesan policies across the United States, National Conference of Bishops, Committee on Marriage

and Family, *Marriage Preparation and Cohabiting Couples* (Washington, DC: USCC, 1999), 10. See also Pontifical Council for the Family, *Marriage, Family, and De Facto Unions* (Rome: Typis Polyglottis Vaticanis, 2000), 4.

44. Robert Schoen, "First Unions and the Stability of First Marriages," *Journal of Marriage and the Family* 54 (1992): 283.

45. Susan McRae, "Cohabitation: A Trial Run for Marriage?," *Sexual and Marital Therapy* 12 (1997): 259.

46. David de Vaus et al., "Does Pre-marital Cohabitation Affect the Chances of Marriage Lasting?" Paper Presented at the Eighth Australian Institute of Family Studies Conference, Melbourne, February 2003, https://melbourneinstitute.unimelb.edu.au/assets/documents/hilda-bibliography/conference-papers-lectures/2003/deVaus_etal_Does_premarital_cohabitation_affect_the_chances_of_marriage_lasting.pdf.

47. Sheri Stritof, "Cohabitation Facts and Statistics You Need to Know," https://www.thespruce.com/cohabitation-facts-and-statistics-2302236.

48. Linda J. Waite, "Cohabitation: A Communitarian Perspective," in *Marriage in America: A Communitarian Perspective*, ed. Martin King Whyte (Lanham, MD: Rowman and Littlefield, 2000), 18. Also Susan L. Brown and Alan Booth, "Cohabitation versus Marriage: A Comparison of Relationship Quality," *Journal of Marriage and the Family* 58 (1996): 668–78.

49. John Paul II, *Familiaris Consortio* 13.

50. *Catechism of the Catholic Church* 1735 and 2352.

51. CDF, *Instruction on Respect for Human Life in its Origin and on the Dignity of Procreation: Replies to Certain Questions of the Day* (Washington, DC: United States Catholic Conference, 1987), II, B, 4, a. Cited henceforth as *Instruction*. In 2008, the CDF issued a more recent Instruction, *Dignitatis Personae*, on Certain Bioethical Questions, which reaffirms the earlier teaching on reproductive technologies. http://www.vatican.va/roman_curia/congregations/cfaith/documents/rc_con_cfaith_doc_20081208_dignitas-personae_en.html.

52. Linda J. Beckman and S. Marie Harvey, "Current Reproductive Technologies: Increased Access and Choice?," *Journal of Social Issues* 61 (2005): 2.

53. The church has not issued a moral judgment on two reproductive technologies that rely on ART but do not violate the inseparability principle: Gamete Intrafallopian Transfer (GIFT) and Low Tubal Ovum Transfer (LTOT).

54. *Instruction*, II, B, 7, emphasis in original.

55. *Instruction*, II, B, 7.

56. *Instruction*, II, B, 5.

57. *Instruction*, Introduction, 5.

58. *Instruction*, II, B, 7, emphasis added.

59. *Instruction*, II, B, 7.

60. *Instruction*, II, B, 7.

61. *Instruction*, II, A, 2, emphasis in original.

62. *Instruction*, II, A, 2.

63. This statement must be qualified in cases of the adoption of children and abandoned cryo-preserved embryos. Such adoptions are loving and just acts.

64. *Instruction*, II, A, 2.

65. *Instruction*, II, B, 4.

66. *Instruction*, II, B, 5.

67. Joseph A. Selling, "Overwriting Tradition: '*Humanae Vitae*' Replaced Real Church Teaching," *National Catholic Reporter* (May 29, 2018), https://www.ncronline.org/news/opinion/overwriting-tradition-humanae-vitae-replaced-real-church-teaching.

68. McCormick, *Critical Calling*, 348.

69. McCormick, *Critical Calling*, 348.

70. See Aristotle, *Generation of Animals* I, 21, 729b; Paige duBois, *Sowing the Body: Psychoanalysis and Ancient Representations of Women* (Chicago: University of Chicago Press, 1988), 39-85; Carol Delaney, *The Seed and the Soil: Gender and Cosmology in Turkish Village Society* (Berkeley: University of California Press, 1991).

71. See Michael G. Lawler, *Marriage in the Catholic Church: Disputed Questions* (Collegeville, MN: Liturgical Press, 2002), 27–42.

72. Lisa Sowle Cahill, *Women and Sexuality* (Mahwah, NJ: Paulist Press, 1992), 75, emphasis in original. Also Thomas A. Shannon, ed., *Reproductive Technologies: A Reader* (New York: Sheed & Ward, 2004).

73. The Ethics Committee of the American Fertility Society accuses the CDF of "barnyard physiology," meaning that the concept of intercourse intended is that of barnyard animals. Cited in Howard W. Jones and Susan L. Crockin, "On Assisted Reproduction, Religion and Civil Law," *Fertility and Sterility* 73 (2000): 449.

CHAPTER 6

1. USCCB, *National Synthesis of the People of God in the United States of America for the Diocesan Phase of the 2021–2023 Synod* (Washington, DC: USCCB, 2023), 6, https://www.usccb.org/resources/US%20National%20Synthesis%202021-2023%20Synod.pdf.

2. USCCB, *National Synthesis*, 8.

3. Robert W. McElroy, "Cardinal McElroy on 'Radical Inclusion' for L.G.B.T. People, Women and Others in the Catholic Church," *America* (January 24, 2023), https://www.americamagazine.org/faith/2023/01/24/mcelroy-synodality-inclusion-244587.

4. See, for example, Southern African Catholic Bishops' Conference, "Synod on Synodality: Bishop's Conference Synodal Synthesis," 5, file:///C:/Users/tas30732/Downloads/SACBC-Synod-Synthesis-FINAL-REPORT.doc.pdf; Canadian Conference of Catholic Bishops, "Synod on Synodality: National Synthesis for Canada (2022)," 17, https://www.cccb.ca/wp-content/uploads/2022/09/Synod-on-Synodality-EN-2022-08-31.pdf; Catholic Bishops' Conference of Malaysia-Singapore-Brunei (CBCMSB), "CBCMSB Synod Synthesis Report," (2022), 5, https://www.todayscatholic.com.my/wp-content/uploads/2022/08/SynodReport15Aug2022-Malaysia-Singapore-Brunei.pdf; Australian Catholic Bishops Conference, "Synod of Bishops: Australian Synthesis" (August, 2022), 37, https://www.sydneycatholic.org/casys/wp-content/uploads/2022/08/Synod-of-Bishops-Australian-Synthesis.pdf; German Bishops' Conference, "For a Synodal Church—Community, Participation, and Mission" (2022), 7, 13, https://www.dbk.de/fileadmin/redaktion/diverse_downloads/presse_2022/2022-114eng-Report-of-the-German-Bishops-Conference-to-the-World-Synod-of-Bishops-2023.pdf.

5. McElroy, "Cardinal McElroy on 'Radical Inclusion.'"

6. Carol Glatz, "Pope: Eucharist Is Bread of Sinners, Not Reward of Saints," *National Catholic Reporter* (June 7, 2021), https://www.ncronline.org/spirituality/pope-eucharist-bread-sinners-not-reward-saints#.

7. Ashley McKinless and Zac Davis, "Cardinal McElroy: Sex and Sin Need a New Framework in the Church," *America* (February 3, 2023), https://www.americamagazine.org/faith/2023/02/03/cardinal-mcelroy-inclusion-sexualty-244650.

8. McKinless and Davis, "Cardinal McElroy." See also James F. Keenan, "LGBT Catholics and 'Disordered' Language: A Biblical Model for Change," *America* (March 12, 2024), https://www.americamagazine.org/faith/2024/03/12/keenan-synod-lgbtq-247472.

9. McKinless and Davis, "Cardinal McElroy."

10. Nicholas A. Livingston et al., "Real-Time Associations between Discrimination and Anxious and Depressed Mood among Sexual and Gender Minorities: The Moderating Effects of Lifetime Victimization and Identity Concealment," *Psychology of Sexual Orientation and Gender Diversity* 7, no. 2 (2020): 132–41.

11. Catholic News Service, "Cardinal Hollerich Says Church Teaching on Gays 'No Longer Correct,'" *Angelus* (February 2, 2022), https://angelusnews.com/news/world/cardinal-hollerich-says-church-teaching-on-gays-no-longer-correct/.

12. Catholic News Service, "German Bishop Calls Current Catholic Teaching on Sexuality 'Too Simple,'" *National Catholic Reporter* (November 10, 2022), https://www.ncronline.org/news/german-bishop-calls-current-catholic-teaching-sexuality-too-simple.

13. Catholic News Service, "German Cardinal Calls for Change in Church Teaching on Homosexuality," *National Catholic Reporter* (March 31, 2022), https://www.ncronline.org/news/theology/german-cardinal-calls-change-church-teaching-homosexuality.

14. Catholic News Agency, "German Catholic Bishops Welcome Initiative Seeking Change in Church Teaching on Sexuality," *Angelus* (January 25, 2022), https://angelusnews.com/news/world/german-catholic-bishops-welcome-initiative-seeking-change-in-church-teaching-on-sexuality/.

15. CDF, *Persona Humana* 8.

16. Daniel A. Helminiak, *What the Bible Really Says about Homosexuality* (San Francisco: Alamo Square Press, 1995), 25–26.

17. *Dei Verbum* 12. See also Pius XII, *Divino Afflante Spiritu, Acta Apostolicae Sedis* 35 (1943): 297–325.

18. This terminology articulates our position that homosexual orientation is neither exclusively genetic nor exclusively social in origin. See John E. Perito, *Contemporary Catholic Sexuality: What Is Taught and What Is Practiced* (New York: Crossroad, 2003), 96.

19. Richard C. Pillard and J. Michael Bailey, "A Biological Perspective on Sexual Orientation," *Psychiatric Clinics of North America* 18, no. 1 (1995): 1.

20. D. Sherwin Bailey, *Homosexuality and the Western Christian Tradition* (New York: Longman's, 1955), x, emphasis added.

21. Donald W. Cory, *The Homosexual in America* (New York: Julian Press, 1951), 8, emphasis in original.

22. See Maria Harris and Gabriel Moran, "Homosexuality: A Word Not Written," in *Homosexuality and Christian Faith: Questions of Conscience for the Churches*, ed. Walter Wink (Minneapolis: Fortress, 1999), 33.

23. See Alfred C. Kinsey et al., *Sexual Behavior in the Human Female* (Philadelphia: Saunders, 1953); Fritz Klein, *The Bisexual Option* (New York: Routledge, 1963).

24. CDF, *Persona Humana* 10; and United States Catholic Conference, *Always Our Children* (1997), passim, https://www.usccb.org/resources/always-our-children.

25. Edward Vacek, "A Christian Homosexuality," *Commonweal* (December 5, 1980): 681–84.

26. Seneca, *Naturales Quaestiones*, 3, 29, 3; Philo, *On the Eternity of the World*, 13, 69. For Greek society, see Paige duBois, *Sowing the Body: Psychoanalysis and Ancient Representations of Women* (Chicago: University of Chicago Press, 1988), 39–85. For Jewish Society, see Sir 26:19; *Mishna*, Ketuboth, 1, 6. For Muslim society, see Carol Delaney, *The Seed and the Soil: Gender and Cosmology in Turkish Village Society* (Oakland: University of California Press, 1991).

27. Bruce J. Malina, "The New Testament and Homosexuality," in *Sexual Diversity and Catholicism*, ed. Patricia Beattie Jung with Joseph Andrew Coray (Collegeville, MN: Liturgical Press, 2001), 163–64.

28. Lev 24:17, 21; Num 35:30; Exod 20:13.

29. Bruce J. Malina and Richard L. Rohrbaugh, *Social Science Commentary on the Synoptic Gospels* (Minneapolis: Fortress Press, 1992), 202.

30. The same system of honor and shame existed among the Greeks. Though it was acceptable for a boy to behave passively sexually, it was not acceptable for an adult male. Taking the female role in sexual activity brought him and his family dishonor. See Michel Foucault, *The Use of Pleasure: The History of Sexuality*, vol. 2 (New York: Pantheon, 1985), 187–225.

31. *Catechism of the Catholic Church* 2357; henceforth CCC. CDF, *Considerations Regarding Proposals to Give Legal Recognition to Unions Between Homosexual Persons*, 4, https://www.vatican.va/roman_curia/congregations/cfaith/documents/rc_con_cfaith_doc_20030731_homosexual-unions_en.html.

32. United States Conference of Catholic Bishops, *Always Our Children*, 4–5. CDF, *Persona Humana* 8.

33. CDF, *Persona Humana* 3.

34. See Michael G. Lawler and Todd A. Salzman, "Human Experience and Catholic Moral Theology," *Irish Theological Quarterly* 76, no. 1 (2011): 35–56.

35. Paul VI, *Humanae Vitae* 11.

36. Paul VI, *Humanae Vitae* 3.

37. *Catechism* 426.

38. Thomas Aquinas, *Summa Theologiae*, I–II, 94, 4.

39. Pope Francis, *Amoris Laetitia* 304.

40. CDF, *Considerations Regarding Proposals* 7, emphasis added.

41. See Michael G. Lawler, *Marriage in the Catholic Church: Disputed Questions* (Collegeville, MN: Liturgical Press, 2002), 27–39.

42. *Catechism* 2357.

43. Margaret A. Farley, *Just Love: A Framework for Christian Sexual Ethics* (New York: Continuum, 2006), 287.

44. *Gaudium et Spes* 49.

45. Gregory D. Smithers, *Reclaiming Two Spirits: Sexuality, Spiritual Renewal, and Sovereignty in Native America* (Boston: Beacon Press, 2022), xix.

46. *Gaudium et Spes* 47.

47. William V. D'Antonio et al., *American Catholics: Gender, Generation, and Commitment* (Lanham, MD: Altamira Press, 2001), 76.

48. D'Antonio, *American Catholics*, 85.

49. D'Antonio, *American Catholics*, 84.

50. Dean R. Hoge et al., *Young Adult Catholics: Religion in the Culture of Choice* (Notre Dame, IN: University of Notre Dame Press, 2001), 59–60.

51. Michael Hornsby-Smith, *Roman Catholicism in England: Customary Catholicism and Transformation of Religious Authority* (Cambridge: Cambridge University Press, 1991); John Fulton, ed., *Young Catholics at the New Millennium: The Religion and Morality of Young Adults in Western Countries* (Dublin: University College Press, 2000).

52. Jeff Diamant, "How Catholics around the World See Same-Sex Marriage, Homosexuality," *Pew Research Center* (November 2, 2020), https://www.pewresearch.org/fact-tank/2020/11/02/how-catholics-around-the-world-see-same-sex-marriage-homosexuality/.

53. *Familiaris Consortio* 5.

54. International Theological Commission, *Theses on the Relationship between the Ecclesiastical Magisterium and Theology* (Washington, DC: USCCB, 1977), Thesis 8, 6.

55. Lawrence A. Kurdek, "What Do We Know about Gay and Lesbian Couples?" *Current Directions in Psychological Science* 14 (2005): 251; "Differences between Partners from Heterosexual, Gay, and Lesbian Cohabiting Couples," *Journal of Marriage and Family* 68 (May 2006): 509–28; "Are Gay and Lesbian Cohabiting Couples *Really* Different From Heterosexual Married Couples?" *Journal of Marriage and Family* 66 (2004): 880–900.

56. CDF, *Considerations Regarding Proposals* 7.

57. See American Psychological Association, *Lesbian and Gay Parenting* (Washington, DC: APA, 2005), 15, https://www.apa.org/pi/lgbt/resources/parenting-full.pdf. See also Marybeth J. Mattingly and Robert N. Bozick, "Children Raised by Same-Sex Couples: Much Ado about Nothing," paper given at the Conference of the Southern Sociological Society, 2001.

58. American Psychological Association, "APA Resolution on Sexual Orientation, Homosexual Gender Identity (SOGI), Parents and Their Children," February 2020, https://www.apa.org/about/policy/resolution-sexual-orientation-parents-children.pdf.

59. See John Courtney Murray, *We Hold These Truths: Catholic Reflections on the American Experience* (New York: Sheed & Ward, 1960), 106.

60. Judith Butler, *Gender Trouble: Feminism and the Subversion of Identity* (New York: Routledge, 1990).

61. Pope Francis, "Address of His Holiness Pope Francis to Participants in the International Conference 'Man-Woman: Image of God. Towards an Anthropology of Vocations'" (March 1, 2024), https://www.vatican.va/content/francesco/en/speeches/2024/march/documents/20240301-convegno-uomo-donna.html.

62. Susannah Cornwall, *Sex and Uncertainty in the Body of Christ* (London: Chelsea Manor Studios, 2010), 29–31.

63. Congregation for Catholic Education, *"Male and Female He Created Them": Towards a Path of Dialogue on the Question of Gender Theory in Education* (2019) (hereafter MFC), 8, http://www.educatio.va/content/dam/cec/Documenti/19_0997_INGLESE.pdf.

64. Virginia Ramey Mollenkott, *OMNIGENDER: A Trans-religious Approach* (Cleveland, OH: Pilgrim Press, 2001), 77.

65. Megan DeFranza, *Sex Difference in Christian Theology: Male, Female, and Intersex in the Image of God* (Grand Rapids, MI: Eerdmans, 2015), 66.

66. Susannah Cornwall, "Intersex and Transgender People," in *The Oxford Handbook of Theology, Sexuality, and Gender*, ed. Adrian Thatcher (Oxford: Oxford University Press, 2015), 671; see also her *Sex and Uncertainty in the Body of Christ: Intersex Conditions and Christian Theology* (London: Routledge, 2016).

67. ISNA, "What is Intersex?," https://isna.org/faq/what_is_intersex/.

68. Thea Hillman, *Intersex (For Lack of a Better Word)* (San Francisco: Manic D Press, 2008), 149.

69. Consortium on the Management of Disorders of Sex Development, *Clinical Guidelines*, 2. These disorders are described in detail in DeFranza, *Sex Difference*, 23–67.

70. M. A. Blackless et al., "How Sexually Dimorphic Are We? Review and Synthesis," *American Journal of Human Biology* 12, no. 2 (2000): 151.

71. United Nations Human Rights, "Intersex People: OHCR and the Human Rights of LGBTI People," https://www.ohchr.org/en/sexual-orientation-and-gender-identity/intersex-people.

72. Dreger, *Hermaphrodites and the Medical Invention of Sex* (Cambridge, MA: Harvard University Press, 1998).

73. John Colapinto, "The True Story of John/Joan," *Rolling Stone* (December 11, 1997): 54–97.

74. Cecelia Dhejne et al., "Long-Term Follow-Up of Transexual Persons Undergoing Sex Reassignment Surgery," *PLoS One* 6, no. 2 (February 22, 2011).

75. Milton Diamond, "Sexual Identity and Sexual Orientation in Children with Traumatized or Ambiguous Genitalia," *Journal of Sex Research* 34 (1997): 199–211; J. J. Van Wyk, "Should Boys with Micropenis Be Raised as Girls?" *Journal of Pediatrics* 134 (1999): 537–38.

76. Pope Francis, *Ad Theologiam Promovendam* (November 1, 2023), 4, https://www.vatican.va/content/francesco/it/motu_proprio/documents/20231101-motu-proprio-ad-theologiam-promovendam.html.

77. Pope Francis, *Ad Theologiam Promovendam* 7.

78. Pope Francis, *Ad Theologiam Promovendam* 8.

CHAPTER 7

1. *Catechism of the Catholic Church* 2358.

2. CDF, *Persona Humana* 8.

3. 116th Congress, "H.R.5—Equality Act," (2019–2020), https://www.congress.gov/bill/116th-congress/house-bill/5/text/eh.

4. IPSOS, "Stonewall Anniversary Poll" (June 6, 2019), https://static.reuters.com/resources/media/editorial/20190612/StonewallFinalResults.pdf.

5. PRRI, "PRRI's American Values Atlas Finds Emerging Public Consensus in Support of LGBT Rights," *Public Religion Research Institute* (May 1, 2018), https://www.prri.org/press-release/ava-emerging-consensus-lgbt-rights/.

6. Quinnipiac, "U.S. Voters Still Say 2–1 Trump Committed Crime, Quinnipiac University National Poll Finds; but Voters Oppose Impeachments 2–1" (May 2, 2019), https://poll.qu.edu/national/release-detail?ReleaseID=2618.

7. Molly Igoe, "Americans Show Widespread Support for LGBT Nondiscrimination Protections and Transgender Rights," *PRRI* (October 1, 2019), https://www.prri.org/spotlight/americans-show-widespread-support-for-lgbt-nondiscrimination-protections-and-transgender-rights/.

8. Daniel Greenberg et al., "America's Growing Support for Transgender Rights," *PRRI* (June 11, 2019), https://www.prri.org/research/americas-growing-support-for-transgender-rights/.

9. Daniel Greenberg et al., "Americans Show Broad Support for LGBT Nondiscrimination Protections," *PRRI* (March 12, 2019), https://www.prri.org/research/americans-support-protections-lgbt-people/.

10. USCCB, "Questions and Answers about the Equality Act of 2019: Sexual Orientation, Gender Identity, and Religious Liberty Issues" (Washington, DC: USCCB, 2019), http://www.usccb.org/issues-and-action/marriage-and-family/marriage/promotion-and-defense-of-marriage/upload/Equality-Act-Backgrounder.pdf; and "Equality Act Letter to Congress" (March 20, 2019), http://www.usccb.org/issues-and-action/marriage-and-family/marriage/promotion-and-defense-of-marriage/upload/Equality-Act-Letter-to-Congress-House-1.pdf.

11. USCCB, "Equality Act Letter to Congress."

12. USCCB, "Questions and Answers about the Equality Act of 2019"; and "Equality Act Letter to Congress."

13. USCCB, "Questions and Answers about the Equality Act of 2019."

14. USCCB, "Questions and Answers about the Equality Act of 2019."

15. Brad Sears et al., "LGBT People's Experiences of Workplace Discrimination and Harassment," September 2021, UCLA School of Law Williams Institute, https://williamsinstitute.law.ucla.edu/publications/lgbt-workplace-discrimination/.

16. Sears et al., "LGBT People's Experiences."

17. Francis DeBernardo, "Employees of Catholic Institutions Who Have Been Fired, Forced to Resign, Had Offers Rescinded, or Had Their Jobs Threatened Because of LGBT Issues," *New Ways Ministry* (September 21, 2021), https://www.newwaysministry.org/issues/employment/employment-disputes/.

18. For detail on the study, see Julie Clague, "Catholics, Families, and the Synod of Bishops: Views from the Pews," *Heythrop Journal* 55, no. 4 (2014): 985–1008.

19. These lengths are scandalously evident in the bishops' opposition to the National Suicide Hotline Designation Act, since the Act includes "special funding for LGBTQ support" (Christopher White, "For US Bishops, LGBTQ 'Anthropology' Rules Out Equality Act Compromises," *National Catholic Reporter* [March 24, 2001], https://www.ncronline.org/news/justice/us-bishops-lgbtq-anthropology-rules-out-equality-act-compromises).

20. USCCB, *Open Wide Our Hearts* (Washington, DC: USCCB, 2018), https://www.usccb.org/resources/open-wide-our-hearts_0.pdf.

21. Pew Research Center, "Leaving Catholicism" (Revised February 2011), https://www.pewresearch.org/religion/2009/04/27/faith-in-flux3/#ftn.

22. Betsy Cooper et al., "Exodus: Why Americans Are Leaving Religion—and Why They're Unlikely to Come Back," *PRRI* (Sept. 22, 2016), https://www.prri.org/research/prri-rns-poll-nones-atheist-leaving-religion/.

23. "History Will Judge the Church Harshly for Its Treatment of LGBTQ Persons," *National Catholic Reporter* (February 9, 2022), https://www.ncronline.org/news/opinion/history-will-judge-church-harshly-its-treatment-lgbtq-persons.

24. Susan Szalewski, "Catholics Urged to Fight Measures Dealing with Sexual Orientation, Gender Identity," *The Catholic Voice* (March 17, 2021), https://catholicvoiceomaha.com/catholics-urged-to-fight-measures-dealing-with-sexual-orientation-gender-identity/.

25. Szalewski, "Catholics Urged to Fight Measures."

26. "A Balancing Act: Catholic Teaching on the Church's Rights—and the Rights of All," *America* (March 5, 2012), http://americamagazine.org/issue/5131/article/balancing-act.

27. See Human Rights Campaign, "The Lies and Dangers of Efforts to Change Sexual Orientation or Gender Identity," https://www.hrc.org/resources/the-lies-and-dangers-of-reparative-therapy.

28. *Dignitatis Humanae* 3.

29. USCCB, "Questions and Answers."

30. See Daniel Horan, "US Bishops Pioneered a Self-Serving Invocation of 'Religious Liberty,'" *National Catholic Reporter* (October 20, 2022), https://www.ncronline.org/opinion/ncr voices/us-bishops-pioneered-self-serving-invocation-religious-liberty.

31. CDF, "Considerations Regarding Proposals to Give Legal Recognition to Unions between Homosexual Persons," (2003) 7, emphasis added, http://www.vatican.va/roman_curia/congregations/cfaith/documents/rc_con_cfaith_doc_20030731_homosexual-unions_en.html.

32. USCCB, "Equality Act Letter to Congress."

33. Paul Sullins, "Invisible Victims: Delayed Onset Depression among Adults with Same-Sex Parents," *Depression and Research Treatment* (May 29, 2016), https://onlinelibrary.wiley.com/doi/10.1155/2016/2410392. The journal that published this article prefaced it with an editorial "expression of concern"; Sullins, "Emotional Problems among Children with Same-Sex Parents: Difference by Definition," *British Journal of Education* 7, no. 2 (2015): 99–120, https://papers.ssrn.com/sol3/papers.cfm?abstract_id=2500537.

34. Sullins, "Invisible Victims."

35. USCCB, "Equality Act Letter to Congress."

36. Mark Regnerus, "How Different Are the Adult Children of Parents Who Have Same-Sex Relationships? Findings from the New Family Structures Study," *Social Science Research* 41, no. 4 (2012): 752–70. Regnerus's study was "rebuked" in a letter signed by 200 social scientists (https://familyinequality.wordpress.com/2012/06/) on the basis of flawed methodologies and the journal itself performed an audit sharply criticizing the peer-review process that accepted the article for publication (https://www.chronicle.com/blogs/percolator/controversial-gay-parenting-study-is-severely-flawed-journals-audit-finds).

37. See American Psychological Association, *Lesbian and Gay Parenting* (Washington, DC: APA, 2005), 15, https://www.apa.org/pi/lgbt/resources/parenting-full.pdf. See also Marybeth J. Mattingly and Robert N. Bozick, "Children Raised by Same-Sex Couples: Much Ado about Nothing," paper presented at the Conference of the Southern Sociological Society, 2001.

38. Joan Laird, "Lesbian and Gay Families," in *Normal Family Processes*, ed. Froma Walsh (New York: Guilford, 1993), 316–17.

39. American Psychological Association, "APA Resolution on Sexual Orientation, Gender Identity (SOGI), Parents and Their Children," February 2020, 4, https://www.apa.org/about/policy/resolution-sexual-orientation-parents-children.pdf.

40. Ann Sullivan, ed., *Issues in Gay and Lesbian Adoption: Proceedings of the Fourth Annual Peirce-Warwick Adoption Symposium* (Washington: Child Welfare League of America, 1995), 24–28.

41. Sullivan, *Issues in Gay and Lesbian Adoption*, 41.

42. Marina Rupp, ed., *Die Lebenssituation von Kindern in Gleichgeschlechtlichen Lebenspartnershaften* (Cologne: Bundesanzeiger-Verlag-Ges, 2009).

43. Ellen C. Perrin, "Promoting the Well-Being of Children Whose Parents Are Gay or Lesbian," *Pediatrics* 131 (2013): e1374–e1383.

44. What We Know Project, "What Does the Scholarly Research Say about the Well-Being of Children with Gay or Lesbian Parents?" Cornell University, https://whatweknow.inequality.cornell.edu/topics/lgbt-equality/what-does-the-scholarly-research-say-about-the-wellbeing-of-children-with-gay-or-lesbian-parents.

45. Nathaniel Frank, "Comment on 'Invisible Victims: Delayed Onset Depression among Adults with Same-Sex Parents,'" *Depression Research and Treatment* (December 2016): 1–2, https://onlinelibrary.wiley.com/doi/10.1155/2016/3185067.

46. "Expression of Concern on 'Invisible Victims: Delayed Onset Depression among Adults with Same-Sex Parents," *Depression Research*

and Treatment (August 22, 2017), https://onlinelibrary.wiley.com/doi/10.1155/2017/4981984.

47. See "What We Know Project."

48. USCCB, "Ministry to Persons with a Homosexual Orientation: Guidelines for Pastoral Care," November 14, 2006, 2, emphasis added, https://www.usccb.org/resources/ministry-to-persons-of-homosexual-iInclination_0.pdf. See CDF, "Letter to the Bishops of the Catholic Church On the Pastoral Care of Homosexual Persons" (1986), 10, https://www.vatican.va/roman_curia/congregations/cfaith/documents/rc_con_cfaith_doc_19861001_homosexual-persons_en.html.

49. See Todd A. Salzman and Michael G. Lawler, *The Sexual Person: Toward a Renewed Catholic Anthropology* (Washington, DC: Georgetown University Press, 2008), 229–30.

50. Human Rights Watch, "Like Walking through a Hailstorm: Discrimination against LGBT Youth in US Schools," 1, https://www.hrw.org/sites/default/files/report_pdf/uslgbt1216web_2.pdf; see also Laura Meckler, Hannah Natanson, and John D. Harden, "In States with Laws Targeting LGBTQ Issues, School Hate Crimes Quadrupled," *Washington Post* (March 13, 2024), https://www.washingtonpost.com/education/2024/03/12/school-lgbtq-hate-crimes-incidents/.

51. James Martin, "How Can Catholic Colleges Welcome the LGBT Person?," *America* (February 3, 2020), https://www.americamagazine.org/faith/2020/02/03/how-can-catholic-colleges-welcome-lgbt-person.

52. Jane McGill, "LGBTQ+ Student at Omaha Catholic Schools," *The Register* (October 13, 2022), https://www.omahacentralregister.com/8978/news/lgbtq-students-at-omaha-catholic-schools/.

53. Skutt Catholic High School, "Mission Statement," https://skuttcatholic.com/about/our-mission/#.

54. McGill, "LGBTQ+ Students at Omaha Catholic Schools."

55. USCCB, "National Synthesis of the People of God in the United States of America for the Diocesan Phase of the 2021–2023 Synod (2022)," https://www.usccb.org/resources/US%20National%20Synthesis%202021-2023%20Synod.pdf.

56. See Katie Collins Scott, "New Catholic Policies across US Create 'Culture of Fear' for LGBTQ Students, Advocates Say," *National Catholic Reporter* (September 15, 2022), https://www.ncronline.org/news/new-catholic-policies-across-us-create-culture-fear-lgbtq-students-advocates-say.

57. Omaha Archdiocese, "Policy on Human Sexuality," https://htv-prod-media.s3.amazonaws.com/files/archdiocese-of-omaha-policy-on-human-sexuality-school-students-parents-and-guardians-pmf-rev-6-22-22-01486445-1661349324.pdf.

58. Congregation for Catholic Education, *Male and Female He Created Them* (Vatican City, 2019), 11, http://www.educatio.va/content/dam/cec/Documenti/19_0997_INGLESE.pdf.

59. *Catechism* 2358.

60. *Catechism* 1935.

61. Parent Pulse, "LB 586 Information," February 27, 2015, https://www.creightonprep.org/cf_news/view.cfm?newsid=1073.

62. Eleuterio F. Fortino, "Dialogue of Charity in the Perspective of the Holy Year," https://www.vatican.va/jubilee_2000/magazine/documents/ju_mag_01071997_p-56_en.html.

63. Betsy Cooper et al., "Exodus: Why Americans Are Leaving Religion—And Why They're Unlikely to Come Back," *PRRI International* (September 22, 2016), https://www.prri.org/research/prri-rns-poll-nones-atheist-leaving-religion/.

64. The Trevor Project, "2022 National Survey on LGBTQ Youth Mental Health" (2022), emphasis in original, https://www.thetrevorproject.org/survey-2022/.

65. James Martin, "Why Should the Church Reach Out to L.G.B.T.Q. People?," *America* (August 2, 2021), https://www.americamagazine.org/faith/2021/08/02/james-martin-lgbtq-catholics-statistics-241139.

66. Katie Collins Scott, "New Catholic Policies."

67. Christopher Well, "Pope: 'Unity with Diversity' a Great Strength for Jesuits," *Vatican News* (August 2, 2018), https://www.vaticannews.va/en/pope/news/2018-08/pope-francis-jesuits-formation-address.html.

68. See Daniel Horan, "Church's Anti-LGBTQ Policies Drive People Away—and the Policies Are Sinful, Too," *National Catholic Reporter* (September 22, 2022), https://www.ncronline.org/opinion/ncr-voices/churchs-anti-lgbtq-policies-drive-people-away-and-policies-are-sinful-too.

69. Jason Welle, "The Shame of Religious Families: Homeless LGBT Youth," *The Jesuit Post* (Sept. 17, 2014), https://thejesuitpost.org/2014/09/the-shame-of-religious-families-homeless-lgbt-youth/.

70. Press Releases, "AMA Adopts New Policies on First Day of Voting at 2019 Annual Meeting," https://nonprofitquarterly.org/american-medical-association-transgender-deaths-are-an-epidemic/.

71. The Tyler Clementi Foundation recently formulated a statement, "God Is On Your Side: A Statement from Catholic Bishops on Protecting LGBT Youth," https://tylerclementi.org/catholicbishopsstatement/. At this time, only 13, three of whom are retired, out of 290 active bishops have signed this statement.

72. *Catechism* 1935.

73. Although the Dicastery for the Doctrine of the Faith's *Dignitas Infinita* (April 8, 2024) (https://press.vatican.va/content/salastampa/en/bollettino/pubblico/2024/04/08/240408c.html) attempts to provide a definition of, and justification for, infinite human dignity, when applied to sexual human dignity this attempt fails anthropologically and methodologically. See Salzman and Lawler, "*Dignitas Infinita*: Anthropologically and Methodologically Consistent?," *Marriage, Families, & Spirituality* 30, no. 1 (2024): 143–53.

CHAPTER 8

1. Cindy Wooden, "Pope Asks Theologians to Help 'De-masculinize' the Church," USCCB, November 30, 2023, https://www.usccb.org/news/2023/pope-asks-theologians-help-de-masculinize-church.

2. Phyllis Zagano, "Does the Catholic Church Really Believe Women Are People?," *U.S. Catholic* (March 1, 2023), https://uscatholic.org/articles/202303/does-the-catholic-church-really-believe-women-are-people/.

3. *Mulieris Dignitatem* (1988), 6, emphases in original, https://www.vatican.va/content/john-paul-ii/en/apost_letters/1988/documents/hf_jp-ii_apl_19880815_mulieris-dignitatem.html.

4. John Paul II, *Familiaris Consortio* 22; *Mulieris Dignitatem* 16; *Letter to Women* (1995), 4, https://www.vatican.va/content/john-paul-ii/en/letters/1995/documents/hf_jp-ii_let_29061995_women.html. See Charles Curran's explanation and critique of John Paul II's position on the dignity and equality of women in *The Moral Theology of Pope John Paul II* (Washington, DC: Georgetown University Press, 2005), 187–95.

5. *Familiaris Consortio* 23.

6. Pope Francis, *Amoris Laetitia* 175. Hereafter cited in parenthetical citations as *AL*.

7. See Elisabeth Schüssler Fiorenza, *In Memory of Her: Toward a Feminist Reconstruction of Christian Origins* (New York: Crossroad, 1983); Elizabeth Johnson, *She Who Is: The Mystery of God in Feminist Theological Discourse* (New York: Crossroad, 1994); Susan A. Ross, "The Bridegroom and the Bride: The Theological Anthropology of John Paul II and Its Relation to the Bible and Homosexuality," in *Sexual Diversity and Catholicism: Toward the Development of Moral Theology*, ed. Patricia Beattie Jung with Joseph Andrew Coray (Collegeville, MN: Liturgical Press, 2001); Phyllis Zagano, *Just Church: Catholic Social Teaching, Synodality, and Women* (Mahwah, NJ: Paulist Press, 2023); Mary E. Hines, "Community for

Liberation: Church," in *Freeing Theology: The Essentials of Theology in Feminist Perspective*, ed. Catherine Mowry LaCugna (New York: HarperCollins, 1993), 161–84; Lisa Sowle Cahill, "Feminist Theology and a Participatory Church," in *Common Calling: The Laity and Governance in the Catholic Church*, ed. Stephen J. Pope (Washington, DC: Georgetown University Press, 2004), 127–49; and Mary Ann Hinsdale, "Beyond Complementarity: Gender Issues in the Catholic Church," in *T&T Clark Handbook of Theological Anthropology*, ed. Mary Ann Hinsdale and Stephen Okey (New York: Bloomsbury, 2021), 357–72.

8. Lisa Cahill, *Sex, Gender, and Christian Ethics* (New York: Cambridge University Press, 1996), 89.

9. John Paul II, *Ordinatio Sacerdotalis* 1; *Mulieris Dignitatem* 26. These arguments based on maleness were first articulated by the CDF in *Inter Insigniores* (Declaration on the Question of the Admission of Women to the Ministerial Priesthood) (1976), https://www.vatican.va/roman_curia/congregations/cfaith/documents/rc_con_cfaith_doc_19761015_inter-insigniores_en.html.

10. Mary Daly, *Beyond God the Father: Toward a Philosophy of Women's Liberation* (Boston: Beacon Press, 1973), 19.

11. Michael Novak, "Women, Ordination and Angels," *First Things* 32 (April 1993), 32. Cited in James F. Keenan, "Current Theology Note: Christian Perspectives on the Human Body," *Theological Studies* 55, no. 2 (1994): 345.

12. *Mulieris Dignitatem* 10.

13. See Anne E. Carr, *Transforming Grace and Women's Experience* (New York: Harper and Row, 1980).

14. See Paige duBois, *Sowing the Body: Psychoanalysis and Ancient Representations of Women* (Chicago: University of Chicago Press, 1988), 39–85; Carol Delaney, *The Seed and the Soil: Gender and Cosmology in Turkish Village Society* (Berkley: University of California Press, 1991); Sirach 26:20; Mishna, Ketuboth, 1, 6.

15. John Gillis, *For Better, For Worse: British Marriages 1600 to the Present* (Oxford: Oxford University Press, 1985), 310.

16. Lynn Jamieson, *Intimacy: Personal Relationships in Modern Societies* (Cambridge: Polity Press, 1998).

17. Karl Rahner, "Theology and Anthropology," in *Theological Investigations*, vol. 9 (London: Darton, Longman, and Todd, 1972), 28.

18. XVI Ordinary General Assembly of the Synod of Bishops, *Synthesis Report* (October 4–29, 2023), III, 15, g, https://www.synod.va/content/dam/synod/assembly/synthesis/english/2023.10.28-ENG-Synthesis-Report.pdf.

19. Hinsdale, "Beyond Complementarity: Gender Issues in the Catholic Church," 357, 359.

20. John Paul II, *Redemptoris Mater* (1987) 20, 23, https://www.vatican.va/content/john-paul-ii/en/encyclicals/documents/hf_jp-ii_enc_25031987_redemptoris-mater.html.

21. John Paul II, *Mulieris Dignitatem* 26, 27.

22. John Paul II, *Familiaris Consortio* 11; and *Mulieris Dignitatem* 17, 21.

23. It is important to note that the distinction between biological sex (male/female) and socially conditioned gender (masculine/feminine) is frequently absent in magisterial discussions of complementarity. Ross, "The Bridegroom and the Bride," 56n5.

24. Curran, *The Moral Theology of Pope John Paul II*, 190–91.

25. Curran, *The Moral Theology of Pope John Paul II*, 190–91.

26. Curran, *The Moral Theology of Pope John Paul II*, 168.

27. John Paul II, "Women: Teachers of Peace: Message of His Holiness Pope John Paul II for the XXVIII World Day of Peace, January 1, 1995," 3, https://www.vatican.va/content/john-paul-ii/en/messages/peace/documents/hf_jp-ii_mes_08121994_xxviii-world-day-for-peace.html.

28. Gudorf, "Encountering the Other: The Modern Papacy on Women," in *Feminist Ethics and the Catholic Moral Tradition*. Readings in Moral Theology No. 9, ed. Charles E. Curran, Margaret A. Farley, and Richard A. McCormick (Mahwah, NJ: Paulist Press, 1996), 75; and Curran, *The Moral Theology of Pope John Paul II*, 192–93.

29. Edward Vacek, "Feminism and the Vatican," *Theological Studies* 66, no. 1 (2005): 173–74, referring to John Paul II, "Authentic Concept of Conjugal Love," *Origins* 28 (1999): 655.

30. John Paul II, "Letter to Women," 7.

31. John Paul II, "Letter to Women," 7, emphasis in original; *Familiaris Consortio* 19.

32. Kevin Kelly, *New Directions in Sexual Ethics* (London: Cassell, 1999), 51. He goes on to critique ontological complementarity as ultimately "oppressive and deterministic" (52).

33. John Paul II, "Letter to Women," 8; *Mulieris Dignitatem* 6.

34. John Paul II, "Authentic Concept of Conjugal Love," 5.

35. John Paul II, "Letter to Women," 7–8.

36. Gareth Moore, *The Body in Context* (London: SCM Press, 1992), 121–27.

37. See John Paul II, *Familiaris Consortio* 23; "Letter to Women," 9; *Mulieris Dignitatem* 18; and "Women: Teachers of Peace."

38. Cristina Traina, "Papal Ideals, Marital Realities: One View from the Ground," in Jung and Coray, *Sexual Diversity and Catholicism*, 284.

39. Traina, "Papal Ideals," 280–82.

40. See Elaine L. Graham, *Making the Difference: Gender, Personhood, and Theology* (Minneapolis: Fortress, 1996).

41. See John Witte Jr., *The Equal Regard Family and Its Friendly Critics: Don Browning and the Practical Theological Ethics of the Family* (Grand Rapids, MI: Eerdmans, 2007); Don S. Browning, *Equality and the Family: A Fundamental, Practical Theology of Children, Mothers, and Fathers in Modern Societies* (Grand Rapids, MI: Eerdmans, 2007).

42. Adrian Thatcher, *Marriage after Modernity: Christian Marriage in Postmodern Times* (Sheffield: Sheffield Academic Press, 1999).

43. Pope Paul VI, *Humanae Vitae* 11.

44. CDF, *Persona Humana* 7.

45. Michel Foucault, *History of Sexuality* (New York: Vintage Books, 1990), vol. 1, 3.

46. See Traina, "Papal Ideals," 281.

47. Traina, "Papal Ideals," 282.

48. NCR Staff, "Letters to the Editor on Women's Ordination," *National Catholic Reporter* (July 21, 2023), https://www.ncronline.org/opinion/letters-editor/letters-editor-womens-ordination-0.

49. Pope Paul VI, "Response to the Letter of His Grace the Most Reverend Dr. F. D. Coggan, Archbishop of Canterbury, Concerning the Ordination of Women to the Priesthood (November 30, 1975)," https://womenpriests.org/church/cant1-correspondence-between-canterbury-and-rome/; *Ordinatio Sacerdotalis* 1.

50. Aristotle, *De Generatione animalium*, II, 3.

51. Aquinas, *Summa Theologiae* 1, 92, 1.

52. Lisa Sowle Cahill, *Sex, Gender, Christian Ethics* (New York: Cambridge University Press, 1996), 205. See John Paul II, *Familiaris Consortio* 23–24; *Mulieris Dignitatem* 14.

53. Hinsdale, "Beyond Complementarity," 357, 359.

54. https://www.vatican.va/roman_curia/congregations/cfaith/documents/rc_con_cfaith_doc_19761015_inter-insigniores_en.html.

55. https://www.vatican.va/content/john-paul-ii/en/apost_letters/1994/documents/hf_jp-ii_apl_19940522_ordinatio-sacerdotalis.html.

56. https://www.vatican.va/roman_curia/congregations/cfaith/documents/rc_con_cfaith_doc_19951028_dubium-ordinatio-sac_en.html.

57. https://www.vatican.va/content/john-paul-ii/en/motu_proprio/documents/hf_jp-ii_motu-proprio_30061998_ad-tuendam-fidem.html.

58. *Inter Insigniores* 5.

59. Pope John Paul II, *Ordinatio Sacerdotalis* 4.

60. *Christifideles Laici* (1988), 50 (emphasis in original), https://www.vatican.va/content/john-paul-ii/en/apost_exhortations/documents/hf_jp-ii_exh_30121988_christifideles-laici.html.

61. CDF, "In Response to Certain Doubts Regarding the Definitive Character of the Doctrine of *Ordinatio Sacerdotalis*" (2018), https://www.vatican.va/roman_curia/congregations/cfaith/ladaria-ferrer/documents/rc_con_cfaith_doc_20180529_caratteredefinitivo-ordinatiosacerdotalis_en.html.

62. Elizabeth A. Johnson, "Forging a Conversation with Colleagues," in *Things New and Old: Essays on the Theology of Elizabeth A. Johnson*, ed. Phyllis Zagano and Terrence W. Tilley (New York: Crossroad, 1999), 108.

63. Second Vatican Council, *Dei Verbum* (1965), 12, https://www.vatican.va/archive/hist_councils/ii_vatican_council/documents/vat-ii_const_19651118_dei-verbum_en.html.

64. See the Pontifical Biblical Commission's Report (1975), https://womensordinationcampaign.org/vatican-documents/2014/2/9/report-of-the-pontifical-biblical-commission-1975. See also John Wijngaards, *What They Don't Teach You in Catholic College: Women in the Priesthood and the Mind of Christ* (Lafayette, LA: Acadian House, 2020).

65. Pope Francis, "Address of His Holiness Pope Francis for the Opening of the Synod" (October 9, 2021), https://www.vatican.va/content/francesco/en/speeches/2021/october/documents/20211009-apertura-camminosinodale.html.

66. *Catechism* 1935; *Gaudium et Spes* 29.

67. Congregation for Catholic Education, *"Male and Female He Created Them": Towards a Path of Dialogue on the Question of Gender Theory in Education* (Vatican City, 2019), http://www.educatio.va/content/dam/cec/Documenti/19_0997_INGLESE.pdf.

68. *Gaudium et Spes* 48.

69. Edward N. Peters, *The 1917 Pio-Benedictine Code of Canon Law: In English Translation with Extensive Scholarly Apparatus* (San Francisco: Ignatius Press, 2001), c. 1081, 2.

70. Megan DeFranza, *Sex Difference in Christian Theology: Male, Female, and Intersex in the Image of God* (Grand Rapids, MI: Eerdmans, 2015), 4n8.

71. For an expanded discussion of this type of anthropology, see Salzman and Lawler, *The Sexual Person: Toward a Renewed Catholic Anthropology* (Washington, DC: Georgetown University Press, 2008), 124–61.

72. Hines, "Community for Liberation: Church," 163–64.

73. See Cahill, "Feminist Theology and a Participatory Church," 133.

74. See Salzman and Lawler, "*Amoris Laetitia*: Towards a Methodological and Anthropological Integration of Catholic Social and Sexual Ethics," *Theological Studies* 79, no. 3 (2018): 634–52.

75. See Zagano, *Just Church*.

76. Cahill, "Feminist Theology and a Participatory Church," 135.

77. See Salzman and Lawler, *Pope Francis, Marriage, and Same-Sex Civil Unions: Foundations for the Organic Development of Catholic Sexual Doctrine* (Lanham, MD: Rowman and Littlefield, 2024).

78. See Rachel DeSantis, "Vatican Says Church Can't Bless Same-Sex Unions Despite Pope's Previous Support: 'Disappointing,'" *People* (March 15, 2021), https://people.com/human-interest/vatican-says-church-cant-bless-same-sex-unions-despite-popes-previous-support/.

79. Associated Press, "Germany's Catholic Bishops Vote to Approve Blessings for Same-Sex Couples," *National Catholic Reporter* (March 10, 2023), https://www.ncronline.org/news/germanys-catholic-bishops-vote-approve-blessings-same-sex-couples.

80. Catholic News Service, "Cardinal Hollerich Says Church Teaching on Gays 'No Longer Correct,'" *Angelus* (February 2, 2022), https://angelusnews.com/news/world/cardinal-hollerich-says-church-teaching-on-gays-no-longer-correct/; Catholic News Service, "German Bishop Calls Current Catholic Teaching on Sexuality 'Too Simple,'" *National Catholic Reporter* (November 10, 2022).

81. "'Instrumentum Laboris' of the 16th Ordinary General Assembly of the Synod of Bishops, 20.06.2023," https://press.vatican.va/content/salastampa/en/bollettino/pubblico/2023/06/20/230620e.html.

82. Pope Francis, *Praedicate Evangelium* (2022), passim, https://www.vatican.va/content/francesco/en/apost_constitutions/documents/20220319-costituzione-ap-praedicate-evangelium.html.

83. James F. Keenan, "Hierarchicalism," *Theological Studies* 83, no. 1 (2022): 84–108.

84. Louis Janssens, "Artificial Insemination: Ethical Considerations," *Louvain Studies* 8, no. 1 (1980): 3–29.

85. Pat Perriello, "The Importance of Complementarity at the Upcoming Synod," *National Catholic Reporter* (June 17, 2015), https://www.ncronline.org/blogs/ncr-today/importance-complementarity-upcoming-synod.

86. Cindy Wooden, "Pope Asks Theologians to Help 'De-masculinize' the Church."

87. Pope Francis, *Ad Theologiam Promovendam*, https://www.vatican.va/content/francesco/la/motu_proprio/documents/20231101-motu-proprio-ad-theologiam-promovendam.html.

88. Pope Francis, *Ad Theologiam Promovendam* 3.

INDEX